LEGENDA

LEGENDA, founded in 1995 by the European Humanities Research Centre of the University of Oxford, is now a joint imprint of the Modern Humanities Research Association and Maney Publishing. Titles range from medieval texts to contemporary cinema and form a widely comparative view of the modern humanities, including works on Arabic, Catalan, English, French, German, Greek, Italian, Portuguese, Russian, Spanish, and Yiddish literature. An Editorial Board of distinguished academic specialists works in collaboration with leading scholarly bodies such as the Society for French Studies and the British Comparative Literature Association.

MHRA

The Modern Humanities Research Association (MHRA) encourages and promotes advanced study and research in the field of the modern humanities, especially modern European languages and literature, including English, and also cinema. It also aims to break down the barriers between scholars working in different disciplines and to maintain the unity of humanistic scholarship in the face of increasing specialization. The Association fulfils this purpose primarily through the publication of journals, bibliographies, monographs and other aids to research.

Maney Publishing is one of the few remaining independent British academic publishers. Founded in 1900 the company has offices both in the UK, in Leeds and London, and in North America, in Boston. Since 1945 Maney Publishing has worked closely with learned societies, their editors, authors, and members, in publishing academic books and journals to the highest traditional standards of materials and production.

Retrospectives

Essays in Literature, Poetics and Cultural History

TERENCE CAVE

EDITED BY NEIL KENNY AND WES WILLIAMS

LEGENDA

Modern Humanities Research Association and Maney Publishing
2009

Published by the
Modern Humanities Research Association and Maney Publishing
1 Carlton House Terrace
London SW1Y 5AF
United Kingdom

LEGENDA is an imprint of the
Modern Humanities Research Association and Maney Publishing

Maney Publishing is the trading name of W. S. Maney & Son Ltd,
whose registered office is at Suite 1C, Joseph's Well, Hanover Walk, Leeds LS3 1AB

ISBN 978-1-905981-95-3

First published 2009

Printed in Great Britain

Cover: 875 Design

Copy-Editor: Richard Correll

CONTENTS

PREFACE

Terence Cave, Neil Kenny and Wes Williams

The previous publications incorporated in this volume in partial, revised and/or translated form have been asterisked in the Bibliography. We thank Cambridge French Colloquia, the Librairie Droz and the Durham Modern Languages Series for permission to reuse material in this way. 'Singing with Tigers' is the only essay reprinted here in a (virtually) unchanged state, with the kind permission of Peter Lang.

Translations are by Terence Cave unless otherwise indicated. No translation is given for foreign-language quotations which appear only in the endnotes. A few of the critical editions used may have been superseded by more recent ones.

For subsidizing this volume's publication costs, we are very grateful to Royal Holloway, University of London; the Sub-Faculty of French, University of Oxford; St Edmund Hall, Oxford; the Department of French, University of Cambridge. We have appreciated the enthusiasm, expertise, and patience with which Graham Nelson of Legenda has steered the volume to publication.

The volume may usefully be twinned with *Pre-Histories and Afterlives: Studies in Critical Method* (edited by Anna Holland and Richard Scholar, also published by Legenda in 2009), which assesses and responds to methods developed in recent years by Terence Cave.

INTRODUCTION

Neil Kenny and Wes Williams

As attempts to look back at the past, acts of reading, of looking at page, screen, or image, are retrospectives of a particularly literal kind. This book investigates the excitement, insights, illusions, and problems involved in reading past texts, especially literary ones. It also studies literary texts as retrospectives in their own right, as attempts to make new sense out of texts and experiences which preceded *them*. Finally, the retrospectives of this book's title designate its author Terence Cave's look back at his own explorations of these issues over some forty years during which the revised studies of which the book consists were first published.

The book is thus an investigation of the retrospection involved in reading the kinds of writing which deploy rhetorical and poetical resources intensively and are generally known now as 'literature' (and in previous periods as 'poetry' in a much broader sense than the term now has). Cave argues that our only hope of being able to understand past literatures in something like their own terms, and of letting them continue to carry traces of vanished experiences, is through a careful, open-ended, never-complete attending to history, to the contexts out of which the texts emerged. The studies gathered here examine both the kinds of relations which literary texts bear to their historical contexts and also the power of certain literary writers to disrupt, exceed, and eventually outlive some of those contexts, while continuing to bear witness to them.

The investigation is in four steps. First, reading is shown to be a practice, or rather a range of practices, which has varied enormously over time. Secondly, the degree to which reading can give access to lost experiences is considered in a number of different contexts and generic forms. ('Experience' is understood as ranging from modes of thought and cognition to specific traumatic events.) Thirdly, the retrospective gaze involved in reading past literature is shown to be often a distorting, anachronistic one, even (or perhaps especially) when it claims to avoid anachronism by using a supposedly neutral historical method. Cave introduces the innovative critical concept and method of 'pre-history' as an adjustment of that gaze, which can sensitize readers to gestures that literary texts make towards lost experiences. Fourthly, he ends by charting — and celebrating — ways in which the distorting retrospective gaze of reading can become imbued with the reader's *own* experience, especially when s/he moves from reading to (re)writing, thereby lending new energy to certain motifs and techniques, and creating 'afterlives' of which their previous exponents could not have dreamt.

These questions are discussed in ways that reveal their applicability to all periods. The epicentre is early modern French culture, but the book extends to that culture's ancient Greek and Roman models, its European contexts, and the afterlives of some of its themes, from Pascal to the present day. The particular attention paid to the extraordinary writing power of the sixteenth-century French trio Rabelais, Ronsard, and Montaigne permits Cave to explore their relation both to past texts — those of Homer, Virgil, Horace, Ovid, and Heliodorus — and to those of later writers from Shakespeare through to Angela Carter, by way of Goethe, George Eliot and others still.

Part I begins with the hypothesis that a new paradigm of reading emerged in many quarters in the sixteenth and seventeenth centuries. It made the practice of reading more prominent, more active, and potentially more independent of authorial control. Montaigne, author of the late sixteenth-century *Essais*, is presented as the most decisive sponsor of this new paradigm, not only through his detailed descriptions of his particular reading practices, but also through the prompts he gives to readers of his own text. His (equivocal) encouragement to them to organize their reading of the *Essais* in terms of *their* experiences, rather than his, points forward within the economy of this volume to the 'afterlives' of Part IV. Part I ends by focusing on one strand within the broad history of reading with which it began: the distinctively early modern practice of excerpting fragments of prestigious and especially ancient discourse in the form of commonplaces before then recycling them in one's own discourse. Cave opens up a research field by drawing attention less to the content of the commonplaces than to the ways in which writers such as Rabelais (the main example here) and others (Montaigne, Molière, La Rochefoucauld) sewed these commonplaces together, thereby revealing cognitive habits which are alien to modern ones, and which often resist modern scholars' attempts to decide categorically whether or not these writers 'believed in' the contents of the commonplaces.

Cognitive habits are one dimension of what Part II is then entirely devoted to, namely, experience. Having treated a characteristically early modern writing practice (commonplacing) as a thinking tool, Cave now does the same for the early modern uses of the fund of images and themes constituted by ancient myth. His main examples are poems written between 1550 and 1563 in which Ronsard represents Bacchus and his attributes. Ronsard is shown to turn the myths associated with this god into a vehicle for his (Ronsard's) own experiences (including passions and imaginings). Much of the poetry's power stems from its blurring of the boundaries between the two levels on which it operates: narration of lived experiences (such as a picnic fuelled by drink and poetry-readings) and the recreation and perpetuation of these particular, contingent experiences through ancient myth.

With an abrupt change of tone, the discussion of experiences then turns to traumatic ones — specifically, rape and bereavement. First, Ronsard's, Rabelais's, and Shakespeare's rewritings of the myth of Philomela's rape are shown to point towards the difficulty — for the first two writers, the impossibility — of even representing an experience that is so alien to them, so unspeakable. Secondly, Joachim Du Bellay's and especially Rabelais's retrospective mid-sixteenth-century lamentations on the death, in 1543, of the leading politician, diplomat, and patron Guillaume Du Bellay are studied for evidence they might provide not so much about what these writers really felt or experienced, as about the modes of representation which were available to them in writing about a loss they seem to have experienced as devastating. Here, those modes of representation involve not myth but other tools also promoted by humanism: '*exempla*, classical *topoi*, adages and analogies'. As with myth, Cave's aim is to go beyond identifying the provenance of particular fragments or 'sources' — important as that is — and to examine instead how they are reworked in the new contexts, woven into elements of lived personal experience.

This discussion of writing about rape and bereavement puts particular emphasis on the otherness of the experiences in question. It is an otherness compounded for modern readers by the historical distance and changes of reading practice which have intervened since. This emphasis leads into Part III's head-on analysis of the formidable (but not total) inaccessibility to us of the energies carried by the literature of the past, which however have the potential to give us information *about* the past that could not be garnered from other sources. When reading past texts, we often miss those energies by retro-projecting onto them conceptual categories that post-date them. Indeed, the label 'early modern', used for convenience in this Introduction, is one of them. There are innumerable others. They include 'scepticism' (in the sense of a worked out philosophical position), 'the self', and (in poetics) 'suspense'. But, if these are anachronistic categories, what immediately preceded them? A set of textual disturbances (argues Cave), which are the historical signs of something that was experienced psychologically, such as 'epistemological uncertainty' and 'ontological or axiological anxiety'. Only when viewed retrospectively can these textual disturbances be seen to indicate the imminent emergence of a new concept or paradigm (such as 'the self'). Opening up a vast field of future research, Cave sets the challenge of writing the 'pre-histories' of these concepts and frameworks. The task is delicate. The very existence of such pre-histories is only revealed by retrospection, which he here calls historical analepsis; but *avoiding* analepsis is also essential when reconstructing past experience and writing pre-history.

The method is then tested through two case studies. First, instead of ana-chronistically attributing either 'scepticism' or 'anti-scepticism' to three neo-Latin mediators of that ancient philosophy (Henri Estienne, Gianfrancesco Pico della Mirandola, Gentian Hervet) and to the vernacular writers Rabelais and Montaigne, Cave examines how these authors 'imagined' scepticism: how their texts carry the traces of disturbed responses to its re-emergence in the early modern period that were not just epistemological but social, moral, and affective too. Secondly, he shows how 'the self' emerged only in the late sixteenth and seventeenth century, its French counterpart *le moi* surfacing especially in Descartes and Pascal — which is to say *not* in Montaigne who, surprisingly, never used the phrase, despite his reputation for having investigated *le moi* more searchingly than any other writer. Cave restores the strangeness of Montaigne's experimentations with the first person by interpreting them as a critical threshold in the pre-history of the self. A second such threshold is detected in the *narrative* experimentations with the first person that are conducted in Rabelais's fictions, particularly at moments where the *je* is half-propelled out of the fictional world and into the crisis-ridden world of experience of 1540s and 1550s France, including Guillaume Du Bellay's death, to which Cave now returns from a different angle.

Whereas writing pre-histories is an attempt to interpret literary and other texts in something approximating to their own terms, writing the 'afterlives' of texts and motifs involves showing how 'their own terms' have been developed, distorted, forgotten, rejected, or parodied by subsequent writers. Part IV begins by combining both approaches. On the one hand, following on from the investigations which conclude Part III, it sketches pre-histories, from antiquity to the sixteenth century, of the notion of narrative suspense, and so to some extent of the kind of novel which keeps readers on tenterhooks before resolving all plot strands at the end; an important threshold is crossed within these pre-histories with Jacques Amyot's 1547 translation and presentation of an ancient Greek fictional narrative, Heliodorus' *Aethiopica*. On the other hand, this discussion of narrative structure can also be interpreted as a study of afterlives (although Cave does not label it as such here). In contrast with the technique of suspense, the technique of endlessly deferring endings — characteristic of medieval romance — was often continued and reworked in seventeenth-century romances or nineteenth-century serial novels. This coexistence of pre-histories and afterlives within one discussion is a reminder that the thresholds crossed in, say, literary history are only ever partial ones: it would be wrong to argue that an 'age of deferred endings' was succeeded by an 'age of suspense' (or 'of suspense satisfied').

Part IV and the book as a whole end by focusing more on afterlives than on pre-histories. Returning to the question of the representation of traumatic experiences, the focus here is on the afterlives of the strangely disturbing figure of Mignon, the mistreated foundling of Goethe's novel *Wilhelm Meisters Lehrjahre* (1796). Having sketched some elements of the pre-histories of this figure, Cave shows how she was radically rewritten by Eliot in *Daniel Deronda* (1876) and by Carter in *Nights at the Circus* (1984). Mignon and her subsequent variant, Eliot's Mirah, are protagonists of recognition plots, which conceal an identity in order eventually to reveal it. Indeed Cave is here analysing afterlives not only of Mignon but of the traditional narrative device of recognition (*anagnorisis*) itself, thus bringing together two of his longstanding preoccupations — with afterlives and with recognitions. Equally, Part IV continues the investigation begun in Parts II and III of the extent to which reading literature can disclose traces of past experiences, in that general sense which includes modes of thought and of cognition. Having earlier examined myth and the recycling of textual fragments as evidence of such modes, Cave now investigates narrative itself as a mode — or rather a repertoire of modes — of attempting to make cognitive sense of a contingent world. In the case of *anagnorisis*, this sense is made retrospectively, as reader and characters look back, in the light of what they now know, at the events they initially experienced in a state of partial or incorrect knowledge. And yet the closing flourish supplied by Carter's postmodern novel calls into question even this kind of retrospective shaping of experience through literature.

The idea for this book came from the editors, who believe that these essays, many of which have hitherto existed only in French or in specialist journals, deserve an even wider readership. As it turned out, a good deal of the hard work for the volume — revisiting the materials and translating thoughts and arguments first conducted in another language and other contexts — was done by Terence Cave himself. In 'curating' *Retrospectives*, the editors have attempted to give some sense of the changing shape of the author's explorations of the questions here addressed. All the essays have been revised for inclusion here, but explorations from quite different moments in Cave's writing career have been deliberately set alongside each other in the four sections; the resulting shifts of emphasis, like the occasional shifts in style, texture, and tone, have been maintained rather than being ironed out, since they are themselves instructive. If it is a logical consequence of the book's own argument that these essays emerged out of particular contexts, then it is also true that they can themselves be read productively in relation to those contexts: now bound by them, now exceeding, even transcending them.

The essays on Bacchus and company (collected for the most part in Part II here) carry traces of Cave's earliest work on poetry and on the classical tradition. Marcel Raymond's extraordinary essay on Ronsard's poetry in *Baroque et Renaissance poétique* first inspired Cave's exploration of the Bacchic theme, and the methodology of the Warburg iconographers, in particular Edgar Wind's landmark study *Pagan Mysteries in the Renaissance*, offered further encouragement. Originally designed as preliminary soundings for a full-length study of Bacchic mythologies in mid-sixteenth-century France, the two essays which are merged and recast here to form a sustained enquiry into a number of Bacchic themes bear witness to a book which remains unwritten: one which would have linked the Bacchic strain of Rabelais's later work, including the *Cinquiesme Livre*, with a series of poems by Ronsard and other contemporary poets. The 'Warburg' method with which these essays engage was interdisciplinary, in that it involved 'reading' images primarily in the light of forerunners from the classical and medieval periods, and doing so in a text-based way. In both respects, it is a method that relishes erudition. For some, erudition and interdisciplinarity function principally as occasions for display — of cultural capital, intellectual mastery, and what Cave here calls 'consumer hermeneutics (or hermeneutic connoisseurship, which amounts to the same thing)'. For others, including Cave himself — as shown by the essays here, and by his first monograph *Devotional Poetry in France, c.1570–1613* (Cambridge: Cambridge University Press, 1969) — the interrelated study of sources and of images at once visual and textual involves rather the serious and imaginative exploration of the differing rhythms and textures of rhetorical, religious, and aesthetic practice over time.

These early soundings were followed by further explorations of Ronsard's mythologies, conducted in a range of articles and editions across the early to mid-1970s.[1] What emerged from these explorations was a recurrent theme: the gap between poetic mastery on the one hand and failure in the realm of human experience on the other. It is a theme which gives the first of Cave's landmark studies, *The Cornucopian Text: Problems of Writing in the French Renaissance* (Oxford: Clarendon Press, 1979), its central, memorable focus. The book's method, like certain of its recurrent themes, carries traces of its post-structuralist moment. The particular ways in which the linguistic and other energies released by writing are there conceived of as *problems*, which is to say as a productive set of questions that writers find themselves asking, not least as readers of their own texts, made powerful sense of the complex insights of Derrida, Barthes, and others. Thirty years on, *The Cornucopian Text* is now recognized as a classic, central to the serious study of early modern writing not only in French and neo-Latin, but also in English, history, and related fields. Translated (with some revisions) into French, its insightful reworking of the legacy of deconstruction remains all the more persuasive for being focused on a particular historical moment, the sixteenth century.

A ghost haunts the *Cornucopian Text*, a phantom study, which could have had been entitled 'Problems of *Reading* in the French Renaissance'. *Retrospectives* includes a number of essays which might in time have led to such a book. The first two essays in Part I, which investigate how reading was both theorized and practised in the early modern period, make a closely linked pair, in so far as 'Representations of Reading' ends with a brief account of the question as it appears in Montaigne's *Essais*, while the second piece explores that terrain extensively. For there are of course constants in Cave's work as well as shifts of theme, method, and tone. The recent work on commonplacing, for instance, can be seen as both a productive reorientation of certain aspects of the 'Warburg' method and a further exploration of how intertextuality and imitation theory are worked out in practice. Likewise, early investigations into the conscription of texts connoting violence in Ronsard's poetry (in particular, elements of a Horatian ode evoking the sufferings of Philomela) led, in time, to a new piece, presented here in English translation, on Philomela's afterlives in Rabelais, Ronsard and Shakespeare.

If problems of reading lurked ghost-like within Cave's work in the 1970s, from the early 1980s onwards they took on a specific shape: the figure of *anagnorisis*. The story of the changing interpretations and representations of this figure, both in theoretical writing and in literary practice, from antiquity to the present day, and across a wide range of European languages, animates Cave's second landmark study, *Recognitions: A Study in Poetics* (Oxford: Clarendon Press, 1988). That this work can in retrospect look dauntingly inclusive in its ambitions and scope tells us much about the consequences of the turn to history of a different kind which marked literary criticism in the years which followed. *Recognitions* is a massive achievement, but there is nothing of the broad brush about it. It lives and breathes detail and is, as a consequence, a continuing inspiration in a wide range of disciplines.

The next stage of Cave's work, adumbrated in his discussion of *anagnorisis*, involved the exploration of how suspense developed both as a topic in sixteenth-century poetics and as a peculiar form of cognitive instrument. The essays 'Imagining Scepticism in the Sixteenth Century' and 'Fragments of a Future Self: The First Person and Narrative in Rabelais', both reworked here, constitute a set of reflections that led to the third of Cave's landmark studies, *Pré-histoires: textes troublés au seuil de la modernité* (Geneva: Droz, 1999). The connecting thread with earlier work was the observation that the rise of a poetics of narrative suspense, together with new models of suspense (especially Heliodorus' *Aethiopica* as presented and translated into French by Jacques Amyot), coincided with the increasingly wide dissemination of Pyrrhonist thought. Cave's peculiar insight is to see the relation between these apparently differing fields of enquiry, between narrative suspense and the Pyrrhonist suspension of judgement (*epochê*), without collapsing the one into the other.

Originally written in French, much of *Pré-histoires* appears here in English for the first time. The Introduction, Chapter 4, and parts of Chapters 5 and 6 have been incorporated in *Retrospectives* in revised and translated form. The selections have been made with regard to the insights they offer into the interrelated concerns highlighted by this book's subtitle, 'Literature, Poetics and Cultural History'. As a consequence, certain sections of *Pré-histoires* (to say nothing of the second volume *Pré-histoires II: langues étrangères et troubles économiques au XVIe siècle* (Geneva: Droz, 2001)) had to be set aside.

One 'missing link' deserves particular mention here. Ronsard's poems of the natural and supernatural worlds and of the connections that they make between different levels of experience have always formed an important part of Cave's imaginary corpus, and he drew on these poems again in Part I of *Pré-histoires* (its Chapters 2 and 3). There, they found themselves in a context where the stress was on the role of cosmic beings (*daimons* in particular) who inhabit the 'middle zone' between human and transcendental experience. At the same time, the aim there was to show how Ronsard and others inserted anecdotes purporting to be from their personal lives in order to make present to the reader an experience of the supernatural. These uses by Ronsard of the first person singular can be seen to anticipate the theme of the self that is explored in Part II of *Pré-histoires*, from which certain of the relevant chapters are translated here. At the same time, the focus on narratives of experience in those Ronsard chapters of *Pré-histoires* revisits questions that reach all the way back to Cave's early essays on Bacchic themes.

It will strike the reader of these essays that much of Cave's recent work has been animated, as he puts it himself, by 'a poetics that is wholly orientated towards history'. The 'poetics' in this phrase (as in our subtitle) is as important as the 'history'. For the rigour of the earlier more explicitly theoretical work is in no way diminished in the later historically oriented studies. Clearly the later work is more obviously animated by the project of recuperating from past texts the fragmentary traces of lost experiences than are the earlier studies, and the essays in *Pré-histoires* certainly pay more sustained attention to non-literary texts than do Cave's earlier books. This, too, can be seen as a response to — and critical, reflective engagement with — the changing critical times, in particular the emergence of new historicism, first as an energetic critical paradigm for the study of Renaissance writing, and then as something close to *doxa*. But as the essays collected in this volume suggest, a number of abiding concerns make sustained sense of Cave's work, even as it maintains its rigorous, enduring methodological ambition: 'not to fill in the blanks — the dark patches — of history'. And even as his recent development of the concept of 'afterlives' — here exemplified by the work on the disturbing figure of Mignon — gives exciting, new, locally attuned life to the old, universal story of influence and originality, so too the argument and the detail of the writing returns us, insistently, to the shifting shapes of particular experiences, ones lived and represented in quite specific times and contexts.

Towards the right-hand side of the image reproduced on the cover of this book — Piero di Cosimo's 'Satyr mourning a nymph' — a dog looks on. Readers of Rabelais's prologues will recognize in the dog an emblem of the curious or engaged reader (or viewer). The fact that another dog — apparently unconcerned — can be glimpsed running along the shoreline in the middle distance only serves to single out this particular beast, its attachment to the scene, and its efforts to make sense of what it is witnessing. A concern with the poetics of witness, as with the particular, the singular even, has always been a mark of Cave's work. So too, on the other hand, has an interest in exemplary or otherwise peculiarly revelatory figures, metaphors, and characters: from the cornucopia through to the cloud-chamber, by way of archipelagos and trans-historical receivers; from Bacchus to Mignon, by way of Philomela. The reader will encounter all of the above in what follows, and each can be read as an emblem, whether of change or of continuity, of the text or of the reader — or of something (or someone) else again.

Note to the Introduction

1. These and all of Terence Cave's publications are listed at the end of this volume.

PART I

Questions of Reading

§1

Representations of Reading in the Renaissance

The hypothesis that I would like to present in this essay is that the sixteenth century, in northern Europe at least, witnesses a major shift in the status of the reader: reading becomes, in various senses, a much more prominent activity.[1] In order to set this hypothesis in motion, it is necessary to suggest, as a preliminary generalization, that relatively low priority is given to the reader in the theories and paradigms of discourse that were dominant at the beginning of the century, whether one is thinking of scholastic or of humanist models. This would certainly be true, for example, of nominalist grammar and logic, with their emphasis on the formal processes of signifying and on the truth-value of propositions. Yet there are a number of apparent exceptions to (or limitations of) the general claim.

In the first place, from the patristic era onward, the problem of how to read correctly gives rise to theories of authorial intention and to complex rules for reading designed to recover the authentic meaning of a text (scriptural or classical).[2] In particular, the techniques of allegory define the reader's activity in considerable detail. Yet the very fact that this activity is prescribed in advance means that reading is assigned a subordinate status. The mimetic task of allegorizing a text (the allegorical rewriting of Ovid's *Metamorphoses*, for example) is at least in principle closed and static, producing a copy of what is presumed to have been hidden inside the original text. *We* may of course regard such readings as transformations, but the theory implied by late medieval allegorical method gives little scope to the transformational potential of texts and small licence to their readers. One might remark also that the product of allegorization is always a series of moral and theological commonplaces. This feature persists in later periods (it is no doubt still with us), but will in certain important instances, as I will try to show, assume a different function.

In the second place, the humanist methods of philological and contextual commentary that are already becoming established by the end of the fifteenth century are also, one might argue, deeply concerned with the activity of reading. Erasmus and other northern humanists interest themselves above all in the education of a skilled reader, prescribing in some cases a lifetime's work as preparation for the supreme exercise of reading Scripture. But here again the text itself would seem to have absolute priority, transcending in its venerable antiquity the local, time-bound and marginal figure of the reader. Indeed, the humanist stress on the priority of the text is the greater in that it is designed to counter what the humanists claimed to be the arbitrary glosses of the scholastics. As an example of this emphasis in the scriptural sphere, one might cite Erasmus's Christocentric theory of reading, in which the reader would ideally be transformed into the text and thus become identified with the divine Logos: Erasmus here owes a great deal to Augustine, whose notion of scriptural reading has as its logical conclusion the disappearance of the reader as a 'wilful', independent subject and the epiphany of grace.[3]

The theory and practice of secular rhetoric more evidently emphasize the act of communication. The notion, for example, that the audience will not be moved and persuaded unless the speaker is himself genuinely moved by his topic[4] dramatizes the production and consumption of discourse; the reader is here explicitly present. The neo-Platonist theory of inspiration, another major *topos* of humanist reflection on discourse, provides a metaphysical version of the same scenario: the poet, like a rhapsode, transmits his supernatural 'enthusiasm' to the listener, who is activated by the energy of the text. The study of rhetoric, however, is designed primarily for writers and speakers, not for readers, and the theory of inspiration is an attempt to explain the production of discourse rather than its consumption.

Finally, it is certainly the case that all three accounts of communication — allegory, rhetoric, neo-Platonist theory — may be considered to be heuristic in the sense that they aim ideally at moral improvement, not by direct instruction but by changing the state of mind or the affections of readers, or giving them a mental discipline that they in the end must put into effect for themselves; this would be true also of the systematic spiritual exercises devised in the sixteenth century and of their medieval antecedents. But the power and privilege of a master text and of its author or speaker remain unshaken: reading is a mimetic act that seeks to restore the totality and integrity of the original discursive performance. Nowhere is this clearer than in the so-called Ciceronian imitation of the Renaissance, where a closed discipline of reading is prescribed in order to guarantee a perfect representation of Ciceronian discourse, and presumably of the Ciceronian *sententia* enclosed within it.

In the course of the sixteenth century, however, other accounts of reading begin to impose themselves, accounts that make the task of the reader more central and correspondingly change the status and function of the text. In a sense, this is perhaps already a generally accepted hypothesis: for example, it is well known that Protestant theories of scriptural reading, as well as humanist stress on the return *ad fontes,* release the reader from the constraints of what one might call institutionalized allegory and glossing. Or again, in a more literary context, studies like those of Walter Kaiser, Barbara Bowen, and Rosemary Colie have demonstrated how such procedures as irony and 'paradox'[5] become dominant in certain sixteenth-century texts, radically changing the nature of the relationship between writer, text and reader.[6] I shall not rehearse those arguments here, although they should be borne in mind in what follows. I shall focus on the ways in which sixteenth-century writing defines or imagines the reader, on the emergence in textual practice of the *figure* of the reader.

Readers in the text

At the most straightforward level, one notices that characters in late Renaissance texts spend a great deal of their time engaged in reading, or in similar activities such as quoting and citing. One might take as an initial paradigm the *Heptaméron* of Marguerite de Navarre (written in the 1540s), where Boccaccio's device of the framework story is expanded to a point at which the game of storytelling is no longer the end but the means: the stories are there to be read and discussed by the *devisants* (narrators who have become readers). A detailed analysis of this example might draw attention to the leitmotif of Biblical readings which run parallel to the secular storytelling, thus multiplying the intertextual possibilities; to the quotation by the storytellers-cum-readers of other texts (the *Roman de la Rose*, Plato, Scripture); to the way in which readings of one story generate the narration of the next story; and to the *mise en abyme* of the whole process in the Prologue, which refers to a 'real', but unrealized, storytelling project proposed by Marguerite de Navarre at the French court, in which all the stories — unlike Boccaccio's — were to be true. In general terms, what is most visible, however, is that while the content of the storytellers' readings may easily be reduced to a set of moral, religious, and courtly commonplaces, this content is presented in such a way as to highlight the heuristic activity of reading. A dialogue of readers has invaded the terrain of narrative.

Among other examples one might cite Erasmus's *Convivium religiosum*. This is a dialogue that transforms interpretation into a pursuit of sense, a mobile scenario in which no reading is ever foreclosed and some readings are ostentatiously unresolved.[7] It is, in fact, another dialogue of readers, although what they are reading is not narrative fiction but a set of emblems and quotations. The mimetic function of the dialogue in this case is not the production of glosses said to represent the true sense of an authoritative text, but rather the representation of reading itself as an activity that can be dramatized, assigned a life of its own beyond the confines of the text or texts being read. These examples seem to me to embody a conception of 'represented reading' that is entirely different from what one finds, for example, in the *Ovide moralisé*, where the allegorizer, having narrated a segment of the narrative, appears on the scene adding his glosses as an external accretion. They are also quite different from the procedure used in the *Roman de la Rose*. There, the lover is certainly a personification of reading as he moves through, and attempts to interpret, his allegorical scenario. But, sealed as he is within the narrative, he is the perfect counterpart of the reader himself, who likewise is obliged to move in linear progression through the arcade of emblems and personifications in search of the single *telos* reserved for him by the text. If the *Roman de la Rose* is regarded as having a heuristic structure, what it encourages the reader to discover is the art of repetition, the virtue of hermeneutic transparency or symmetry. The unfinished and generative readings of the Renaissance examples, by contrast, while still rehearsing *topoi*, begin to assert the otherness, the irreducible asymmetry or discontinuity of reading, and the ultimate priority of the reader.

The enactment of reading in Rabelais may be said to work in the same way, and the first meeting between Pantagruel and Panurge in *Pantagruel* 9 (1532) provides a graphic demonstration of the importance of this issue on the very threshold of Rabelais's writing career.[8] The episode is narrated in dialogue form as an instance of non-communication. Pantagruel asks questions to which Panurge replies in a series of foreign languages that his interlocutors cannot understand. It thus highlights the role of the reader: unsuccessful reading necessarily makes the content of the text subordinate to the attempt at comprehension. Panurge's foreign-language speeches are of course not a narrative or a poem or a scriptural text in need of elucidation, so that the word 'reading' might seem misplaced here. However, the relation of the whole episode to reading emerges when one observes, first of all, that what Panurge enunciates in disguised form is a number of quotations, *sententiae*, and adages: in other words, excerpted readings. In the second place, it can be shown that the encounter is a parodic inversion of a recurrent episode in the *Odyssey*, namely, the reception of a stranger by a host who invariably offers hospitality before asking the stranger who he is and where he comes from (Pantagruel does the reverse). Thus the shadow of a displaced narrative, itself a consecrated text, falls across the dialogue: its absence allows an activity to take the stage that would be germane to glossing, were its product not also partially occulted (the product being Panurge's set of *topoi* on the themes of charity and the priority of moral action over language). The whole episode might thus be reconstituted by the reader as an evangelical humanist gloss on the *Odyssey*, except that what is represented here is not the inner meaning of a venerable text, since the charade performed by the characters peremptorily changes the terms of reference of reading. The visibly imperfect reading within the text obliges us as readers to play an active role: not simply the solving of a riddle, although that paradigm has some relevance, but the rehearsal of the characters' performance at one or more removes. A similar function can arguably be ascribed to the 'misreadings' of Panurge in the *Tiers Livre*, although there the heuristic procedure is still more apparent because its repetition structures the greater part of the book.

In Montaigne's *Essais*, too, the reader is personified, not only through Montaigne's often ironic second-person asides, but through the writer's self-personification as a reader of other texts and of his own. I shall be returning to this question shortly, but I prefer to approach it by way of imitation theory, which is undoubtedly central, whether as cause or as symptom, to the shift we are considering here.

Reading and imitation

The debate over the imitation of consecrated authors — the classics, Scripture, a few moderns such as Petrarch — necessarily implies contrasted views of what reading is and does. The so-called Ciceronian position, represented in the sixteenth century by writers such as Dolet and Scaliger, stresses the universality of nature as located in, and perceived by, the human mind; this universal may be more or less perfectly represented in discourse, so that the reader's task is to seek out and dwell on its most perfect representation. Thus, as we saw earlier, reading is for the Ciceronian the repetition of a perfect or near-perfect discourse; the reader should, as it were, disappear or be effaced in favour of the paradigm text. By contrast, the anti-Ciceronian position, which is developed in its most detailed and penetrating form by Erasmus,[9] extends virtually *ad infinitum* the range of texts to be read and stresses, not universal nature, but the individual nature of the reader as the agent by which this assemblage of materials is gathered, selected, and given meaning. This is probably the most pervasive single aspect of the reorganization of discourse in terms of the subject that is generally attributed to Renaissance humanism. In Erasmian theory, nature is plural and protean; it shifts to the side of the imitator or of the 'copy,' generating new meanings and new texts.

It is important to notice, however, that Erasmus does not quite say that each reading of a text displaces that text in a direction determined by the context and nature of the reader: the displacement occurs for him at the moment of rewriting. The reverence for ancient texts and for their original, authentic meaning, which is an equally potent part of the humanist approach, here provides a constraint. What I think it possible to argue is that imitation as a theory of writing contributes to a change in habits of reading. If venerable texts are to be fragmented and eventually transformed by the process of rewriting, it becomes visibly less necessary to regard them as closed and authoritative wholes.

Evidence for the decline of the authoritative status of such texts is provided by the work of Antoine Compagnon and Marc Fumaroli. Compagnon discerns in the sixteenth century a shift from the citing (*allégation*) of *auctoritates*, a procedure akin to glossing, to free quotation. In one case, readers of ancient texts see their own reading and their own discourse as wholly subservient: it is a humble activity carried on very precisely in the margins. In the other case, of which Montaigne is the prime example, the reader as an independent subject is beginning to impose himself and his own discourse as primary: the quotation is integrated into a new context authorized by the rewriter. According to Compagnon, this is a transitional stage: by the later seventeenth century, the signs of 'borrowing' will have virtually disappeared, and the new text will thus be wholly the responsibility of its author. Marc Fumaroli corroborates this hypothesis from another point of view by his discussion of 'quotation rhetoric,' which he regards as the predominant mode of writing among the *magistrature* of the later sixteenth century, but which becomes outmoded in the course of the seventeenth.[10]

The production of new texts in the late Renaissance according to the principles of Erasmian imitation or quotation rhetoric might, then, be said to give the reader an entirely new role. Precisely because such new texts contain (and, as it were, enclose) fragments of *auctoritates*, reading can no longer consist of systematic glossing or of mimetic repetition. The gloss has swollen to the point where it has visibly engulfed the master text. What works such as Montaigne's *Essais* represent is not an inert original meaning but a process, a displacement or transformation. This is already true of certain of Erasmus's works (the *Adages*, for example), and of Rabelais's fiction, where innumerable fragments of canonical writings are cited and quoted by both narrator and characters in constantly shifting contexts, often provocatively unexpected ones. Rabelais's strategies of citation imply that whatever may be of value in these fragments can only be realized by a positive act of appropriation on the part of the reader. The displacement mimed by the text provokes the reader to carry out a further displacement beyond its margins.

Montaigne and reading

Reading thus becomes a kind of rewriting, because what is read is itself perceptibly a reading in something like the modern sense — that is to say, a provisional exercise.

This possibility is most explicitly envisaged by the *Essais* of Montaigne (published from 1580 onwards). Montaigne preserves the notion of an original, intended meaning and attacks glossing as a deviation. But what he objects to is perhaps that the gloss, instead of recognizing that it is a deviation, claims perfectly to represent the master text. In virtually all of Montaigne's accounts of reading, deviation is accepted and recognized as potentially productive. The appropriation of alien texts adumbrated in the imitation theory of Erasmus and vigorously promoted by French vernacular writers such as Du Bellay is systematically put into practice in the *Essais*. Montaigne misquotes, disguises his quotations, quotes without identifying the text, provides a radically new context for his quotations, and in addition makes all these operations explicit.

This subject has been explored by Compagnon, Lino Pertile, and Mary McKinley, so I will not cite specific examples here.[11] I would like instead to indicate two aspects of the way in which the *Essais* imagine their own reader. The first is the oscillation between strategies of obstruction and exclusion on the one hand and the theme of desire for an ideally sympathetic and alert reader on the other. Montaigne speaks of his text as being only suitable for his family and friends, as being not worthy of the reader's attention, as being difficult to read, and as requiring a reader who falls into no pre-existing category. At the same time, he persistently addresses his readers, courts them, and plays the game of irony with them; he says that he is 'affamé de [se] faire connoistre' [hungry to make himself known] and hopes that the book may eventually find for him a sympathetic friend to replace the one he lost in Étienne de La Boétie. This oscillation undermines the conventions of reading that contemporary readers were familiar with and begins to open up a space — still hypothetical and on the horizon of Montaigne's perception — for a different kind of reading. Such a reading would at once be uniquely attuned and sympathetic to the displacement enacted by the *Essais,* and for that very reason be capable of a new and as yet unpredictable displacement. An example that embodies these characteristics, although it is not one in which Montaigne is speaking explicitly about the reception of the *Essais*, is a passage from I.35 ('D'un defaut de nos polices').[12] Montaigne here reports his father's suggestion that every town should have a register in which people could announce their reciprocal needs and thus contact one another, as for example 'Je cherche à vendre des perles, je cherche des perles à vendre. [...] tel s'enquiert d'un serviteur de telle qualité; tel d'un maistre' [I want to sell some pearls, I want to buy some pearls [...] so-and-so seeks a servant of such-and-such a type; someone else seeks a master]. He even uses the word 'advertir,' thus anticipating verbally as well as by the general conception the system of advertisement. Like an entry in the personal columns of a modern newspaper, the *Essais* is a text in search of exactly the right reader.[13]

The second point concerns Montaigne's use of what one might call a *topos* of textual appropriation. When he says 'Je ne dis les autres que pour d'autant plus me dire' [I only speak others in order better to speak myself] (I.26, p. 148), and later in the same chapter 'Ce n'est plus selon Platon que selon moy, puisque luy et moy l'entendons et le voyons de mesme' [It's no more Plato's idea than it is my own, since he and I understand and see it the same way] (p. 152), he is rephrasing Seneca's remark

a product for leisure consumption and for university study. Nevertheless, I would propose that a great deal of what we now understand as the activity of reading is made possible by the shifting representations of the reader in the Renaissance. It appears indeed that, in parallel with the widely acknowledged rise of the figure of the author in this period, the status of the reader also undergoes a profound change and the activity of reading comes to the fore as a key shaping force.

Notes

1. I am concerned here primarily with Latin humanism and the French vernacular. For a similar approach, see Cathleen M. Bauschatz, 'Montaigne's Conception of Reading in the Context of Renaissance Poetics and Modem Criticism,' in *The Reader in the Text*, ed. by Susan R. Suleiman and Inge Crosman (Princeton: Princeton University Press, 1980), pp. 264–91; also Michel Charles, *Rhétorique de la lecture* (Paris: Seuil, 1977).
2. See my account of this question in *The Cornucopian Text: Problems of Writing in the French Renaissance* (Oxford: Clarendon Press, 1979), I.3; the articles by Eugene Vance, Kevin Brownlee and Marina Brownlee in *Mimesis: From Mirror to Method, Augustine to Descartes*, ed. by John D. Lyons and Stephen G. Nichols, Jr. (Hanover and London: University Press of New England, 1982), the volume in which the article reproduced here was originally published, are also relevant.
3. See *The Cornucopian Text*, pp. 79–86.
4. Here, as elsewhere in this essay, I have used the exclusive masculine pronoun where the use of the feminine pronoun cannot be justified on historical grounds (in this case, because the theory and practice of rhetoric from Antiquity to the Renaissance always predicates a male speaker).
5. On the definition of 'paradox', see below, p. 40.
6. See Walter Kaiser, *Praisers of Folly: Erasmus, Rabelais, Shakespeare* (London: Victor Gollancz, 1964); Rosalie Colie, *Paradoxia Epidemica: The Renaissance Tradition of Paradox* (Princeton: Princeton University Press, 1966); Barbara C. Bowen, *The Age of Bluff: Paradox and Ambiguity in Rabelais and Montaigne* (Urbana: University of Illinois Press, 1972).
7. See *The Cornucopian Text*, pp. 102–08.
8. This example is discussed in my article 'Panurge and Odysseus', in *Myth and Legend in French Literature*, ed. by K. R. Apsley, D. M. Bellos and P. Sharratt (Edinburgh: Edinburgh University Press, 1982), pp. 47–59. See also Gérard Defaux, 'Une rencontre homérique: Panurge noble, pérégrin, et curieux,' *French Forum*, 6 (1981), 109–22, which corroborates my conclusions with regard to the Homeric paradigm. I return to the same episode at some length in *Pré-histoires II*, Part I.
9. It is necessary to point out, however, as I failed to do in *The Cornucopian Text*, that Erasmus at many points exploits material derived from his Italian predecessors in the debate. In particular, the notion of 'self-expression' occurs in a letter by Angelo Poliziano published before the end of the fifteenth century: see Marc Fumaroli, *L'Âge de l'éloquence: rhétorique et 'res literaria' de la Renaissance au seuil de l'époque classique* (Geneva: Droz, 1980), pp. 81–83; cf. *The Cornucopian Text*, pp. 42–43.
10. Antoine Compagnon, *La Seconde Main, ou le travail de la citation* (Paris: Seuil, 1979), pp. 235–317; Fumaroli, *L'Âge de l'éloquence*, especially pp. 464–66.
11. Lino Pertile, 'Paper and Ink: The Structure of Unpredictability,' in *'O un amy!' Essays on Montaigne in Honor of Donald M. Frame*, ed. by Raymond C. La Charité (Lexington, KY: French Forum Monographs, 1977), pp. 190–218; Mary B. McKinley, *Words in a Corner: Studies in Montaigne's Latin Quotations* (Lexington, KY: French Forum Monographs, 1981).
12. Michel de Montaigne, *Les Essais: édition conforme au texte de l'Exemplaire de Bordeaux*, ed. by Pierre Villey and V.-L. Saulnier (Paris: PUF, 1965), I.35, p. 223. The page numbers given below for the *Essais* refer to this edition.
13. The application of this example to the *Essais* is perhaps the more legitimate in that the later part of the same chapter reveals that Montaigne's father kept a record of daily domestic events.

Montaigne adds that he wishes he had done the same; but the *Essais* become, of course, just such a record, although of the author's 'fantaisies' or 'imaginations', not of external events.

14. II.17, p. 657. For a more detailed discussion of this passage, see below, pp. 32–33.

15. Michel Beaujour's *Miroirs d'encre: rhétorique de l'autoportrait* (Paris: Seuil, 1980) has some excellent things to say on this topic.

16. Blaise Pascal, *Pensées*, in *Œuvres complètes*, ed. by Louis Lafuma (Paris: Seuil, 1963), p. 591, no. 689.

17. My remarks on this configuration of texts, and in particular on Pascal's transformed quotation of Montaigne, are indebted to Frederick G. Hodgson, 'Pascal's Conversion of Montaigne's *Essais*' (unpublished doctoral dissertation, University of California, Santa Barbara, 1979).

18. Stanley Fish, whose *Self-Consuming Artifacts* (Berkeley: University of California Press, 1972) raises questions similar to those discussed here, would perhaps not agree with me as far as *Pilgrim's Progress* is concerned.

Problems of Reading in Montaigne's *Essais*

All literature, it may be argued, depends for its existence on the literary texts which preceded it, whether or not it draws directly on them as its sources, and the proposition is nowhere more palpably true than in the *Essais*. Montaigne quotes, alludes to and borrows from other writers at every turn. In 'Sur des vers de Virgile', having discussed explicitly the question of literary imitation, he claims that he is going to leave books on one side and speak 'plus materiellement et simplement' [more materially and simply]; but in the very next sentence, he refers to Zeno and Cratippus and quotes Claudian; shortly after, there is a quotation from Horace, a reference to Plato, and paraphrases of sayings of Alexander and Aristotle (III.5, pp. 877–78). The Montaigne of the *Essais,* as opposed, for example, to the Montaigne who was mayor of Bordeaux, is above all a reader: a highly intelligent one whose dialogue with the books he reads is instructive more — as he himself would say — for its method than its matter. Indeed, reading is one of the themes to which Montaigne recurs most often in the *Essais,* taking its place next to such major concerns as virtue, happiness and death. He discusses his preferences and deficiencies as a reader, the difficulty of discovering the correct meaning of a text, the dangers of over-interpretation, the question of authorial intention, and many other aspects of the topic which are still debated in our own day. In consequence, the practice of reading, and reflections on that practice, form an integral part of Montaigne's self-portrait.

The example cited above already suggests that reading is not always the innocent and straightforward activity it may at first sight appear to be: it presents problems. In particular, it refuses to be tied down or relegated to a subordinate domain. Even when Montaigne thinks (or we think) it has been set aside, it infiltrates everything he writes; likewise, precisely because the question of reading is inherent in the fabric of the *Essais* as a whole, our own reading of the text is fraught with problems which are the more acute because they are often hidden. These problems cannot be finally solved, for reasons which will become apparent in due course. They can be explored and elucidated; the rest is up to the reader.

This essay will consider two principal aspects of the question of reading as it appears in the *Essais*. The first section will present a sketch of Montaigne's practice of reading: the kinds of books he avowedly read and preferred, the uses to which he puts his reading, and the evaluative or descriptive comments he makes. The second section considers how the *Essais* themselves are offered to the reader. As the very notion of a self-portrait implies, Montaigne is no less conscious of his own readers than he is of himself as a reader: he approaches them with disarming gestures, he uses devices like irony and paradox to outwit their conventional responses, he at once ignores and embraces them. Reflection and practice are thus in a constant relationship with one another in Montaigne's writing; Montaigne's 'theory' is so intermittent, so deliberately unsystematic, that to attempt to make of it a coherent structure of thought which could be used to explain his practice would be to ignore and falsify the character of his discourse.

The chronological development of the *Essais* will be taken into account as far as clear evidence exists and where it is relevant to the question. It can be shown, for example, that Montaigne had different reading habits and incorporated his reading into the *Essais* in a somewhat different way in his later years. But the three principal strata of the text as indicated in modern editions only provide a rough guide to chronology.[1] In many respects, the decisive development occurred in the period 1572–80. What came later is undeniably rich and, for modern readers at least, intellectually and aesthetically satisfying; but the essentials of Montaigne's method, his range of themes, and the notion of self-portraiture are established by 1580, as is the crucial invention of the title. What the later versions provide above all is an endless series of examples of the way in which Montaigne read his own text and incorporated it, as it were, into a new and expanded body of writing.

Montaigne's practice of reading

If many of Montaigne's remarks give the impression that he adopted a nonchalant and even facile method of reading,[2] others make it clear that he was well aware of the rarity of discriminating literary judgement. The most extended of these occurs in 'De l'art de conferer' (III.8, pp. 936–37) but a similar observation is made in relation to poetry in 'Du jeune Caton' (I.37, pp. 231–32) and the idea is already present in embryo in the 1580 edition, where Montaigne speaks of Aesop as an 'autheur de très-rare excellence et duquel peu de gens descouvrent toutes les graces' [an author of the rarest excellence, whose merits are fully discerned by very few people] (II.37, p. 769). It is precisely because Aesop would not normally be classed as a difficult author that the remark has the widest of implications.

In his own reading of texts, Montaigne's frame of reference is predominantly ethical. The vast collection of anecdotes, examples and sayings which he culls from other texts in order to weave them into the *contexture* of the *Essais* has the function above all of illustrating the infinite variety of forms of human behaviour. It is the training ground of the judgement, seen here as a faculty of moral discrimination. Since the potential discrepancy between language and moral substance (or language and action) is one of the most insistent of Montaigne's topics, it is not surprising to find that he frequently explores the relationship between an author's writings and his life. Thus in 'Un traict de quelques ambassadeurs', he claims that he pays particular attention, in a writer's works, to those matters in which the writer was expert: in this instance, an anecdote recounted by the diplomat Guillaume Du Bellay, Sieur de Langey, about the way François Ier's ambassadors reported a defiant speech by the Emperor Charles V (I.17, pp. 73–74). The principle established here is exemplified also in II.34, which analyses the superiority of Caesar's writings on war among books suitable for 'chefs de guerre'. Such instances concur with Montaigne's concern to find reliable and authoritative witnesses rather than ones who may distort their report by adding their own interpretations (see I.31, III.6).

The most characteristic examples, however, are the ones in which Montaigne infers the moral character of an author from his works, or uses external evidence to reconstruct that character and then bring it to bear on the writings. The chapter on Caesar itself contains an example of this procedure: 'il me semble lire en plusieurs de ses exploits une certaine resolution de se perdre, pour fuyr la honte d'estre vaincu' [in several of his exploits, it seems to me that I can read a certain resolution to lose his own life in order to flee the shame of being defeated] (II.34, p. 740); another occurs in 'De l'art de conferer', on Tacitus: 'Si ses ecris rapportent aucune chose de ses conditions, c'estoit un grand personnage, droicturier et courageux, non d'une vertu superstitieuse, mais philosophique et genereuse' [If his writings tell us anything about his character, he was a great man, upright and courageous, whose virtue was not over-scrupulous but philosophical and noble] (III.8, p. 942); and more fleetingly, in 'De la moderation', a poet is presumed to be suffering from sexual frustration because he tells a story of Jupiter succumbing to an unusually vigorous access of passion for his spouse Juno (I.30, p. 199). In 'De la gloire', external evidence is used to corroborate Montaigne's impression that a letter dictated by Epicurus just before his death betrays the concern for reputation which Epicurus had decried in his writings (II.16, p. 620). The principle is, of course, most acutely relevant where writers on ethics are concerned, and in 'De la colere', Montaigne not only judges the relative sincerity of Cicero, Seneca, Plutarch and others, but also describes his method explicitly: 'Je ne voy jamais autheur, mesmement de ceux qui traictent de la vertu et des offices, que je ne recherche curieusement quel il a esté' [I never read an author, particularly any of those who discuss virtue and duties, without carefully investigating what kind of a man he was] (II.31, p. 716; see also II.32).

A similar procedure is apparent in Montaigne's assessment of Amyot's translation of Plutarch at the beginning of 'A demain les affaires':

> je n'entens rien au Grec; mais je voy un sens si beau, si bien joint et entretenu par tout en sa traduction, que, ou il a certainement entendu l'imagination vraye de l'autheur, ou, ayant par longue conversation planté vivement dans son ame une generale Idée de celle de Plutarque, il ne luy a aumoins rien presté qui le desmente ou qui le desdie [...] (II.4, p. 363)

> [I understand no Greek; but I see everywhere in his translation such a beautifully coherent and sustained sense that he must either have had a secure grasp of his author's true conception or, having a general Idea of Plutarch's mind vigorously planted in his own through long converse with his text, he has at least grafted on to it nothing that betrays or contradicts him [...]]

The remark implies an acceptance of the central principle of sixteenth-century translation theory, namely, that the translator should strive to capture the author's thought or meaning rather than to produce a word-for-word version. But it also suggests that, in reading the works of a given author, Montaigne applied a criterion of internal coherence in order to determine the sense. This does not, it must be stressed, necessarily mean that he believed that literary works are only meaningful if they are wholly consistent. It will become apparent later that Montaigne was perfectly able to conceive of inconsistent or even fragmentary works (the *Essais*, for example) as having their own authenticity. But it does suggest that he believed a work to be imprinted by its author with characteristic features which, when discovered, provide the key to the reconstruction by the reader or translator of its true meaning.

As an instance of reading, the case of Amyot's Plutarch (and, it should be noted, of Montaigne's Amyot) transcends the moral domain. It does, however, fit exactly into the moralist's constant desire to discern the underlying mechanisms or patterns of human behaviour. The literary text is viewed here as the discourse of a man whose independent existence confers meaning on it; its quality is judged on the one hand by its consonance with its author's life, on the other by the extent to which it is functional in suggesting norms of moral behaviour to the reader. The reading of a text is, in this respect, parallel to the interpretation of the comportment of other people still living, except that in the latter case visible action, facial expressions and so on provide a part of the evidence. The parallel emerges with especial clarity in a passage in 'De l'experience' where Montaigne claims that his long experience in judging himself has given him a happy capacity to judge others:

> à mes amys je descouvre, par leurs productions, leurs inclinations internes; non pour renger cette infinie variété d'actions, si diverses et si descoupées, a certains genres et chapitres [...] (C) Les sçavans partent et denotent leurs fantasies plus specifiquement, et par le menu. Moy, qui ny voy qu'autant que l'usage m'en informe, sans regle, presente generalement les miennes, et à tastons. Comme en cecy: (B) je prononce ma sentence par articles descousus, ainsi que de chose qui ne se peut dire à la fois et en bloc. La relation et la conformité ne se trouvent poinct en telles ames que les nostres, basses et communes. (III.13, p. 1076)

> [I uncover in my friends, through their behaviour and actions, their internal inclinations; not in order to classify those actions, so infinitely various, so diverse and disconnected, under certain types and headings [...] (C) The learned divide up and set out their ideas more specifically and in detail. As for me, since I see in them only what custom tells me about them, following no rules, I present mine in general terms, groping my way forward. As in this book: (B) I utter my opinion in disjointed segments, as if it were something that cannot be said all at the same time and as a whole. Consistency and conformity are not to be found in minds such as ours, the low and common ones.]

By representing his interpretation metaphorically as a book explaining the 'inclinations internes' of his friends, Montaigne nicely discloses his tendency to seek a correlation between living human behaviour and written texts.

All this will, no doubt, not seem very surprising to a modern reader, who can hardly have avoided at some point using the 'life and works' approach to literature. But it is important to stress that methods of reading are not timeless and universal: they have their own history, and Montaigne is a major contributor to the success of the view of literature indicated above. If humanist readers did not themselves invent these procedures, they certainly revived them and gave them an enormous and lasting impetus at a time when quite other methods were well established.[3] The same might be said of Montaigne's exercises in 'practical criticism', the most celebrated of which are the comparison of Latin poets in 'Du jeune Caton' and the analysis of a passage from Lucretius in 'Sur des vers de Virgile'.[4] Using a metaphorical and emotive vocabulary based, initially at least, on classical Latin accounts of literary effect, Montaigne colourfully conveys his response to both subject matter and style. He is able to point with great precision to the word or phrase which determines a given effect, as well as to command the reader's assent by his strategy of carefully graded comparison. Once again, Montaigne is helping to forge a discourse of literary appraisal based on a presumption of shared good taste and fine discrimination, rather than on methodical application of rhetorical categories.

But, to return to the biographical principle, it may also be argued that the equivalence between reading texts and reading people is not as straightforward as at first appears. The passage from 'De l'experience' quoted above asserts the difficulty of making judgements which are other than piecemeal, such is the diversity and discontinuity of human behaviour. In a subsequent development, the point is made still more clearly:

> Je laisse aux artistes, et ne scay s'ils en viennent a bout en chose si meslée, si menue et fortuite, de renger en bandes cette infinie diversité de visages, et arrester nostre inconstance et la mettre par ordre. Non seulement je trouve mal-aisé d'attacher nos actions les unes aux autres, mais chacune à part soy je trouve mal-aysé de la designer proprement par quelque qualité principalle, tant elles sont doubles et bigarrées à divers lustres. (III.13, pp. 1076–77)

> [I leave it to the Masters of Arts — and I don't know whether they will succeed in something so mixed, so fine-grained and accidental — to arrange that infinite diversity of aspects sequentially, to pin down our inconstancy and impose an order on it. Not only do I find it difficult to connect our actions one with another, but I find it difficult to designate each separate one correctly by some principal quality, so ambivalent are they, so many-coloured and many-faceted.]

Montaigne's image of man as a creature of chance and circumstance, the image which dominates the celebrated opening passage of 'Du repentir', renders at least problematic the model of a text made coherent by the character of its author. Two potential exceptions are allowed: superior souls — Cato and Socrates, perhaps — unlike our 'low and common' ones, may aspire to consistency; and scholastic philosophers ('artistes') may succeed in imposing order on the wealth of human experience. But even these exceptions are suspect. The word 'artistes' strongly recalls the opposition between art and nature which is one of Montaigne's fundamental themes. 'Art' is artifice; it deals in surfaces, appearances; it is the realm of the specious.[5] Nature may have its own profound pattern; but if so, it is mostly hidden from us, and can be perceived only in glimpses, after long and cautious probing. Even the harmony of superior souls may be only an effect of art. For the most part, the phenomena of human behaviour present themselves to us discontinuously. Furthermore, whereas the circumstantial analysis of one's friends' behaviour is subject to a criterion of sorts (we can ask them if they agree), this is not the case in the reading of texts by dead authors. All we can do is examine in turn their shifting 'visages' and 'lustres', and make provisional, unresolved judgements. There can be no unequivocal guarantee for our readings.[6]

One might juxtapose with this late passage a brief chapter in Book I where Montaigne considers some of the ways in which chance can create effects of rationality or of aesthetic purpose. The theme is already elaborated with several examples in the 1580 text, but it is most pithily expressed in a late insertion: 'Semble il pas que ce soit un sort artiste? Constantin, fils d'Helene, fonda l'empire de Constantinople; et, tant de siècles après, Constantin, fils d'Helene, le finit' [Does it not seem that chance is behaving in this case like a rhetorician? Constantine, the son of Helena, founded the Empire of Constantinople; and, so many centuries later, Constantine, the son of Helena, brought it to an end] (I.34, p. 221). Once again, the effects described here are specious; they are governed by no unifying intention. But if the history of Constantinople has only a fortuitously aesthetic symmetry, might not the same be true of much historical narrative? Chance, as an artist, can rival the 'artistes' of 'De l'experience' who make neat patterns out of the confusion of actions and events. One of the most striking features of Montaigne's view of history is precisely the absence of cause-and-effect narrative, or of speculations about the necessary order of things. His reading of history is always fragmentary; episodes taken from quite different periods and national contexts are juxtaposed according to the temporary (and random) perspective of the reader. The factual status of his examples is not paramount: probability provides an adequate basis for the operation of the moralist's judgement (see the conclusion of I.21). On the other hand, not surprisingly, Montaigne tends to be suspicious of fiction. In 'De trois bonnes femmes', he condemns fiction explicitly, and suggests that it would be valuable to compose an amalgam of 'true' (i.e. plausible) stories, loosely linked like Ovid's (implausible) *Metamorphoses* (II.35, p. 749). This is, in effect, what he himself is doing in 'De trois bonnes femmes'; indeed, it is not too far removed from the character of the *Essais* as a whole. The writer, like the reader, recreates the workings of 'fortune' without too many of its miraculous coincidences.

It is clear, then, that Montaigne's practice of reading is subject to the same oscillations and apparent contradictions as his thought in general. In some contexts, the intuitive conviction of right judgement, or the sense of an underlying continuity, will predominate. In others, certainty crumbles, and the world dissolves into a heterogeneous collection of ambiguous 'visages' and 'lustres'; chance infiltrates all of our attempts to make sense of things (see the (C)-text which concludes I.47). The presence of an original, authentic intention which stabilizes the meaning of any text is always presupposed, and may in some cases be uncovered with confidence; on the other hand, the reader — and above all perhaps the discerning reader — will often find a text to be elusive and equivocal, hiding its true intention and thus giving rise to many possible reconstructions.

A group of passages may be taken to illustrate briefly the consequences of this uncertainty. The earliest is a 1580 passage in 'Des livres', where Montaigne blames the weakness of his judgement when he is unable to discern the value of one of Plato's dialogues:

Il s'en prend à soy, et se condamne, ou de s'arrester à l'escorce, ne pouvant

> penetrer jusques au fons, ou de regarder la chose par quelque faux lustre [...]
> Il pense donner juste interpretation aux apparences que sa conception luy
> presente; mais elles sont imbecilles et imparfaictes. (II.10, p. 410)

> [It blames and condemns itself, either for stopping at the outer shell, incapable
> of piercing through to the essence, or for considering the question from some
> false angle [...] It thinks it is giving a correct interpretation of the appearances
> that its conception presents to it, but they are feeble and imperfect.]

In this instance, the hidden value is guaranteed by the reputation of the author, and
the reader's interpretation is considered defective. Also in the (A)-text, but greatly
elaborated after 1588, is an application to reading of the sceptical arguments of the
'Apologie de Raimond Sebond': 'il n'est aucun sens ny visage, ou droict, ou amer,
ou doux, ou courbe, que l'esprit humain ne trouve aux escrits qu'il entreprend de
fouiller' [there is no meaning or angle of vision, whether straight or bitter or sweet
or curving, that the human mind cannot find in the writings that it undertakes
to explore] (II.12, p. 585). The difficulty of grasping the true sense of Scripture
is presented as a first example, followed by the ambiguity of oracles and 'fables
divinatrices' [prophetic myths]; subsequently, a (C)-text, embroidering on a reference
to Homer in the 1580 version, asks whether Homer could possibly have intended
all the meanings attributed to him by different readers.[7] The argument as a whole
is designed to show that we perceive everything in our own terms, that we read
into texts meanings which suit our own preoccupations and meet our own needs.

A slightly different account of the problem of over-interpretation is given in
the opening pages of 'De l'experience'. Here the target is the mania for writing
interpretative commentaries, setting in train an infinite regression from the original
sense of the text: 'Nous ne faisons que nous entregloser' [All we do is gloss one
another] (III.13, p. 1069). It is a celebrated passage, requiring no further analysis here.[8]
Together with the examples from 'Des livres' and the 'Apologie', it demonstrates
that Montaigne was sharply conscious of the apparently infinite capacity of a text
for generating meanings. The tone is pejorative in every case: these supplementary
meanings are said to be spurious and even pernicious (in the case of Scripture). But
it should be remembered that Montaigne's negative arguments are seldom a blind
alley. They have a habit of opening up avenues in unexpectedly positive directions.

In 'Divers evenemens de mesme conseil' (and already in the (A)-text), the
argument that works of art owe much to fortune is sketched out. A mild irony
towards artists is apparent here, as in 'La fortune se rencontre souvent au train de la
raison' (I.34; cf. also III.8, p. 927), but the conclusion of the passage turns the irony
to the advantage of the reader:

> la fortune montre bien encores plus evidemment la part qu'elle a en tous ces
> ouvrages, par les graces et beautez qui s'y treuvent, non seulement sans l'in-
> tention, mais sans la cognoissance mesme de l'ouvrier. Un suffisant lecteur
> descouvre souvant ès escrits d'autruy des perfections autres que celles que
> l'autheur y a mises et apperceües, et y preste des sens et des visages plus riches.[9]

> [Fortune reveals still more clearly her share in all these works by the strokes of
> elegance and beauty that they contain, not only without the intention but even
> without the knowledge of the author. A competent reader often finds in other

people's writings brilliant qualities other than those that the writer put there
and was aware of, and richer meanings and aspects.]

Here it is the capable reader, not the inadequate one, who discovers in a text
meanings other than those the author put there. The vocabulary is markedly
positive ('suffisant', 'perfections', 'plus riches'): the imaginative reader can make
capital out of chance. Likewise, in 'De l'institution des enfans', a post-1588 addition
develops Montaigne's earlier assertion that history should not be learnt but judged
by suggesting that this is the subject 'à laquelle nos esprits s'appliquent de plus diverse
mesure. J'ay leu en Tite-Live cent choses que tel n'y a pas leu, Plutarque en y a leu
cent, outre ce que j'y ay sceu lire, et, à l'adventure, outre ce que l'autheur y avoit
mis' [to which our mind applies itself in the most diverse measure. I have read in
Livy hundreds of things that someone else didn't read, Plutarch has read hundreds
more than I could, and, perhaps, more than the author had put there] (I.26, p. 156).
Montaigne is here claiming to be a 'suffisant lecteur', while acknowledging that
Plutarch can do even better.

Thus the plurality of readings to which texts can be subjected may appear as
a rich and fertile phenomenon. It is worth recalling here that earlier humanists
had taken the view that privileged texts such as the Bible or Homer's epics are
infinitely pregnant with meaning. Erasmus asserts (following Augustine) that, even
if a meaning was not certainly intended by God, it is valid, provided always that it
is consonant with evangelical doctrine and the rule of faith. Montaigne, too, has
his criterion of validity, although it is secular rather than sacred. It is clear from
his practice of interpretation, if not from his overt statements, that any reading is
acceptable if it is profitable to the reader, that is to say if it prompts self-awareness or
helps to train the judgement. In other words — and here we return to Montaigne's
extension of the humanist doctrine of imitation — the coherence of an individual's
reading materials lies ultimately in their application to his own character and
circumstances, rather than to those of the defunct author. No doubt he will
attempt to judge other writers through and in their works, just as he will attempt
to judge his contemporaries through their speech and actions; but the appropriation
and digestion of all these materials for his own benefit remains his primary aim.
Speaking of the way a teacher should ideally instruct his pupil, Montaigne says:

> Qu'il ne luy demande pas seulement compte des mots de sa leçon, mais du sens
> et de la substance, et qu'il juge du profit qu'il aura fait, non par le tesmoignage
> de sa memoire, mais de sa vie. Que ce qu'il viendra d'apprendre, il le lui face
> mettre en cent visages et accommoder à autant de divers subjets, pour voir s'il
> l'a encore bien pris et bien faict sien. (I.26, p. 151)

> [Let him demand from him an account not only of the words of his reading,
> but of its meaning and substance, and let him judge the profit he has drawn
> from it by the testimony not of his memory, but of his life. Let him get him
> to put what he has just learnt into a hundred different perspectives and adapt
> it to as many diverse subjects to see if he has yet grasped it aright and made it
> fully his own.]

This principle governs the whole field of reading as envisaged by Montaigne.

The *Essais* and their reader

The way in which Montaigne presents his own readings in the *Essais* is an important aspect of the way in which he presents his text as a whole to be read by others: indeed, there are few works in which the problems of reading so clearly have this double character. It is as if the text were situated exactly at the mid-point between the writings it echoes and its potential readers, looking in both directions simultaneously; or as if it were the catalyst in a chain reaction which displayed some of the characteristics of reading and re-reading as a perennial activity.[10]

Broadly speaking, Montaigne's directions to the reader, whether explicit or implicit, may be divided into two categories. The first consists of those which bear on the response to the book as a whole, and in particular on the notion of a self-portrait; the second, of those concerning meaning and form in the *Essais*, the intellectual and aesthetic character of the text. In one case, Montaigne speaks as a man exposing himself, with some irony and not a little anxiety, to the public gaze; in the other, he draws attention to features of his writing such as digression, ellipsis, obscurity, obliqueness, in order to encourage an intelligent and productive reading of his text.[11]

The reader's attitude to the 1580 edition is of course most cogently affected by the preface 'Au lecteur', a text which may be regarded as a sharply ironic extension of the 'humility *topos*',[12] by means of which the author disclaims any lofty ambitions for his book. Erasmus's *Praise of Folly* had been presented in this way, as the work of idle moments spent on a journey to England; Du Bellay's *Regrets*, too, are proffered in this spirit. The *topos* is not meant to be taken literally: it is above all a generic indication, assigning the work loosely to the domain of satire, miscellanies, epistles and the like. It may be particularly useful in an age of repressive censorship, where the author may thus conventionally avoid being read as a serious contributor to theological or political debate; in Montaigne, it rather has the function of excluding the text from the realm of systematic philosophical or pedagogical writing, and distracting attention from what is said to the way it is said. When in the concluding sentence Montaigne tells his readers that they needn't waste their time on the *Essais*, he is attempting to discourage, not all readings, but conventional or pedantic readings.

Even when one takes account of the crucial reference in it to self-portraiture, the preface as a whole has a primarily emblematic function: it is designed to indicate the angle from which the text should be viewed, rather than to give a literal account of its contents.[13] In order to test this, one need only attempt to read the first twenty or so chapters of the 1580 version as if one had never seen the preface or the later versions, as if Montaigne had never said 'Ainsi, lecteur, je suis moy-mesmes la matiere de mon livre' [Thus, reader, I am myself the subject matter of my book] (I, 'Au lecteur', p. 3). Once readers have been given appropriate instructions, they will compose the 'self-portrait' for themselves as they read; if they — like many of the book's earlier readers — ignore the instructions, they will no doubt treat the *Essais* as a more or less attractively composed miscellany.

The reader's construction of the self-portrait will consist in giving special attention to the writer's first-person observations, whether in the form of opinions, self-analysis, or familiar anecdote, and however sporadic they may be. Passages which echo the preface, such as the extended development in 'Du dementir' on the *Essais* as a memento for friends, will appear as particularly significant and serve to reinforce the construction. Widely scattered passages will have to be drawn together and treated as parts of a coherent whole. Chapters like 'De l'amitié', 'De l'exercitation', 'De la præsumption', will be singled out as focal points and their themes extrapolated to give meaning to other quite different chapters. My point here is not that the notion of the self-portrait is less significant than is normally believed, nor that one is mistaken in accepting Montaigne's instruction to read the *Essais* as if its author were the 'matter of his book'. I would simply insist that the participation of readers, their collusion with the author, is an indispensable factor in the elaboration of such a reading.

In the later editions, the perspective is somewhat different. The project of self-portraiture is now clearly formulated in advance and will determine major features of presentation such as the placing of 'De l'experience' at the end as a final conspectus of the self-portrait, or the inclusion of a chapter ('Sur des vers de Virgile') which seems to put into practice Montaigne's remark in 'Au lecteur' that he would have liked to present himself naked to the reader. The author's habits, tastes and experiences become a much more pervasive theme of the book, infiltrating the chapters of the 1580 edition in order to create a retrospective unity. Furthermore, by 1588 Montaigne knew that the *Essais* were a success: the earlier editions had been widely read and had already conferred a degree of fame on their author.

The image of the *Essais* as a 'private' text presented to a circle of intimates persists, but its figurative character becomes increasingly evident:

> J'escris mon livre à peu d'hommes et à peu d'années. Si ç'eust esté une matiere de durée, il l'eust fallu commettre à un langage plus ferme [...] Pourtant ne crains-je poinct d'y inserer plusieurs articles privez, qui consument leur usage entre les hommes qui vivent aujourd'huy, et qui touchent la particuliere science d'aucuns, qui y verront plus avant que de la commune intelligence. (III.9, p. 982)

> [I write my book for few people and few years. If its subject had been a lasting one, I would have had to cast it in a more durable language [...] I am therefore not afraid to insert into it a number of private matters that will use up their currency among those who are alive today and that touch on the particular knowledge of certain people, who will see more there than is possible for people of common understanding.]

This special group of readers now diminishes almost to vanishing point amid the public at large, a public whose anonymity appears at times as a source of anxiety for the writer: in 'Consideration sur Ciceron', having said that he might have published his thoughts in letter form if he had had someone 'à qui parler', he continues: 'J'eusse esté plus attentif et plus seur, ayant une addresse forte et amie, que je ne suis, regardant les divers visages d'un peuple' [If I had had someone to write for to whom I was strongly attached, I would have been more attentive and more confident than I am, confronting as I must the different gazes of a public audience] (I.40, p. 252). The need to assess the function and value of self-portraiture at this level becomes much more acute: the difficulty of the enterprise, its bizarre and extravagant character, the good faith of the writer and his trust in the reader's judgement, the writer's admission of his own fluctuating judgement of his book — all of these are signs to the reader that normal reading habits are inadequate here. Even the pronouncements which would seem to emerge from the depths of the author's psyche — 'Je suis affamé de me faire connoistre' [I am hungry to make myself known], 'je crains mortellement d'estre pris en eschange' [I am mortally afraid of being taken for something other than I am] (III.5, p. 847) — may also be taken as provocative signals, alerting readers to the singularity of the enterprise, and inviting them to understand it as a probing reassessment of the nature of self-knowledge. Thus, when Montaigne says that he hopes his book may attract to him, during his lifetime, a new friend who shares his 'humours', and who will be in complete sympathy with him, he is offering an emblem of the perfect reader, who is also a rare (if not non-existent) reader (III.9, p. 981). This imaginary figure would no doubt play the role assigned to Montaigne's lost friend La Boétie, with whom he claimed to enjoy mutual comprehension (I.28). Once again, Montaigne is no longer writing for the figure of a casual friend or relative. His book invites the reader to separate himself or herself from the anonymous crowd by the application to the text of an especially rigorous and sustained insight. A singular reader is required for this singular enterprise.

Many other features of the book may be seen as inviting his readers, however obliquely, to reflect on their own status and attitude. Montaigne is acutely sensitive to the ways in which language is proffered and received: he writes about conversation, oratory, storytelling, lying, diplomacy, letter-writing, eye-witness reports and above all, of course, *essai*-writing. The treatment of such themes helps the reader to clarify the view that should be adopted of the equivocations and para-doxes which are endemic in the *Essais*: they motivate the use of a mode of writing which might otherwise seem gratuitously elusive. Or again, the passages in which Montaigne refers now to his cultivation of solitude, now to his sociability and love of conversation (see especially III.3 and III.8), provide a framework within which the reader may comprehend the presentation of a highly personal book for public consumption. When at the end of 'De trois commerces' Montaigne says that he returns to his books as his most faithful friends, he is not excluding his own reader; on the contrary, he is endorsing precisely the activity that his reader is engaged in.

While waiting for the ideal reader, Montaigne himself reads and re-reads the *Essais*. This activity appears in the same light as his reading of other books in at least one important respect: just as he forgets where he has found his quotations and examples, or fails to discover on re-reading the qualities of a book he once found attractive, so in reviewing his own text the original meaning may escape him:

> (B) En mes escris mesmes je ne retrouve pas tousjours l'air de ma premiere imagination; je ne sçay ce que j'ay voulu dire, et m'eschaude souvent à corriger et y mettre un nouveau sens, pour avoir perdu le premier, qui valloit mieux. (II.12, p. 566; see also I.10, p. 40)

> [Even in my writings I cannot always rediscover the character of my original thought; I don't know what I meant to say, and I often expend my energies in correcting and adding a new meaning because I've lost the first, which was worth more.]

These passages form a complex variant of the rule according to which a reader may legitimately find more in a text than the author was conscious of inserting. In one sense, the notion of an original 'correct' sense is preserved; but the author's own loss of contact with that sense, its appropriation by other readers who can quote Montaigne to himself or tell him what he meant, calls into question the very notion of a single correct sense. Perhaps the first sense was already a particular reading, to which the author brought his own momentary preoccupations, and which was dissipated as the author–reader shifted his perspective. There would thus be no moment of perfect unity of text and meaning, presided over by a god-like author, only a set of words that can be read in various different ways by different readers.

No doubt Montaigne does not go quite as far as this. But the equivalence between writer and reader which at certain moments he is prepared to entertain is none the less striking. As will shortly become apparent, it might seem to invite the reader reciprocally to 'rewrite' the text. For the moment, however, one may observe from the second passage quoted that Montaigne's reading of the *Essais* is intimately linked with his own rewriting of the text. He claims on more than one occasion that he never corrects the *Essais*, only adds to them (II.37, p. 758; III.9, p. 962). But this is not quite true, even in the literal sense: minor alterations, over and above the verbal adjustments demanded by the insertion of a new development, are quite frequent (one of the disadvantages of the modern 'three-layer' presentation of the text is that it obscures them).

More centrally, the addition of new material can and does affect the meaning. In 'Du parler prompt ou tardif', the writer's own spontaneity in speech or writing is never directly mentioned in the (A)-text. It is perhaps hinted at in 'Je cognois, par experience, cette condition de nature' [I know by experience that natural disposition] (I.10, p. 40), but this could equally be a reference to his experience of others. A (B)-text inserted immediately before the final sentence attaches the topic unambiguously to the first person singular, and in the process shifts the balance of the preceding passage from observation of others to personal experience; furthermore, it adds a new charge of irony to the final sentence: the reader is in this version made acutely conscious that the writer gives oral spontaneity priority over the more laborious and 'prepared' mode of writing. The (C)-addition which imposes a new ending on the chapter picks up the theme of writing and twists it in an unexpected direction: the reader in person appears on the stage as the 'estranger' who may more easily recognize Montaigne's meaning than Montaigne himself. The result (for the reader who can identify the three layers) is a complex interaction between the first text, Montaigne's rewritings, and the explicit theme of the author's discontinuous self-reading. Similar effects may be observed throughout the *Essais*, although not always with this degree of overt reflection on the processes involved.

We must turn now to the way in which the *Essais* characterize the intellectual problems of reading, the kind of attention it demands of the reader. Montaigne's preferred discourse is one which discards theoretical preambles, prefatory apostrophes and rhetorical padding, and in consequence requires an alert reader:

> Je veux qu'on commence par le dernier point [...] il ne me faut point d'alechement
> ny de sause: je menge bien la viande toute crue; et, au lieu de m'esguiser l'apetit

broken down and adapted to the individual's needs. Montaigne wants his reader
to pay attention in order to see that the *Essais* are not just another amalgam of
auctoritates.

This passage from 'De la vanité' implies, then, that the *Essais* are ultimately
coherent, even if their coherence has to be reconstructed by the reader. In a rich
(C)-passage from 'Consideration sur Ciceron', the density and discontinuity of the
text are presented from a somewhat different angle:

> Si suis je trompé, si guere d'autres donnent plus à prendre en la matiere; et,
> comment que ce soit, mal ou bien, si nul escrivain l'a semée ny guere plus
> materielle ny au moins plus drue en son papier. Pour en ranger davantage, je
> n'entasse que les testes. Que j'y attache leur suitte, je multiplieray plusieurs fois
> ce volume. Et combien y ay-je espandu d'histoires qui ne disent mot, lesquelles
> qui voudra esplucher un peu ingenieusement, en produira infinis Essais. (I.40,
> p. 251)

> [And I am much mistaken if many others provide more to get hold of in their
> subject matter; and, however it may come out, for good or ill, if any writer has
> scattered it on his paper more substantially or at least more thickly. In order to
> get more in, I only heap up the headings. If I attached the rest, I would multiply
> the size of this volume several times over. And how many anecdotes have I
> poured out that remain silent, whereas if someone wanted to interpret them
> with a little subtlety, they would produce an infinite number of Essais.]

This striking image of the almost infinite extensibility of the *Essais* in the reader's
hands is closely bound up with the function of Montaigne's *exempla,* quotations and
citations, as the continuation makes clear:

> Ny elles, ny mes allegations ne servent pas tousjours simplement d'exemple,
> d'authorité ou d'ornement. Je ne les regarde pas seulement par l'usage que j'en
> tire. Elles portent souvent, hors de mon propos, la semence d'une matiere plus
> riche et plus hardie [...]

> [Neither they nor my citations always serve merely as an example, a source of
> authority or an ornament. I don't consider them only in terms of the use I make
> of them. The often carry, beyond my purpose, the seeds of a richer and bolder
> subject matter [...]]

The 'borrowed' elements, then, instead of referring back to an authoritative
corpus, become the seedbed of new and unforeseen meanings to be generated by
the reader.[14] Likewise, the discontinuous, densely packed fragments of Montaigne's
own text as a whole — which of course includes all the *exempla* and quotations —
signal, as it were, not to one another but to other invisible texts and contexts in the
reader's mind.[15]

We thus come to the point at which the *Essais* move beyond the writer's control.
The image of the self-portrait now begins to dissolve, since the perfect reader is the
one who, in following the traces of the self-portrait and understanding their function,
learns that whatever of value is to be gained from the text must be organized in
terms of his or her own experience, not Montaigne's. The sceptical argument of the
'Apologie', it will be recalled, proposes that meaning is the product of the reader's
subjective awareness rather than an essence residing in the text. In 'De l'experience',

the point is more moderately, but still very strikingly, put in the formulation 'La parole est moitié à celuy qui parle, moitié à celuy qui l'escoute' [Language belongs half to the speaker, half to the listener] (III.13, p. 1088). Whether expressed in terms of a dialogue or of an extension or regeneration of meaning, this theme is one which allows for a dynamic and expansive conception of the act of reading. The text remains perpetually an open question; the reader embarks on an endless quest.

The writer's intermediary role between his readings and his readers is powerfully embodied in a reworking, in the 'Apologie', of the commonplace image of the bear that licks its young into shape:

> les sciences et les arts ne se jettent pas en moule, ains se forment et figurent peu à peu en les maniant et pollissant à plusieurs fois, comme les ours façonnent leurs petits en les lechant à loisir: ce que ma force ne peut descouvrir, je ne laisse pas de le sonder et essayer; et, en retastant et petrissant cette nouvelle matiere, la remuant et l'eschaufant, j'ouvre à celuy qui me suit quelque facilité pour en jouir plus à son ayse, et la luy rends plus souple et plus maniable.[16]

> [the sciences and the arts are not cast in a mould; they are rather formed and shaped gradually by being handled and polished time and time again, as bears fashion their young by assiduous licking: when my powers cannot uncover something, I don't stop probing and testing it; and, as I mould and knead this new material, working it and warming it, I give those who follow me a better chance of enjoying it at their leisure; I make it more supple and easier for them to handle.]

The communication between writer and reader is part of a chain of metamorphoses; meaning passes along the chain as one text after another assembles itself, then disintegrates to be reassembled in a new form by a new generation.[17]

The topic of reading opens an avenue of approach to all of the central features of the *Essais*: their sources, themes, structure and style, their character as a self-portrait, their literary self-consciousness, as well as the question of the reader's image as projected by the text. One might even say that the intrinsic interest of Montaigne's book is more intimately bound up with the question of what reading is and how it is done than with any other. And if reading is, for Montaigne, always a stage to be transcended, we as readers are none the less incessantly drawn back to the *Essais* in an attempt to make visible the linking thread (see below, pp. 39–40, 45).

When regarded in a historical context, the fact that Montaigne should have reflected at such length and in such complex ways on the problems of reading is in itself of considerable importance. The gradual fragmentation and dissolution of the humanist ideal of an encyclopaedia of knowledge based on classical literature and thought may be perceived at an advanced stage in the *Essais;* at the same time, questions of the utmost historical significance — the status of 'authorities', the relationship between a text and its gloss, the capacity of a text for generating an indefinite range of meanings — re-emerge in Montaigne's writing in a literary form which changes their character. The change, it may be argued, had been anticipated by Erasmus, Rabelais and others; the Renaissance love of dialogue, enigma, paradox, emblems and adages provides many of the threads that Montaigne wove into his contexture. But the fluidity of the *Essais*, their intrinsic capacity for revealing different aspects of a topic and suggesting far more than are revealed, goes beyond anything one finds in Montaigne's forerunners.

Likewise, the acute and many-sided view the *Essais* give of reading as a pre-eminently difficult activity (while yet not a metaphysically obscure one) would be hard to match from any work, ancient or modern. Perhaps only Pascal has in this respect ever taken Montaigne up at his own pitch. Modern theorists would no doubt have little difficulty in detecting inconsistencies and deficiencies in Montaigne's account: he does not, for example, fully face the problem of where, if texts can be re-read and reinterpreted indefinitely, we draw the line between legitimate and illegitimate readings. How far is the original, intended sense recoverable, and if at all recoverable, how far does it determine the limits of what a text can mean? But, once again, Montaigne is not a theorist. What the *Essais* demand is not passive assent to a set of propositions or to a body of doctrine, but active engagement: they define their readers by manipulating and provoking them, by pre-empting their role. It is in this sense that the *Essais* invite nothing less than a reassessment of the whole activity of reading.

Notes

1. The letters (A), (B) and (C) refer to the three main strata of the *Essais* according to the chronology of their composition: all text following (A) was present in the first edition of the work (1580); text marked (B) first appeared in the 1588 edition; text marked (C) was added subsequently.
2. See for example II.17, p. 637; III.12, p. 1056.
3. I am thinking here of allegorical commentary as practised in both the Middle Ages and the Renaissance; also of rhetorical analysis: cf. 'Du jeune Caton' (I.37, p. 231), where Montaigne speaks dismissively of judging poetry 'par les preceptes et par art'.
4. I.37, pp. 231–32; III.5, pp. 872–73. Cf. also the judgements Montaigne makes in 'Des livres' (II.10, *passim*). Richard Sayce, *The Essays of Montaigne: A Critical Exploration* (London: Weidenfeld and Nicholson, 1972), pp. 46–49, and Dorothy Gabe Coleman, *The Gallo-Roman Muse* (Cambridge: Cambridge University Press, 1979), especially pp. 163–65, discuss Montaigne's practical criticism.
5. Cf. III.5, p. 874: 'Si j'estois du mestier [sc. speculative philosophy], je naturaliserois l'art autant comme ils artialisent la nature'; also III.12, p. 1056: 'Nous autres naturalistes estimons qu'il y aie grande et incomparable preferance de l'honneur de l'invention à l'honneur de l'allegation', where 'naturalistes' implies 'artistes' as its antithesis.
6. Note that in I.38 Montaigne argues against the naïve assumption that human responses are coherent and consistent: it is possible, he suggests, to feel two different emotions simultaneously, as one perceives two different aspects of a given situation.
7. This passage should be compared with Rabelais's questioning of Homer's allegorical intention in the prologue to *Gargantua*.
8. This passage, and Montaigne's view of interpretation in general, are intelligently discussed by Steven Rendall in '*Mus in pice*: Montaigne and Interpretation', *Modern Language Notes*, 94 (1979), 1056–71; see also the same author's *Distinguo: Reading Montaigne Differently* (Oxford: Clarendon Press, 1992). I have myself given a more detailed account than is possible here in *The Cornucopian Text*, pp. 313–20.
9. I.24, p. 127. See Michel Charles, *Rhétorique de la lecture* (Paris: Seuil, 1977), pp. 289–90, for a detailed analysis of this passage.
10. The section that follows develops in greater detail certain of the points in the section 'Montaigne and reading' above, pp. 14–18.
11. A brief sketch of the first of these topics will be found in Hugo Friedrich, *Montaigne*, trans. by Robert Rovini (Paris: Gallimard, 1968; German original, Berne: Francke, 1949), pp. 331–34; it is usually dealt with as a secondary aspect of self-portraiture in the *Essais*. The second topic is

dealt with by Sayce, Friedrich, Coleman and others in the context of Montaigne's use of form and style. My purpose here is to show how far the two domains are linked when seen from the point of view of the reader (or, more precisely, Montaigne's image of the reader).

12. For a comparison between Montaigne's and Horace's use of this device, see Coleman, *The Gallo-Roman Muse*, pp. 116–34.

13. Cf. the concluding section of II.37, addressed to Madame de Duras, which acts as an epilogue to the 1580 edition, complementing the preface.

14. Note that appropriate readers are subsequently specified as 'ceux qui rencontrent mon air' — those who will abound in Montaigne's sense, one presumes, rather than imposing alien constructions of their own. McKinley, *Words in a Corner*, treats the whole question of quotation in the light of Montaigne's conception of the 'diligent lecteur'; for further remarks on quotation, see above, pp. 14–16, and below, 'Thinking with commonplaces', pp. 39–40. For a detailed account of Montaigne's practice of quotation, see the full version of the present essay in *Montaigne: Essays in Memory of Richard Sayce*, ed. by I. D. McFarlane and Ian Maclean (Oxford: Clarendon Press, 1982), pp. 133–66 (pp. 144–53).

15. Montaigne here applies to the *Essais* a view of reading he had earlier recommended as suitable for Plutarch: 'il guigne seulement du doigt par où nous irons, s'il nous plaist, et se contente quelquefois de ne donner qu'une attainte dans le plus vif d'un propos. Il les [sc. the more condensed passages] faut arracher de là et mettre en place marchande' (I.26, p. 156). See also the earlier part of this passage, quoted above, p. 27.

16. II.12, p. 560. McKinley (*Words in a Corner*, pp. 20–26) points out the allusion to the story of Pygmalion implied by this passage and by the quotation from Ovid's *Metamorphoses* which immediately follows it.

17. A striking example is provided by the series of sentences discussed above, pp. 15–16, and below, pp. 139–40, where Pascal echoes Montaigne who echoes Seneca on the question of the appropriation of material from other writers.

§3

Thinking with Commonplaces:
The Example of Rabelais

We have come a long way in the understanding of the commonplace culture of the early modern period since the pioneering work of Ernst Robert Curtius.[1] A quarter of a century ago, Walter J. Ong could still deplore the absence of a study 'situating the commonplace tradition in the broader perspectives of noetic history';[2] his own brief sketch of such a study has now been amply replaced by Ann Moss's *Commonplace Books and the Structuring of Renaissance Thought*,[3] and negative assumptions of the kind still common when Ong wrote his article are now happily rare.[4] Despite these advances, it remains difficult for us to evaluate, even to *read* commonplace as a feature of individual texts. The difficulty is historical but also aesthetic, and it resides in the space between two theoretical polarities: commonplace may be perceived, on the one hand, as a dead place from which all meaning has been drained by constant use or, on the other, as a repository of authoritative knowledge or wisdom.[5]

This essay will first review the different ways in which meaning can be attributed to commonplace, both as a broad cultural phenomenon and as a feature of particular texts; it will then consider some of the ways in which commonplace materials function in one such text which belongs neither to the realm of pedagogy, nor to that of the faculty disciplines (theology, law, medicine), nor again to that of poetry or rhetoric, but to the in-between domain of a fictional discourse where instances of *doxa* emerge tantalizingly, as if pointing towards some ultimate truth, only to disappear again before they have had time to establish themselves. It must be admitted that the text in question — that of François Rabelais — is so particular as to be positively idiosyncratic. It is, however, undeniably a historical phenomenon, an object belonging to early modern history, and thus potentially bearing witness to that history; and it is a test-case, not because it represents the generality, but precisely because, by skewing the general pattern in unexpected ways, it reveals aspects of commonplace culture that might well remain hidden in other texts. It thus functions like a cloud chamber rendering visible the passage of a reality (an 'experience', one might say) too remote to be grasped directly.

In tracing the sedimentation of classical *topoi* in medieval Latin culture and their transmission thence to early modern and modern European culture, Curtius was concerned solely with a phenomenon of literary history. He did not seek to interpret this phenomenon as an indicator of deep changes at the level of what later historians called *mentalité* or *epistêmê*, nor was he even interested in the change from script to print. The same is true of R. R. Bolgar's seminal work on the techniques of transmission elaborated by Renaissance humanists, the *copia* method and the 'copy-book' in their many and various forms. Whatever one thinks of Ong's McLuhan-inspired notion of the technological and cognitive shift brought about by the advent of print culture, it is to Ong that we owe the first serious attempt to interpret the Renaissance obsession with the gathering and classification of commonplaces in terms of a long-term anthropological-historical perspective. Rather than just a pedagogical device (although it was certainly also that), the compilation of *topoi* becomes in that perspective a core activity of human cultural evolution, simultaneously preserving, recycling, extending and reassessing a corpus of potentially usable data. As Moss's book confirms, the present-day electronic revolution makes us particularly sensitive to those activities and to the way they can be transformed by technological change. But while a history in the *longue durée* mode may afford understanding of the phenomenon as a whole, it does not necessarily resolve the question of how one reads particular uses of commonplace materials. A *moyenne durée* perspective would stress the horizon of expectation of readers innocent of our obsession with originality and for whom the recognition of commonplaces was potentially both an aesthetic and a cognitive pleasure; and we have certainly become proficient, in the last half-century, at identifying *topoi* in Renaissance texts, no doubt discovering aesthetic and cognitive pleasures of our own in the process. Yet this too has its limitations. Ong's analysis of a Shakespeare sonnet in his article 'Commonplace Rhapsody' boils down in the end to a list of epithets Shakespeare arguably 'borrowed' from Ravisius Textor or a similar source. Of course, in the reading of a poem as of any text viewed in its literary aspect, the assimilation and recognition of a commonplace lexis is a primary and indispensable move. Once one knows the lexis, one becomes sensitive to all kinds of inflections and micro-variations, just as one needs to learn the idiom of late Renaissance music in order to hear what Lassus or Gabrieli or Monteverdi does with that idiom. Yet it is clear that such familiarization can be no more than the starting point of an interpretative enquiry.

Since Ong's article was published, considerable progress has been made in this direction, primarily by scholars working within the wider field of *imitatio*. One model for a more nuanced assessment of the ways in which a *topos* may be appropriated was offered by Thomas M. Greene, who distinguished, in his seminal study *The Light in Troy*, between four modes of *imitatio* ranging from respectful citation to antagonistic reaction or parodic distortion.[6] The precise borderlines between these categories are less important here than the principle of a virtual range of functions. Similarly, Antoine Compagnon's *La Seconde Main* brought into focus in a different segment of texts crucial distinctions between citation (*allégation*), quotation (*citation*) and what Montaigne refers to as his *emprunts*;[7] Compagnon also traces a history of such practices in which the relation to authority implied by citation is progressively eroded and the writing subject assumes responsibility for everything that it writes.

In any such history, Montaigne is likely to figure as a central point of reference: he after all famously (and of course ironically) characterized his *Essais* as a *florilège*, an 'amas de fleurs estrangeres' for which he had only supplied the binding thread.[8] Sensitive work has been done on the relation between his quotations and their context,[9] while André Tournon has not only shown the importance for an understanding of the *Essais* of contemporary practices of legal commentary, but also argued that the Montaignian *essai* may be regarded as a productive transformation of the Pyrrhonian notion of a perpetual enquiry (a 'zététique').[10] In this last instance, a 'commonplace-book' becomes an indefinitely extensible horizon within which fragments of stored potential wisdom, juxtaposed with materials from the writer's own experience, remain perpetually in suspense according to the Pyrrhonian principle of *epochê*.

Yet even with these refined instruments of analysis at their disposal, scholars remain divided on certain of the most fundamental questions raised by the use of commonplace materials, and in particular on the question of conviction or belief. When Montaigne rehearses the orthodox *topoi* of Christian faith, is he presenting his readers with a statement of a deeply held position? When Ronsard deploys classical *topoi* implying the permanence of matter or the immanence of divinity in the world, is he indulging in a provocative use of poetic ornament or something more? That such essentialist questions can never be finally answered is undeniable, but it does not necessarily follow that the questions are invalid. Some answers, at least, can be shown with reasonable certainty to be wrong or at the very least highly implausible; others stand up to a greater or lesser extent to the test of iterability (they work well in different contexts and for different bodies of material), or of interpretative reach (they account satisfactorily for many features of a given text or group of texts).

In texts falling within the disciplines of theology, law and medicine, or in pre-Cartesian philosophical writing, where debate over commonplaces is conducted formally and professionally, the problem is much reduced, since in most cases their authors are overtly professing opinions or convictions. Inherited formulas are here of the essence, even if they are amended or challenged, as is shown by the emergence in the sixteenth century of collections of paradoxes (in the strict sense of propositions running counter to the *doxa* on a given question).[11] The paradox is, as it were, the negative *alter ego* of the commonplace.

Even here, however, the long-term rise and fall of what one might call a culture of the commonplace reveals a problem that progressively proves unmanageable: the increasingly labyrinthine modes of organization of the commonplace-book itself are attempts to handle an exponential proliferation of possible opinions and observations. The *doxa* is no longer a reasonably stable store either of garnered lore and wisdom, or of authoritative professional opinion, but a potential breeding ground for the unorthodox and the heterodox. This is the phenomenon to which the *Essais* bear such eloquent witness, and which will be countered in the seventeenth century by assertions of the need for a radical clean sweep. When Fontenelle, writing in 1688, optimistically predicts the rapid progress of human knowledge and addresses the problem of potential overload by positing a parallel development of method, he is of course referring not to the invention of new indexes for commonplace-books but to the refinement of Cartesian method.[12] Thereafter, and despite some notorious counter-examples (Bayle is one), philosophies and systems of discursive knowledge will become less radically open and plural, and consequently more susceptible of univocal interpretation.

Meanwhile, over a period of at least a hundred and fifty years, texts that we regard as primarily literary exhibit in a dazzling variety of ways the phenomenon of doxological fragmentation and — where assertions of conviction or belief or their opposite emerge amid the stream of fragments — a capacity to leave unsatisfied the most energetically pursued hermeneutic enquiries. In the 1660s and 1670s, La Rochefoucauld's book of *Maximes*, with its teasingly condensed encapsulations of *doxa* and paradox, could be said to be a late example of this phenomenon; so could Molière's comedies, where the voice of the so-called *raisonneur* reiterates prudential commonplaces in opposition to what are often themselves deformed commonplaces (Arnolphe's moralizing discourse, the Jesuitical arguments of Tartuffe, the discourse of the doctors and of Argan himself in *Le Malade imaginaire*), or paradoxes (*Dom Juan*), or again commonplaces exacerbated to the point of paradox (*Le Misanthrope*).

Let us now return to an earlier phase — before Molière, and before Montaigne — when the fervour for commonplace 'rhapsodizing' (as Ong calls it, evoking the etymological sense of 'rhapsody' as a 'sewing together') was still new and creative, the age of Erasmus and of Ravisius Textor himself. Rabelais's comic narratives seem at times to be the fictional equivalent of a commonplace-book, an encyclopaedic gathering of references, quotations, legal, medical and theological citations, classical anecdotes and *exempla*, Biblical allusions, adages, proverbial sayings and popular stories. Gargantua and (especially) Pantagruel, with their omnivorous appetites, are the primary vehicles of this material, although other characters, as well as the narrator himself, provide plenty of their own. The overlapping of oral, manuscript and print cultures is also highly visible in Rabelais, and indeed provides much of the imaginative momentum from the outset. The giants read voraciously, taking advantage of the rising tide of printed books, but when they write it is mainly to send letters, presumably hand-written; their learned culture is retained above all in their capacious memories, ready to be applied in the appropriate context. In other words, Rabelaisian characters, together with Alcofrybas Nasier and his narratorial successor in the third and fourth books, regularly think with commonplaces.

All this is no doubt evident and well enough known, in a general sense. What has never to my knowledge been undertaken is a comprehensive study of the ways in which allusions, quotations and other *topoi* are introduced into the text, and in particular of the phrasings used by the various Rabelaisian speakers to recall, enumerate, assert confidently, advance cautiously, throw doubt upon, present as questions, bear witness to, ruminate on, speculate with, show reverence for, take pleasure in, make fun of, inculcate, advise against, use communicatively, use playfully, emphasize the abundance of — in short, rhapsodize with — common-places. This is not the place for such a comprehensive study: I shall simply offer two examples in order to point the way.

The first is taken from the *Tiers Livre* (1546), where the deluge of commonplace is at its height, partly because narrative is here reduced to a minimum, partly because the investigation of a wide range of different types of potential knowledge provokes a virtuoso display of stored materials which might (or might not) throw light on their relative validity. When Panurge consults Epistemon on the marriage question, telling him that he has made a vow not to wear spectacles or a codpiece until his uncertainty has been resolved, Epistemon first comments on the vow itself, enumerating examples from both antique and modern sources. Rather than considering their content, let us simply note the expressions the speaker uses to refer to his own production of *topoi*:

(1)   Vous entendent parler, me faictez souvenir du veu des Argives [...] du veu aussi du plaisant Hespaignol Michel Doris [...]

(2)   Et ne scay lequel des deux seroit plus digne et meritant [...]

(3)   Car lisant icelluy long narré, l'on pense que doibve estre commencement [...] mais en fin de compte on se mocque [...]

(4)   La mocquerie est telle que de la montaigne d'Horace [...][13]

The first of these shows that the citation of *topoi* arises from a communicative encounter, and that it is resourced by an act of memory; the second indicates relative evaluation of the two instances mentioned; the third reconstructs the act of reading one of the examples cited; the fourth uses the supposed reader's response in order to introduce a further commonplace, which illustrates that response rather than the original topic (vows made to do or not to do something until some other matter is resolved). This part of Epistemon's reply is secondary, its function being limited to underscoring the absurdity of Panurge's. Yet it transpires that Epistemon puts considerable cognitive effort into the recovery of this set of *topoi*.

Once Panurge puts his question head-on ('Me doibz je marier ou non?' [Should I get married or not?]), the intensity of the second-order expressions[14] in Epistemon's reply increases visibly. Let us once more enumerate them:

(1)   Certes [...] le cas est hazardeux, je me sens par trop insuffisant à la resolution.

(2)   Et si jamais feut vray en l'art de medicine le dict [...] JUGEMENT DIFFICILE, il est en cestuy endroict verissime.

(3)   J'ai bien en imagination quelques discours moyennant les quelz nous aurions determination sus vostre perplexité. Mais ilz ne me satisfont poinct apertement.

(4)   Aulcuns Platonicques disent que [...] Je ne comprens pas bien leur discipline, et ne suys d'advis que y adhaerez. Il y a de l'abus beaucoup.

(5)   J'en ay veu l'experience en un gentil homme [...]

(6)   C'est le poinct premier. Un aultre y a.

(7)   Si encores regnoient les oracles [...] Je seroys d'advis [...] y aller [...]

(8)   (paradvanture non seroys)

(9)   Mais vous sçavez que tous sont devenuz plus mutz que poissons [...]

(10) Ores toutesfoys qu'encores feussent en regne, ne conseilleroys je facillement adjouster foy à leurs responses. Trop de gens y ont esté trompez.

(11) D'adventaige je me recorde que Agripine [...][15]

These interventions, by their sheer quantity, would almost outweigh the cited materials themselves, were it not for the long list of superannuated oracles. As a purveyor of *topoi* relevant to Panurge's situation, Epistemon is not merely prudent, he is positively anxious. Nervousness, especially in the face of the possibility of calling up diabolical powers, is in fact a characteristic of his behaviour throughout the *Tiers Livre*,[16] but in this instance there is an additional element which seems to anticipate the arrival on the scene of Trouillogan, and hence of Pyrrhonism, the philosophy of hyperbolical doubt. The first three utterances listed above sound like an echo of the Pyrrhonist *epochê*; the seventh and the tenth construct a double counter-factual conditional ('If they were [...] my opinion would be [...] but they are not'; 'and even if they were [...] I would not [...]') which simultaneously opens up possibilities and denies them. To the first of these conditionals is added yet another in parenthesis, which itself potentially negates the sentence in question.[17] And into these structures are inserted adverbials ('paradvanture', 'facillement') which nuance the expression still further.[18]

This packaging of the *topoi* Epistemon cites would bear further analysis in relation to the thematic and epistemological structure of the *Tiers Livre* (Rabelais's character is perhaps not named at random). I am more interested here in the way in which a commonplace 'rhapsody' becomes a series of communicative propositions, in the sense that they presuppose and invoke the presence of an interested interlocutor, rather than items in a commentary: one need only mention the rhetoric of the 'Pantagruelion' episode to make the difference palpable. Of course all the usual indicators are there: the reference to a well-known *sententia* ('le dict'), the reporting of what is authoritatively claimed ('Aulcuns disent que'), the appeal to experience, the act of recalling from the store of memory. But in addition to these, Epistemon's caution, and the means he uses to bring the relative value of the cited materials home to Panurge, elicit some graphic representations of the process of thinking with commonplaces. Of these, the one with the broadest resonance is undoubtedly the third: 'J'ai bien en imagination quelques discours [...] Mais ilz ne me satisfont poinct apertement' [I indeed have some arguments in my imagination [...] But they don't entirely satisfy me]. The word 'imagination' must here refer to the faculty which calls up materials from the memory, with no connotations of unreliability or fictive activity; as is plain from the context, 'discours' denotes not simply rational arguments, but ready-made discursive items; 'apertement' has the literal sense 'patently', hence 'unambiguously'. The sentence thus invokes a mental space stocked with many potentially usable materials (*topoi*), and a mental searching process which remains, for the moment at least, unresolved.

We move now to the 1552 *Quart Livre* and to the very different commonplace rhapsody enunciated by Pantagruel in the episode of the 'frozen words'. Here again, words whose meaning cannot at first be resolved unambiguously emerge into an imagined space. At the primary level, the 'space' is that of the fiction itself, within which the words take on a physical embodiment; the characters in the fiction become aware of them as sounds rather than as mental concepts. Yet, in Pantagruel's case at least, a mental space is imposed on the physical, as if the two were perfectly analogous. The process is facilitated by an initial visual examination, accompanied by a conjecture ('Par adventure [...]') and by an evocation of the gigantic range of Pantagruel's vision: 'Voyons premierement quelz gens sont. Par adventure sont ilz nostres. Encores ne voy je persone. Et si voy cent mille a l'entour' [Let us first see what kind of people they are. Perhaps they are countrymen of ours. I still can't see anyone. And yet I can see all round for a hundred miles].[19] As this initial scan that movement through and beyond the commonplace culture (or the 'quotation rhetoric') which Compagnon, Fumaroli and others have traced. Yet that assumption of responsibility is infinitely and delicately nuanced by the linguistic and rhetorical devices Montaigne regularly deploys in conjuring up and presenting his 'borrowed' materials: the very sentence I have just quoted is presented as something someone else might say: 'Comme quelqu'un pourroit dire de moy [...]'. Once again, as in the case of Rabelais, an analysis of this *outillage* is arguably a more productive historical exercise — and one less open to potential anachronism — than an attempted extrapolation of the actual 'positions' expressed or implied in the *Essais*, be they Stoic, Pyrrhonistic, 'fideist', post-Tridentine Catholic, or proto-agnostic.

One can confidently say that Rabelais's fictions and Montaigne's *Essais* are in their different ways transformations of the commonplace-book. More precisely, they are collections of commonplace materials torn out of the pedagogical culture of the period and brought into contact with real issues and real experiences. We no longer have access to the experiences themselves, and the commonplace-book as an inert repertory may seem moribund to us. Yet the intricate work of sewing that mobilizes the *topoi* is available to us, if only we can learn to focus on it, rather than regarding it as mere packaging. One might then even imagine a history of commonplace cognition, stretching back into the medieval period and forward through the seventeenth century, and culminating in Flaubert's *Bouvard et Pécuchet* (together, of course, with the *Dictionnaire des idées recues*) as its final landmark. What else do Bouvard and Pécuchet do, after all, than attempt — comprehensively, disastrously, but with a strangely moving effect — to think with commonplaces?

Notes

1. Ernst Robert Curtius, *European Literature and the Latin Middle Ages*, trans. by W. R. Trask (London: Routledge & Kegan Paul, 1953; German original, Berne: Francke, 1948).
2. Walter J. Ong, 'Commonplace Rhapsody: Ravisius Textor, Zwinger and Shakespeare', in *Classical Influences on European Culture, AD 1500–1700*, ed. by R. R. Bolgar (Cambridge: Cambridge University Press, 1976), pp. 91–126 (p. 92).
3. Ann Moss, *Printed Commonplace-Books and the Structuring of Renaissance Thought* (Oxford: Clarendon Press, 1996).
4. Ong opens his article with a disparaging remark by P. O. Kristeller ('Commonplace Rhapsody', p. 91).
5. For this latter view, see for example M. A. Screech, 'Commonplaces of Law, Proverbial Wisdom and Philosophy: Their Importance in Renaissance Scholarship (Rabelais, Joachim Du Bellay, Montaigne)', in *Classical Influences*, ed. by R. R. Bolgar, pp. 127–34.
6. Thomas M. Greene, *The Light in Troy: Imitation and Discovery in Renaissance Poetry* (New Haven and London: Yale University Press, 1982), pp. 38–47.
7. Compagnon, *La Seconde Main*. The habit which seems to have spread recently among Anglophone writers familiar with French of using the Gallicism 'citation' in the sense of 'quotation' runs the risk of blurring this important distinction.
8. Montaigne, *Essais*, III.12, p. 1055. The irony is apparent in the illocutionary framing of the sentence: 'Comme quelqu'un pourroit dire de moy [...]' (see above, p. 45).
9. See in particular McKinley, *Words in a Corner*.
10. André Tournon, *Montaigne: la glose et l'essai*, rev. edn (Paris: Champion, 2000 [1983]); 'L'Argumentation pyrrhonienne: structures d'*essai* dans le chapitre «Des boiteux»', *Cahiers Textuel*, 2 (1986), 73–85.

11. This terrain is mapped out in detail by Agnieszka Steczowicz in 'The Defence of Contraries: Paradox and the Late Renaissance Disciplines' (unpublished D.Phil. dissertation, University of Oxford, 2006).

12. Fontenelle, *Digression sur les anciens et les modernes*, in *Entretiens sur la pluralité des mondes; Digression sur les anciens et les modernes*, ed. by Robert Shackleton (Oxford: Clarendon Press, 1955), pp. 172–73.

13. François Rabelais, *Œuvres complètes*, ed. by Mireille Huchon, Bibliothèque de la Pléiade (Paris: Gallimard, 1994), p. 425.

14. By this I simply mean the expressions that indicate the speaker's own 'rhapsodizing' activity or his attitude to the materials presented.

15. Rabelais, *Œuvres complètes*, pp. 425–26.

16. This chapter ends with a flat refusal by Epistemon of Panurge's suggestion that they visit the supposed oracle of Saturn: 'C'est [...] abus trop evident, et fable trop fabuleuse. Je ne iray pas' (p. 427). See also ch. XVI (*Œuvres complètes*, pp. 400–02), ch. XLIIII (p. 489), and Epistemon's reaction to Panurge's sample of *lanternois* (p. 496; see also *Pantagruel*, IX, pp. 247–48).

17. Although grammatically the *incise* could be read as '[tu] non seroys', it must in fact be read as 'paradvanture [je] non seroys', since Epistemon and Panurge consistently use the 'vous' form in their dialogue.

18. For a linguistic study of such expressions, and in particular of 'à l'avanture' (a synonym for Rabelais's 'paradvanture'), see Kirsti Sellevold, *'J'ayme ces mots ...': expressions linguistiques de doute dans les 'Essais' de Montaigne* (Paris: Champion, 2004). It was Dr Sellevold's study that first drew my attention to the importance of these linguistic markers.

19. Rabelais, *Œuvres complètes*, p. 668.

20. Ibid., pp. 668–69.

21. This element is confirmed by the pilot's reply at the beginning of chapter LVI: 'Seigneur, de rien ne vous effrayez' (p. 669). This remark is only comprehensible if Pantagruel had indeed shown signs of alarm at this strange phenomenon.

22. See the references provided in *Œuvres complètes*, p. 1571 (p. 667, note 5).

23. See Tournon, *'En sens agile': les acrobaties de l'esprit selon Rabelais* (Paris: Champion, 1995), pp. 9–16.

1

Ronsard's Bacchic Fresco

The figure of Bacchus and his attributes play a major role in the iconography of the later Renaissance. In Italy, the Bacchic myths were variously represented and interpreted by poets, artists and thinkers from Ficino and Poliziano to Titian and Flaminio, while in France in the mid-sixteenth century they enjoyed a heyday of comparable splendour, at least in the literary domain. The presence of Bacchus is felt throughout the works of Rabelais, reaching a peak in the *Quart Livre*; he became the subject of extended poems by Du Bellay, Pontus de Tyard, Olivier de Magny and Rémy Belleau; and Ronsard, between 1550 and 1563, wrote a series of major Bacchic poems. Read as a group, these form a mythological fresco where different scenes from the myth are taken up, combined and echoed from one segment to another in order to celebrate not only the god but also the poet, his powers, his *familia* and his patrons. The fresco never appears in this form in the collected editions of Ronsard's works; to think of them thus is a retrospective reconstruction. Yet such reconstructions are commonplace in art galleries and exhibitions, and in this instance the rationale for reading the poems as a related cluster seems inarguable.

In the reading that follows, the *Hinne de Bacus* will be given pride of place as the culmination of a series of three major poems — the *Bacchanales* (1552), the *Dithyrambes* (1553) and the *Hinne de Bacus* (1554) — which share a common mythological imagination. The first two celebrate particular events: the well-known fêtes organized by Ronsard and his fellow-students, the picnic in honour of Dorat and the 'pompe du bouc' [ceremony of the goat] in honour of Jodelle's *Cléopâtre captive*,[1] both of which took place at Arcueil; they are predominantly exuberant in mood, and give plenty of scope to intoxication in its literal sense while remaining in touch with higher levels of Bacchic enthusiasm. The *Hinne de Bacus* shares no anecdotal point of departure with its predecessors, yet it develops comparable themes in the context of a more overt control and seriousness. Indeed, many of the cardinal passages of the hymn are clearly a reworking of similar material in the *Dithyrambes*, while the later parts of both poems draw substantially on the *Hymnus Baccho* of the sixteenth-century Latin poet Marullus. Some ten years later, the figure of Bacchus featured in another fresco, that of the Seasons, where it appears in a less extensive form but is placed at a climactic moment in the hymn to Autumn. This and other poems of the 1560s will be considered here as a kind of epilogue to the primary fresco of the 1550s. First, however, it will helpful to review some of the ways in which Bacchus was represented in the half-century before Ronsard began to write, for the most part in texts — classical and other — which he is likely to have known.

The triumph of Bacchus: an iconographical theme

Amid the vast quantity of Bacchic material which was known to the sixteenth century, one image or group of images may be distinguished as a focal point, representing one of the principal areas of significance within which the myth operates. It is the image of a Bacchic triumph, around which much of Ronsard's hymn is built and which is particularly amenable both to visual representation and to allegorical interpretation. A youthful Bacchus, crowned with a wreath of vines or ivy, is seated in a chariot drawn by tigers or lynxes, and accompanied by satyrs, maenads and the ancient Silenus on his donkey. The procession is a turbulent one, suggesting the orgiac rites of the god, or his conquest of India, or the regal descent on Naxos which is the subject of Titian's 'Bacchus and Ariadne'. More perhaps than any other figure in the classical pantheon, Bacchus is a god who travels, and who more particularly travels at speed: his trajectory and the disturbance that accompanies it are central to the myth and will be thoroughly exploited by Ronsard.

The main features of the triumph were popularized by Ovid, and to a lesser extent by Catullus and Statius; and these writers invested them with a significance which corresponds to one of the oldest and most fundamental aspects of the myth. In the *Metamorphoses*, Bacchus appears as a god of youthful, almost childlike, beauty, who nevertheless brings terror and destruction to those who offend him; in Ovid's *Ars amatoria* and in Catullus, his procession carries him to Ariadne, who is forced to submit to his divine power; while Statius portrays him returning in triumph from India, surrounded by the violent companions who put his enemies to flight.[2] In each case, he embodies an irresistible and irrational force, intoxicating yet perilous; and this combination of qualities recurs throughout the Bacchic literature of Greece and Rome, from Hesiod and Euripides onwards. Hence, like Venus or Diana, Bacchus is an ambiguous god: as Horace puts it, his influence is a 'lene tormentum' [gentle torment], a 'dulce periculum' [sweet peril].[3]

This antithetical interpretation was schematized in didactic fashion by the medieval mythographers.[4] As the god of wine, Bacchus now begins to personify gluttony, lust, sloth or wrath. Few of the deadly sins are unknown to him; yet at the same time he inspires courage, vigour and perspicacity. The double direction is clearly represented in Boccaccio's *De genealogia*, where the lynxes and tigers, which both appear in the Statius passage quoted by Boccaccio, are glossed antithetically:

> Lynxes are attributed to him, so that it may be understood that wine, when consumed in moderation, increases strength, boldness and perspicacity. And tigers pull his chariot to show the savagery of drunkards.[5]

Boccaccio has also included here the need for moderation, which rationalizes the antithesis and reduces it to the literal sense of intoxication; and this interpretation of Bacchus as the god of moderate drinking recurs in many other late medieval and Renaissance works where the allegorical tradition persists — in the *Ovide moralisé*, for example, and in Alciati's emblem book.[6]

In the course of the mythographical tradition, the image of Bacchus in triumph thus tends to become fragmented, divorced from its literary context, and limited to the morality of drinking. The ambiguity of the god's powers loses the tension which it derived in Greek and Latin literature from the explicitly religious aspect of the myth. At the same time, however, the interpretation of Bacchus as a symbol of divinity is not excluded from the medieval commentaries. Most of the variants of the *Ovide moralisé*, for example, represent him both as the god of *vinolentia* (and thence of various deadly sins), and as the divine intoxication of grace, the triumph of virtue.[7] It is true that these two glosses are mutually exclusive, and that in consequence there can be no real tension between them; on the other hand, it is important that the allegorical tradition should have preserved the sense of a divine force which was endemic in the classical representations, while converting it to an explicitly Christian theology.

When Jean Lemaire de Belges, in the *Illustrations de Gaule* (1510–13), describes the arrival of the Bacchic procession at the marriage feast given by the gods for the wedding of Peleus and Thetis, he uses the same triumphal image, together with the allegorization provided by Boccaccio:

> Le gentil Bacchus Dieu du vin [...] sen venoit en grand triomphe sur son chariot, trainé par Lynces, qui sont bestes ayans le regard si agu, quil perce les murailles, et par Tigres, qui sont bestes tresfurieuses: en signifiance que quand lhomme prend du vin raisonnablement, on en voit plus cler en ses affaires: et quand il en prend oultre mesure, on perd lusage de raison.[8]

> [The noble Bacchus, god of wine [...] was arriving in great triumph on his chariot drawn by lynxes, beasts whose eyes are so sharp that they can see through walls, and by tigers, who are wild, raging beasts: signifying that those who take wine in reasonable quantities have a clearer insight into their affairs, and that those who drink immoderately lose the use of their reason.]

This passage, like many of the other allegories in the same chapter, is derived principally from the *De genealogia*, as Jean Lemaire himself admits; and by using the wedding of Peleus and Thetis as a centrepiece for the first book of the *Illustrations de Gaule*, Lemaire is aligning himself implicitly with the *Ovide moralisé*, which gave prominence to the same story. The allegorical glosses have the same limitations as their source, bearing primarily on the effects of wine and the need for moderation, although an association is made in passing between the ivy crown, the vigour of wine, and poetry. However, the moral lesson illustrated by the lynxes and the tigers is not wholly gratuitous: it takes on a wider resonance in the context of the *Illustrations* as a whole. The work is intended not only as a nationalistic history, but also as a moral allegory in which the judgement of Paris plays a central part. Jean Lemaire is concerned throughout with the difficult choice between good and evil, between chaste love and uncontrolled passion: the love of Paris for Pegasis Œnone is passionate but legitimate, while his love for Helen is lustful and destructive. Thus love, like wine, is shown to be morally ambiguous, and Lemaire expounds in his own terms the distinction between the good and evil Venus.[9] It seems likely, then, that the interpretation he gives of Bacchus is not merely a gratuitous imitation of Boccaccio but a calculated part of the moral mosaic he is constructing.

In spite of the ambiguity indicated in the allegorization, Bacchus is presented here in a predominantly favourable light: he arrives in triumph at a feast which 'ne valoit rien sanz luy' [was worthless without him]; he is the last of the gods to come, having been specially sought out by Mercury; and he is honoured by all the gods and goddesses. Although Jean Lemaire refers, like Ovid, to the comic behaviour of Silenus and the satyrs, his Bacchus is not a god of ribaldry and red noses. He is essential to the enjoyment of the feast, yet he is one of the most respected guests. This emphasis is important, since it preserves the unity of the presentation. The figure of Bacchus is no longer fragmented into a series of isolated attributes and interpretations: it appears as a coherent visual and literary image, corresponding with the integration of the moral itself into the overall pattern of the work. Lemaire's *Illustrations* could not be mistaken for a mythological handbook. It respects and makes use of the traditions of moral and mythological allegory, but its author is aiming at a relatively wide public: he uses the vernacular, and is clearly concerned with the accessibility of his story and his style. Thus the description of the Bacchic procession which Boccaccio quotes from Ovid and others as part of a catalogue of attributes is recast here in a fully literary context. The didactic message is retained, but disguised in a rich tapestry of rhetoric.

The *De genealogia* and similar works continued to be read and respected in the sixteenth century; and the handbooks of the newer mythographers, of Conti or Giraldi, whose techniques are fundamentally much the same, will be consulted and exploited by the French poets of the second half of the century.[10] Thus Jean Lemaire's acceptance of the allegorical interpretation of myth is as valid in the sixteenth century as it would have been in the fourteenth or fifteenth. Moreover, there is undeniably a discrepancy of tone between his image of the Bacchic train and its moralization: the whole allegorical tradition assumes a rigid separation of the various established levels of significance, and Lemaire's work is clearly affected by this technique. All this must be stressed if one is to grasp the essential continuity of method between the medieval and the Renaissance presentation of myth. Yet Lemaire's interpretations arise from images which have already established themselves independently on the visual level: his Bacchus, his Mars and his Venus have a plastic, sensual mode of existence, not merely a schematic one, so that they embody in dynamic form the meanings which the glosses then elaborate. This is crucial, since if the use of mythology in Renaissance literature is characterized by a decline of allegory, this is not because there is a transference of myth from an allegorical to a decorative function; it is rather because there is a movement towards metaphor, towards a more complete identification of the poetic image and its inner meaning. In the poetry of Ronsard, Bacchus will appear not merely as a classicizing image, but as a metaphor which has subsumed the traditional allegorical content and endowed it with a new and broader significance.

'Bacchanales' and 'Dithyrambes'

A restaging of the Bacchic trajectory is already apparent in the title of the first poem in Ronsard's Bacchic fresco, the *Bacchanales ou le folastrissime voyage d'Hercueil*.[11] The materials of the poem operate on two levels: the first is the narration of the picnic which, one presumes, actually took place at Arcueil one summer's day in 1549; the principal feature of this new experiment is the use of a free metre, which bodies forth the intoxication and the unchecked enthusiasm provoked by Bacchus. Indeed, the adoption of this metre coincides with the attempt to produce an effect of dynamic disorder at all levels of the poem, structural, stylistic, and even syntactic:

> Evoé, Pere, Satyre,
> [...]
> Ta fureur me gette
> Hors de moy,
> Je te voy, je te voy,
> Voi-te-cy,
> Rompsoucy:
> Mon coeur, bouillonnant d'une rage,
> Envole vers toy mon courage.
> Je forcene, je demoniacle,
> L'horrible vent de ton oracle,
> J'entens l'esprit de ce bon vin nouveau,
> Me tempeste le cerveau. (lines 73–88)

> [Euoi, Father, Satyr,
> [...]
> Your divine fury hurls me
> Out of myself,
> I see you, I see you,
> Here you come,
> Care-breaker:
> My heart, boiling with a raging fury,
> Sends my wild thoughts flying up towards you.
> I rave like a *daimon*,
> The terrible wind of your oracle
> (I mean the spirit of this good new wine)
> Storms through my brain.]

This passage, with its blend of simple ejaculatory phrases, erudite allusions, quasi-elevated language and fragmented syntactical units, mirrors the texture of the poem as a whole. On the one hand, Ronsard exploits a vein of Bacchic comedy, evident in images like that of the poet 'haletant à grosse alaine' as he follows the Bacchic procession. On the other hand, in the later part of the poem Bacchus becomes explicitly the object of a religious cult: there are references to the poetic initiation of his priest, to his righteous anger against the profane, to his functions as a god of natural fertility, civil order and cosmic balance, and finally to his role as a mediator between man and the divine mysteries. It is true that all this material is adapted from the *Hymnus Baccho* of Marullus, which in fact supplies the basis for the whole of the dithyrambic hymn placed in the mouth of Jodelle. However, Ronsard's use of the same material in the *Hinne de Bacus* suggests that the borrowing is far from gratuitous; indeed, it seems likely that he found in the Bacchic motifs formulated by the neo-Latin poet a means of extending and enriching his own interpretation of the myth. One needs constantly to bear in mind here that the distancing effect that the medium of Latin creates for modern readers would not have been apparent to Ronsard; Marullus was in fact a poet of considerable range and power.

The poem as a whole, with its change of emphasis from a predominantly comic and anecdotal tone to the panegyric themes of the concluding hymn, embraces a much wider sphere of activity than the *Hymnus Baccho*. Its central implication seems to be that the forces of the personality which are expressed in gaiety and drunken festivity may, under the right conditions, provide access also to the divine mysteries, since they are deeply connected with the principles which govern nature and the universe. These latter themes are presented far more explicitly and in greater detail in the *Dithyrambes* than in the *Bacchanales*, but the fundamental pattern is similar: a continuity is demonstrated between the hedonistic mood of the festival and the most profound aspects of poetic creativity. Moreover, on the level of style and structure, this pattern operates in both poems through the adoption of an 'improvised' manner, by the deliberate avoidance of an obtrusive order or consistency. The dynamic forward movement of the festive mood and of Bacchic inspiration must be caught in full flow.

The 'Hinne de Bacus'

If the *Dithyrambes* replays the motif of poetic inspiration already featured in the *Bacchanales* by presenting in quasi-improvisational mode the raw material of the dithyrambic *fureur*, the *Hinne de Bacus*[14] reworks the same material within a more controlled and unified poetic form. There is in this instance no real event which forms the point of departure: a considerable proportion of the poem is on the level of mythological narrative, albeit addressed in the second person to Bacchus himself; and when the dithyrambus finally begins, the poet's companions are exclusively mythological. Nevertheless, the connection with an easily recognizable experience is maintained. The mood of Bacchic comedy and of ordinary drunkenness still recurs from time to time, and a passage in which Bacchus is credited with the origin of a vineyard in Vendôme provides a characteristic means of transition from the narrative to the dithyrambus.

Whereas the two earlier poems had contained encomiastic elements, the *Hinne* is presented wholly as an encomium: Ronsard explicitly selects versions of the myth which are favourable to Bacchus. A defence so carefully prepared implies in Ronsard a sensitivity to the kind of criticism which his own 'paganizing' activities, together with their expression in verse, could easily invite (see, in particular, lines 83–96 and 149–64); and it gives a new emphasis to the Marullan panegyric, which again — recast now in eloquent alexandrines — forms the climax of the poem. More clearly than in the *Dithyrambes*, the overall structure is oriented towards this climax. A single reference to Bacchus's chariot in the *Dithyrambes* (line 362) is expanded here to form a major principle of unity, for the procession narrative begins (lines 109 ff.) with a magnificent image of the Bacchic train: after a preliminary section in which the birth and youth of Bacchus are described, the god mounts his chariot and initiates a movement which is carried through to the end of the poem.

Most of the details of the procession in the *Hinne* — the chariot, the lynxes, Silenus on his donkey, the maenads, thyads, Pans and sylvans, the horns and drums, the wreaths of serpents, the thyrsus — occur in Ovid, Horace or Catullus, and are thus standard; furthermore, the whole of the concluding phase of the poem is

La superbe majesté,
La force, et la gravité,
Et la chaste continence,
Sont sous le joug de tes loix:
Et les sages, et les Rois,
Le murmure, et le silence.

La sanglante cruauté,
L'odieuse verité,
L'obscur oubli, la memoire,
La discorde, et l'amitié,
La rigueur, et la pitié,
Accompagnent ta victoire.[23]

[Proud majesty,
Power, and solemnity,
And chaste continence,
Are under the yoke of your laws,
As too are the wise, and Kings,
Murmuring and silence.]

[Cruelty red with blood,
Odious truth,
Dark forgetfulness, memory,
Discord and friendship,
Severity and pity,
Accompany your victory.]

It will be noticed that the positive attributes are heavily emphasized at the outset, so that when more dubious qualities appear in the following stanza — 'la sanglante cruauté', 'la discorde' — they can hardly be interpreted in an exclusively pejorative sense, just as the overall encomiastic tone of Ronsard's poem excludes an interpretation of his personifications on the level of moral censure. The attribution to Bacchus of these qualities, each taken individually, could be glossed without much difficulty by reference to the classical and medieval traditions; furthermore, Ronsard may well have had Pontus's list in mind when he adapted Statius, since some of Ronsard's figures appear in Pontus but not in Statius. However, what is of primary importance here is that Bacchus is once again responsible for drawing together and harmonizing antithetical moral qualities, although Pontus fails to convey the total effect of this harmony.[24] The breathless momentum of Ronsard's procession bodies forth in physical terms the confident energy which Bacchus represents, whereas Pontus's triumph is abstract and static. Where Ronsard clothes Bacchus in Tyrian purple, Pontus refers to his 'superbe majesté'; likewise, 'la force, et la gravité' are realized by Ronsard in the wreath of ivy and vine leaves.

Olivier de Magny's *Hymne de Bacchus*, dedicated in 1559 to Ronsard, clearly owes much to the example of the master. In this instance, the image of the triumphal procession has disappeared entirely, leaving the interpretative structure even clearer than in Pontus's poem:

Il tient en paix en nous les discordans acordz,
Il chasse nostre crainte et croist nostre courage,
Il chasse la paresse, et fait bien davantage,
Car d'une saincte force il fait veoir à noz yeux
Les poles, les cerceaux, et les Astres des cieux,
Il faict veoir de Phebus la flambante carriere,
Il faict veoir de Phebé l'inconstante lumiere,
Les douleurs d'Orion, l'extréme ardeur du chien,
Et les deux plains tonneaux et de mal et de bien.[25]

[He keeps the peace in us between discordant accords,
He puts our fear to flight and increases our courage,
He puts idleness to flight, and does much more,
For with a sacred power he gives us the vision to see
The poles, the orbits, and the stars of the heavens,
He shows us the blazing path of Phoebus,

He shows us the inconstant light of Phebe,
The sufferings of Orion, the extreme heat of the dogstar,
And the two full barrels of evil and good.]

The first line of this passage endorses the hypothesis that, for both Pontus and Ronsard, Bacchus has the function of establishing a *discordia concors*, and thus of giving positive expression to conflicting inward passions. Magny rationalizes the antitheses still more clearly than Pontus, and the qualities he mentions (although no longer personified as companions of Bacchus) are equally close to Ronsard's. Yet he seems to feel that certain of these qualities ('creinte' and 'paresse') must be explicitly rejected: if Bacchus is to remain morally intact, he must be shown to drive out fear and idleness, not to encourage them. Hence an element of moral categorization is reintroduced, and this emphasis is confirmed by the concluding line, where Magny attributes to Bacchus the power of making us distinguish clearly between 'mal' and 'bien' by showing us the Homeric twin barrels which stand at the gate of Jove.[26] By contrast, Ronsard's Vice and Virtue, swept along together in the midst of the procession, suggest a moral insight of a different order. Bacchus is not a didactic moralist who insists on sharp distinctions between evil and good; in his triumph, the two extremes cooperate in a movement and purpose which are superior to conventional morality.

The related yet divergent moral allegories of Ronsard and his contemporaries need not surprise us in a period in which the formal categories of Christian ethics are still very much alive but are supplemented by more flexible moral criteria drawn in part from classical thought. Erasmus' *Praise of Folly* — in which the praise of Bacchus and his gifts is much in evidence — is rich in moral implications of this kind; and the Erasmian 'anti-Stoicism' exploited by Rabelais in his earlier work may have made its impact on Ronsard himself.[27] Likewise, the problem of reconciling a secure morality with a hedonistic outlook was familiar to the Florentine Academy and to the painters who gave plastic form to many of its concepts.[28] Thus it seems likely that Ronsard, faced with the same problem as many of his humanist predecessors — that of exploiting and at the same time justifying the morality of 'pagan' literature — produced a similar answer. The Bacchus of the *Hinne* is not the god of drunkenness, or at least he is only partially so. He is a god who utilizes the forces of the human personality, even those which a stricter code would condemn as potentially sinful: *Ira*, for example, whom Ronsard transferred from Statius, is a deadly sin according to medieval Christian tradition, but might be interpreted in other contexts as the noble quality of righteous anger.[29] On a more general level, the liberation of the mind and of passionate impulse from conventional limitations is clearly implied — and endorsed — by the whole processional motif of the *Hinne*: indeed, as we shall see shortly, this impulse becomes the motive power by which the mind may be raised to the contemplation of divine things.

In retrospect, the distance between Ronsard's image of the triumph and Jean Lemaire's is considerable, in terms of both visual impact and intellectual penetration; nevertheless there is a direct line of affiliation between the two. Boccaccio's — and hence Jean Lemaire's — juxtaposition of details from both Ovid and Statius is still valid for Ronsard, although the spectrum is widened both by additional classical

> Par toi, Pere, chargés de ta douce ambrosie,
> Nous elevons au ciel l'humaine fantasie,
> Portés dedans ton char, et d'homes vicieux,
> Purgés de ta liqueur osons monter aux cieus,
> Et du grand Jupiter nous assoir à la table. (lines 277–81)

> [Thanks to you, Father, sated with your sweet ambrosia
> We raise up to heaven the human fantasy;
> Borne in your chariot and no longer sinful
> Now that we are purged by your liquor, we dare to climb to the heavens
> And sit at the table of the great Jupiter.]

The triumphal image established at the outset is taken up once more in the reference to the chariot: but now it is we who, thanks to the mediating power of Bacchus, are carried upwards by the chariot in a spiritual ascent towards the table of Jupiter. The movement is at this point clearly a transcendental one, but the continuity between human and divine is maintained by the parallel between the previously established metaphor of human intoxication and the image of a divine feast. For Ronsard, the two levels are inseparable, and this is further demonstrated by the specification of the 'humaine fantasie' as the faculty which is elevated by Bacchus. As a faculty closely related to and often identified with the imagination, the fantasy represents precisely that level of experience which, according to Ficino's *Symposium* commentary and Pontus's *Solitaire premier*, is transcended through the mediation of Bacchus.[35] It seems likely, then, that Ronsard is consciously proposing the vindication of a faculty which had often been considered in a pejorative light, but which at the same time was a key faculty for the poet.[36] If this is so, he has here altered the sense of the Platonist ascent. For Ficino, and for Pontus, the fantasy and the imagination belong to the lower regions of the soul and must be left behind in the spiritual ascent: Bacchus does not exalt the imagination, he represents one step in the movement that eventually transcends it. Once again, then, Ronsard is stressing the validity of the whole range of human experience: the 'fantasie', the power of creating many and varied images, remains an integral part of the progress towards divine insight. He thus gives a human content not only to the neo-Platonist *raptio*, in which the contemplator is possessed by the power which emanates from God, but also to the *remeatio*, which reunites the soul with its divine origin.[37] And likewise, just as the moral theory which underlies the poem justifies the ambiguous morality of the myth on which it is based, so the elevation of the fantasy justifies the act of poetic creation itself, which can use fictive and even frivolous material to embody fundamental insights. Finally, it is significant that Ronsard strongly emphasizes in this same context the purgation of vices through the 'liqueur' of Bacchus, thus making the connection between the psychological and the moral levels perfectly clear: the consciousness of his intention in these respects is confirmed by a comparison with his model Marullus, who mentions neither the fantasy nor the moral purgation.[38]

The *Hinne de Bacus*, when seen in the context of Ronsard's poetic production of the early 1550's, appears both as the culmination of an intensive interest in the myth of Bacchus and as a first exercise in the method of the 'hymn', a genre which synthesizes a variety of elements — philosophical, mythological, Christian — in a single poetic unity. After a series of experiments in a predominantly pagan and hedonistic vein, Ronsard seems to have felt the need to give definitive expression to his Bacchic material in a form which strongly implied its vindication. Hence the pleasure of drinking and feasting, the Bacchic sense of humour, the harmony of music and dance, the Anacreontic lilies and roses, Youth, Love and the Graces, are all worked into the fabric of the hymn, where they are seen as part of a wider pattern.

Just as such hedonism required justification against the accusation of the didactic moralists — whether of an earlier age or of Ronsard's own time — so also did the passions which motivate Ronsard's Bacchic procession; for his poetry, particularly in these earlier poems, was much concerned with the representation of passion, whether in the 1552 *Amours*, in the *Odes*, or in the Bacchic poems themselves. Pontus, in the *Solitaire premier*, speaks of poets as those who

> si vivement representent les celestes puissances et humaines passions, que dedans leurs vers reluisent les celestes grandeurs, que par leurs vers la vertu est montrée amiable, le vice horrible, et encores les affections paintes de leurs vrayes et non feintes couleurs. (p. 73)

> [so vividly represent the celestial powers and human passions that the grandeur of the heavens shines forth in their verses, virtue is shown by their verses to be worthy of love and vice to be horrible, and the emotions too depicted in their true, unfeigned colours.]

And it is precisely by showing how human passion is intimately related to divine forces that Ronsard defends such representation. Its dangers are acknowledged: the darker forces of human nature are not easily handled. But at the same time they constitute the powerful impulse which, properly directed, can unite the soul with its divine source.

Ultimately Ronsard's view is not Platonic, as has often been pointed out: he is too attached to the abundance and diversity of the physical world. Indeed, this poem concludes not at the table of Jupiter, but with a salutation of a decidedly this-worldly nature. Nevertheless, he uses the Platonist framework for his own purposes, the purposes of a poet concerned for the value of his art; and it is here that the central inspirational passages and the exaltation of the 'humaine fantasie' come into their own. It is the poet's function to be moved and to move;[39] his work is the medium through which the unified divine force of inspiration is bodied forth in the spectrum of human passions. But the 'energy' or 'enthusiasm' which is his motive force also reconnects the diverse and the human with its original source; and this re-ascent is the central theme of the *Hinne de Bacus*.

Finally, the fantasy is vindicated as a faculty because the true poet, although dealing with images which might be condemned as fictions, uses these very fictions as a cloak in which to convey the hidden truth. Yet it is not necessary to see the *Hinne* as the working-out of some pedantic, outmoded allegorical system. In a characteristic manner, Ronsard has borrowed themes, images and ideas from all manner of different sources and welded them together into a whole which has its own significance. Nor has he forgotten that the 'fabuleux manteau' must be richly and beautifully made:[40] much of the detail of the poem, superfluous to the 'allegory' itself, is justified by its sensuous appeal. Indeed, the movement away from allegory in the strict sense and towards metaphor has been brought about in part at least by this exploitation on a visual, decorative and rhythmic level of images which had earlier been treated schematically. At the same time, these images inevitably retain some of the allegorical associations which they had acquired through centuries of mythographical commentary; on a more general level, Ronsard clearly perceived the enduring value of myth as a means of embodying profound insights into both the human world and the cosmos. What he has achieved, in this poem and in many others, is a breakdown of the distinction between the literal and the figurative levels: in the last analysis the 'cloak' and the underlying significance are inseparable.

Furthermore, it is precisely the same tendency which is reflected in the presentation of the moral and inspirational themes. Whereas Pontus retains a strict sense of hierarchy within these realms, Ronsard is interested in exploring the continuity of experience, in demonstrating the fundamental unity which underlies both the 'celestes puissances' and the 'humaines passions'. As a poet, he cannot afford to abandon either the human or the transcendental order; similarly, he must achieve a fusion between the fabric of his poem and the significance it embodies. The triumph of Bacchus is thus for Ronsard the triumph of mediation and reconciliation on every level — moral, aesthetic, psychological, spiritual, and cosmic. The hierarchical system of the mythographers, with its rigid distinctions between form and content, virtue and vice, human and divine, is transcended. Out of the confusion of fragmentary images and interpretations of Bacchus handed down by tradition, Ronsard has created a harmonious synthesis, a synthesis which embodies much of what is fundamental to his poetic theory and practice.

Bacchus and the seasons

The *Hymne de l'autonne*[41] seems at first sight to present a rather different interpretation of the Bacchic myth. There is now no dithyrambus: the mythological section of the poem is cast in a third-person narrative form and contains no explicit reference to Ronsard himself, to the Vendôme, or to any contemporary setting. Isolated from its context, this section appears indeed to be simply a seasonal allegory, sumptuously decorated. However, the 'fable' proper is preceded by a discourse on the nature of fables and of poetic composition, a discourse in which Ronsard's own conception of himself as a poet is prominent. Thus, whereas in the three earlier poems a consciousness of the poet's activity was clearly implied — and sometimes stated — through the myth itself, the structure of the *Hymne de l'autonne* places the commentary and the myth in two separate, independent compartments. Since they nevertheless combine to form a single poem, one might reasonably expect the fable to illustrate the prologue, a hypothesis which is supported circumstantially by the preoccupations of the earlier Bacchic group; but if so, the relationship between the two 'halves' remains oblique and problematic until further evidence, both internal and external, has been examined.[42]

The introductory discourse, which centres on an analysis of the poetic *fureur* and the conditions under which the poet receives it, is at times curiously similar in theme and even in phrasing to the *Hinne de Bacus*. The 'Daimon' who mediates the *fureur*

[...] me haussa le cueur, haussa la fantasie,
M'inspirant dedans l'ame un don de Poësie,
Que Dieu n'a concedé qu'à l'esprit agité
Des poignans aiguillons de sa divinité. (lines 9–12)

[raised my heart, raised my fantasy,
Inspiring in my soul the gift of Poetry,
Which God has granted only to the spirit that is moved
By the sharp goads of his divinity.]

The phrase 'agité [...] divinité', apart from the possessive pronoun which attributes the inspiration to God rather than Bacchus, occurs in exactly the same form in the *Hinne* (lines 187–88). This resemblance suggests that Ronsard considered Bacchus to have a close affinity with God himself as mover of the poet's soul, and thus indicates how seriously he understood the origin of this divine force: the Apolline 'Daimon' of this poem, like Bacchus, symbolizes one of the specific areas of experience through which the divinity becomes apparent to humankind. In this context, the elevation of the 'fantasie' once again assumes an important role, particularly as Ronsard's 'esprit fantastique' is referred to twice (lines 39 and 62). Furthermore, the rites of purification which the poet must undergo in order to prepare himself for the gift of insight into nature and the divinity are here specified as 'oraison,' 'jeune' and 'penitence': the Christian overtones of these words make it clear that Ronsard is thinking in terms of a divine power which could readily be rephrased in the language and beliefs of his own day. Yet at the same time the transference of this theme to a mythological frame of reference is an easy one; for, some twenty lines later, Euterpe is pictured as leading him through precisely the same kind of initiation by washing him nine times in the Castalian spring. Here, too, there is a parallel with the *Hinne de Bacus*, in which the purification motif is stressed; and the parallel is supported by the rejection of tyranny, malice, impudence and ambition, which recalls the righteous anger of Bacchus towards the Giants, Pentheus and others in the earlier hymn.

The role played by Bacchus in the mythological section of the *Hymne de l'autonne* is likewise analogous in certain respects to his function in the earlier poetry: he confers value on a problematical realm of experience which embodies potentially unproductive and even destructive qualities. In this instance, the qualities are those of the autumnal season, summarized by Nature just before the appearance of Bacchus (lines 357–68*)*. Yet Bacchus is not characterized predominantly as the bringer of grapes, of the vintage that redeems autumn's place in the natural cycle. It is his youth and energy which are stressed at the outset, and, then, at the conclusion of his own speech, his power, authority, and, divine origin:

Je ne suis pas un Dieu foretier ny champestre,
Je suis ce grand Bachus, des Satyres le maistre,
Qui ay cent mille autels, qui ay cent mille noms
Tant craint et reveré par tant de nations.
[...]
Jupiter est mon pere, et quand je monte aux cieux
J'ay mon trosne eslevé entre les plus hauts Dieux. (lines 425–28, 435–36*)*

the much-quoted reference to the use of fable as a cloak for truth which concludes the prefatory section implies at least an awareness that the material of the myth is charged with meaning beyond the literal, surface level. Thus it seems legitimate to read the fable as a richly developed metaphor which — elaborating in a different mode those explored in the earlier poems in this Bacchic sequence — tells one a great deal about Ronsard's view of the value of his own poetic activity as a compensation for the sterility and debility of other aspects of his life.

Between the *Bacchanales* and the *Hymne de l'autonne*, the mood has changed radically: the notion of the Bacchic fury as consecrating the gaiety and paganizing hedonism of Ronsard's earlier career has been supplanted by a Bacchus whose function is to redeem an erosive melancholy. Yet there is a common underlying structure. Confronted by two divergent and even conflicting realms of experience, human and divine, transient and eternal, the poet invokes Bacchus as a guiding *daimon* and mediator. In this sense, he represents an ideal of the poetic activity itself. Unlike the Muses or even Apollo, however, his range of significance is not limited to a purely aesthetic plane. As an embodiment of pleasure and festivity, of creative energy and of autumnal plenitude, he spans a widely recognizable range of cultural values, thus enabling Ronsard to reaffirm the function of poetry as a vehicle for both human and transcendental insights, and hence to present, *sub specie aeternitatis,* essential aspects of his own experience.

Notes

1. Ronsard and his fellow poets regarded Jodelle's play as the first French tragedy to be composed according to ancient Greek models.
2. Ovid, *Metamorphoses*, IV.i, et seq.; *Ars amatoria*, I.525–64; Catullus, LXIV.251–64; Statius, *Thebaid*, IV.656–63.
3. *Odes*, III.xxi.13; xxv.18.
4. For this tradition as a whole, see Jean Seznec, *The Survival of the Pagan Gods: The Mythological Tradition and its Place in Renaissance Humanism and Art*, trans. by B. F. Sessions (New York: Pantheon, 1953; French original, London: Warburg Institute, 1940). The authors and texts mentioned in the present section all play a major role in the mythographical tradition as it was handed down to the sixteenth century, and readers unfamiliar with them should consult Seznec for further details.
5. 'Lynces autem illi attribuuntur, ut intelligatur vinum moderate sumptum vires, audaciam et perspicaciam augere. Tigres autem ideo currum trahunt, ut ebriorum ostendatur sevitia' (*De genealogia*, 61a; I refer to the edition in the *Scrittori d'Italia* series, no. 200: *Genealogie deorum gentilium libri*, vol. 1 (Bari: G. Laterza, 1951); all the references given in the present study are to book 5, ch. 25 unless otherwise stated).
6. See, for example, the prose *Ovide moralisé*, ed. by C. de Boer, in 'Verhandelingen der Koninklijke Nederlandse Akademie van Wetenschappen, Afdeeling Letterkunde', *Nieuwe Reeks*, 61:2 (Amsterdam: North-Holland, 1954), p. 147: 'Bacchus desprise moult les glotons de boyre trop de vin, et si fait il ceulx qui point n'en boyvent.' Cf. also ibid., p. 129. For a parallel in Alciati, see the emblem *In statuam Bacchi*, in *Andreae Alciati Emblematum fontes quatuor*, facsimile ed. by H. Green, Holbein Society, vol. IV (London: Truebner, 1870); from the 1534 Paris edition, pp. 71–72. A classical source is provided by Seneca, *De tranquillitate animi*, XVII.8–11; cf. Horace, *Odes*, III.21, on the beneficial effects of drinking. In a further Bacchic emblem published in the 1546 Venice edition of Alciati, Bacchus and Pallas are shown standing together on a pedestal: 'Vino prudentiam augeri' is the motto (fol. 40$^\text{v}$ of the facsimile edn in the collection referred to above).
7. See, for example, Pierre Bersuire (Petrus Berchorius), *Reductorium morale, liber XV, cap. I. De*

Formis figurisque deorum, (Utrecht: Institute for Late Latin, 1960; after the Paris edn of 1509), fol. XIII^v. Cf. C. de Boer's edn of the *Ovide moralisé* in the series referred to above, vol. XV (Amsterdam: North-Holland, 1915), pp. 353–56, 357–61.

8. Jean Lemaire de Belges, *Œuvres*, ed. by J. Stecher, vol. I, *Les Illustrations de Gaule et Singularitez de Troye, Premier Livre* (Louvain: J. Lefever, 1882), p. 210.
9. See *Œuvres*, vol. II, prologue to the second book of the *Illustrations*, pp. 2–5.
10. See Seznec, *The Survival of the Pagan Gods*, Book II, sections I and III.
11. The *Bacchanales* was first published in 1552 at the end of the fifth book of Ronsard's *Odes*. All references to Ronsard are to the edition in 20 volumes by Paul Laumonier and others (Paris: Hachette/STFM, 1914–75); here, vol. III.
12. Cf. an important early variant of line 72: 'ce Hanap [...] / Dont la pance / *Fait bruncher mes compaignons*' becomes '[...] / *Sert d'oracle aus conpagnons.*' Whether or not this is a conscious echo of Rabelais's 'dive bouteille,' the reference to the oracular function of wine should perhaps not be interpreted in an exclusively burlesque sense.
13. For this poem, see the Laumonier edition, vol. V.
14. For this poem, see the Laumonier edition, vol. VI.
15. *Michaelis Marulli Carmina*, ed. by A. Perosa (Turin: Thesaurus mundi, 1951), pp. 115–16 (quotations given below are from this edition). See Laumonier's tabulation of the parallels between the *Hymnus Baccho* and Ronsard's *Dithyrambes* and *Hinne de Bacus*, in his *Ronsard, poète lyrique* (Paris: Hachette, 1909), pp. 736–42.
16. This and subsequent quotations from the *Hinne de Bacus* are taken from the text of Laumonier's edition, vol. VI.
17. Lines 149–64; cf. Horace, *Odes*, II.19. In another passage (lines 93–96), Ronsard professes amazement at the sacrifice of the goat at Bacchic festivals. This is consistent with the 1563 *Response aux injures et calomnies*, where Ronsard insists that the goat was not sacrificed at the 1553 *cérémonie du bouc* (Laumonier, XI, 141–42): he seems in both poems anxious that the thoroughly pagan motif of a sacrifice should be dissociated from his poetry; cf. the first *Ode à la fontaine Bellerie*, where again Ronsard suppresses the sacrifice and blood which are central in the *Fons Bandusiae*. Likewise, although Ronsard makes use of Statius in the description of Bacchus's followers, he omits Statius's reference to the 'Mimallones' bearing 'semineces lupos' and 'scissas ursas' (*Thebaid*, IV.659–60); again, in his adaptation of Marullus, he suppresses the sequence of two and a half lines in which Marullus refers to the 'sancta Mimallonum / Cohors' who tear apart living calves in their fury (*Hymnus Baccho*, lines 46–48). All this makes it clear that Ronsard wishes to exclude the wantonly destructive aspects of Bacchus's power from his own image of the god.
18. cf. *Ars amatoria*, I.549–50: 'Iam Deus e curru, quem summum texerat uvis, / tigribus adiunctis aurea lora dabat'; *Metamorphoses*, IV.24–25: 'tu biiugum pictis insignia frenis / colla premis lyncum'; and *Thebaid*, IV.656–58: 'et iam pampineos materna ad moenia currus / promovet; effrenae dextra laevaque secuntur / lynces, et uda mero lambunt retinacula tigres.'
19. *Thebaid*, IV.661–63: 'nec comitatus iners: sunt illic Ira Furorque / et Metus et Virtus et numquam sobrius Ardor / succiduique gradus et castra simillima regi.' The juxtaposition of 'le Somme' and 'le Discord' after a reference to 'la Creinte' — and indeed the group as a whole — also recalls the personifications which stand at the gate of hell in *Aeneid*, VI.273–81 ('Metus', 'Sopor' and 'Discordia demens' appear in the company of 'mala mentis Gaudia', 'mortiferum Bellum', etc.). Virgil's group is expanded in Boccaccio's *De genealogia, liber primus*, ch. 14 et seq., as children of Erebus; similar personifications are given as children of the Night at the opening of Hyginus's *Fabulae* (published at Basle in 1535 and 1549 in a collection of mythographical handbooks which also includes the *Mythologiae* of Fulgentius; see Seznec, *The Survival of the Pagan Gods*, pp. 307–09).
20. Tibullus I.vii.45 and 47. In Philostratus, *Imagines*, I.15, Bacchus is depicted wearing a red cloak and a wreath of roses as he approaches Ariadne; the author points out that these attributes indicate his amorous intent. Cf. Titian's 'Bacchus and Ariadne', in which the red cloak appears also. Lilies, roses and other flowers in association with wine occur in the *Anacreontea*, nos. 5–6, 18A, 43, 44, 50, 53, 55 (numbered according to the edition in the Loeb Classical Library, *Elegy and Iambus with the Anacreontea* (London and Cambridge, MA: Loeb, 1961)).

21. Cf. the often reprinted edition of the *Metamorphoses* with commentaries by Petrus Lavinius and Raphael Regius and the summaries of Lactantius: *P. Ovidii Nasonis metamorphoseos libri moralizati cum pulcherrimis fabularum principalium figuris* (Lyon: J. Huguetan, 1518), fol. 57^v.

22. M. Raymond, *Baroque et Renaissance poétique* (Paris: José Corti, 1955), pp. 97–100. The polarization of moral values on the one hand, and the sense of a controlled energy on the other, were embodied also in the Platonic image of the charioteer and his good and bad (white and black) horses (*Phaedrus*, 246b and 249 ff). Ficino's gloss on this image occurs immediately after his interpretation of the four Platonic furies (in which Dionysus represents the second fury), and reduplicates it thus: 'Primus itaque furor, *bonum equum*, id est, rationem opinionemque, a *malo equo*, id est, a phantasia confusa et sensum appetitu distinguit. Secundus malum equo bono, bonum *aurige*, id est, menti subicit.' (Marsilio Ficino, *Commentaire sur le Banquet de Platon*, ed. by R. Marcel (Paris: Les Belles Lettres, 1956), p. 259). On this image in Pléiade poetry, see R. V. Merrill and R. J. Clements, *Platonism in French Renaissance Poetry* (New York: New York University Press, 1957), pp. 81–90. The Seneca passage referred to above also contains a 'chariot' image illustrating the impetus of the inspired and liberated mind: 'efferatur et mordeat frenos et rectorem rapiat suum'. Moreover, a similar pattern appears in certain of the allegorical triumphs of the Renaissance; see, for example, Dürer's series of woodcuts, 'The Large Triumphal Car of Emperor Maximilian', in *The Complete Woodcuts of Albrecht Dürer*, ed. by W. Kurth (New York: Dover, 1963), plates 312–17.

23. Pontus de Tyard, *Œuvres poétiques complètes*, ed. by J. C. Lapp (Paris: Didier, 1966), pp. 168–69.

24. It is perhaps relevant to note that Pontus introduces in a previous stanza the *discordia concors* theme in its specifically musical sense ('Quel accor discordant bruit, / S'entremesle, et s'entrefuit, / Qui mes esprits espouvante?' (*Œuvres poétiques complètes*, pp. 167–68)).

25. *Les Odes d'Olivier de Magny*, ed. by E. Courbet, 2 vols (Paris: A. Lemerre, 1876), II, 56.

26. Cf. D. and E. Panofsky, *Pandora's Box* (New York: Harper and Row, 1965), pp. 48–54. The relationship that the Panofskys establish in this book between iconography and poetry in a French context is highly relevant to the present study, particularly as it centres on questions of moral attitude. Magny's emphasis on moral clear-sightedness recalls the 'perspicacia' of Boccaccio; on the cosmic functions of Bacchus, also referred to in this passage, see above, p. 65, and below, note 34.

27. See *Desiderii Erasmi operum omnium tomus quartus* (Hildesheim: Olms, 1962; facsimile of the 1703 Leiden edition), cols. 411–12, 412–13, 417–18, 429–30 (from the *Praise of Folly*). For evidence of Ronsard's contacts with Erasmianism, see P. de Nolhac, *Ronsard et l'humanisme* (Paris: Champion, 1921), p. 37, and p. 243; see also J. C. Margolin, 'L'Hymne de l'Or et son ambiguïté', *Bibliothèque d'Humanisme et Renaissance*, 28 (1966), 290–93.

28. See E. Wind, *Bellini's 'The Feast of the Gods'* (Cambridge, MA: Harvard University Press, 1948), pp. 45–55 and 56–63. Wind's analysis of the Bacchic mysteries in *Pagan Mysteries in the Renaissance* (London: Faber and Faber, 1958), chs. XI and XII, is also relevant to the present study. The Florentine engraving of Bacchus and Ariadne reproduced above, pp. 52–53, originates in this same milieu.

29. Cf. Wind, *Pagan mysteries*, pp. 69–71; Kaiser, *Praisers of Folly*, pp. 52–83.

30. Cf. *Natalis Comitis Mythologiae sive explicationis fabularum libri decem* (Padua: Tozzi, 1616), p. 273, col. I. See also below, note 36.

31. Pontus de Tyard, *Œuvres poétiques complètes*, p. 168. Cf. Olivier de Magny, *Odes*, II, 6; Pontus de Tyard, *Solitaire premier*, ed. by S. F. Baridon (Geneva: Droz, 1950), pp. 17–19 (cf. also pp. 41–42).

32. Du Bellay, *Deffence et illustration de la langue françoyse*, ed. by H. Chamard (Paris: Didier, 1948), p. 106; Pontus de Tyard, *Solitaire premier*, pp. 22, 73–74; Ronsard, *Ode à Michel de l'Hôpital*, in *Cinquième livre des odes*, Laumonier, III, 143, 144–45. Cf. G. Castor, *Pléiade Poetics* (Cambridge: Cambridge University Press, 1964), p. 35.

33. See Merrill and Clements, *Platonism in French Renaissance Poetry*, pp. 10–12.

34. Marullus makes no reference to the dance and has no equivalent for 'animal': 'tu libras pondera machinae / Medioque terram suspendis in aere stabilem' (*Carmina*, p. 116, lines 53–54). The point is further confirmed by an important variant of lines 274–76 of the *Hinne* which appears in all the editions from 1578: 'tu restaures le monde / De ta longue jeunesse et de ta tresse blonde: /

Tousjours un sans estre un, qui te fais et desfais, / Qui meurs de jour en jour, et si ne meurs jamais.' The identification of Bacchus with the world-soul is an Orphic motif which is derived from the story of Bacchus's dismemberment by the giants and which was subsequently given a cosmic interpretation by Macrobius and others.

35. Pontus de Tyard, *Solitaire premier*, section 3 (pp. 12–21; especially pp. 17, 19). Cf. above, note 22, quotation from *Symposium* commentary; in Marcel's edition, Ficino's analysis appears in chs. 13–14 (pp. 257–60).

36. See Castor, *Pléiade Poetics*, especially chs. 13–17; cf. also p. 189, on Ronsard's sense of an order underlying the flux of the world, and the connection of this view with the interpretation of *imagination*. Cf. Alciati, *Emblemata cum commentariis* (Padua: Tozzi, 1621), p. 133: 'Sic veteres Bacchum Musis adiunxerunt, quia vino non minimum vires ingenii excitentur [...] moveantur phantasiae, addatur impetus, subministretur fiducia.' Finally, a similar function of Bacchic inspiration is implied in Ronsard's expansion of Marullus's phrase 'tu robur addis consilio' to 'tu marie au conseil / De celuy qui te croit un pouvoir non pareil' (*Hinne*, lines 267–68). Cf. also Milton's poem 'At a Solemn Musick', which speaks of 'our high-rais'd phantasie' (line 5) as the medium through which the combined sounds of 'voice and verse' are able to communicate an experience of the divine.

37. Cf. Wind, *Pagan Mysteries*, p. 40. The 'pagan' nature of the Bacchic myths is in the last analysis redeemed (as in the case of other myths) by this 'theological' allegory, according to which they embody a truth consonant with Christian belief.

38. Marullus, *Hymnus Baccho* (in *Carmina*), lines 55–57: 'Per te remota coeli procul ardua colimus, / Nimio diffusi praecordia nectare gravia, / Tu das deorum sanctis accumbere dapibus.'

39. Cf. Du Bellay, *Deffence et illustration*, pp. 36–37, 105, 179; and Pontus's *Solitaire premier*, p. 25.

40. I refer to the well-known passage in the *Hymne de l'autonne* (Laumonier, XII, 50, lines 81–82). The image of the 'fabulous cloak' forms a central strand in my essay 'Ronsard's Mythological Universe', in *Ronsard the Poet*, ed. by T. Cave (London: Methuen, 1973), pp. 159–208.

41. For this poem, see Laumonier, XII.

42. See the analysis of this hymn, together with the other seasonal hymns, by Donald Stone, in *Ronsard's Sonnet Cycles: A Study in Tone and Vision* (London and New Haven: Yale, 1966), pp. 107–20; also D. Wilson, *Ronsard: Poet of Nature* (Manchester: Manchester University Press, 1961), pp. 102–05.

43. On the history of melancholy as a temperament, see R. Klibansky, B. Panofsky and F. Saxl, *Saturn and Melancholy* (London: Nelson, 1964). Laumonier notes that the list of sicknesses in this hymn seems to derive from Folengo, who places them specifically under the sign of Saturn.

44. See Wilson, *Ronsard*, pp. 94–105.

45. Wilson, *Ronsard,* p. 96, n. 1.

46. Laumonier, XI, 159. Cf. the image of the wind which accompanies the Bacchic fury in the *Hinne de Bacus*, lines 129–30, 144–46 and particularly 191–94.

47. *La Lyre*, Laumonier, X, 293–94.

48. The 'dual psychology' of this hymn is closely paralleled by a passage in *Les Daimons* (Laumonier, VIII, 126–27), describing the contrary properties of good and evil *daimons*. Bacchus himself is, precisely, a good *daimon*.

2

'Tua facta loquar': Philomela's Afterlives in Rabelais, Ronsard and Shakespeare

It is difficult to speak of rape: difficult for the victim, especially, but also for others, including those who take it upon themselves to narrate it. The difficulty begins no doubt with the silence of a victim traumatized not only by her physical wounding but also by the degradation and imputation of guilt that the nature of the wound brings upon her in a patriarchal society. From there, the inability to speak is propagated, like a referred pain, throughout society itself, taking the form of an age-old taboo: of all crimes, rape is the most *secret*. The story of Philomela as it is told or cited in the Western literary tradition preserves the taboo even while breaking it, since its narrative always articulates a radical silence, a deprivation of the power of speech. It may thus be regarded as the paradigm of what is at stake when someone undertakes to recount an experience so alien that it is unspeakable.

Let us begin, then, by giving 'Philomela' the chance to speak. It will of course not be the woman herself who speaks: her words are imagined here by a male poet. What is more, she speaks a foreign language — Latin — rather than her native Greek. Such mediations are however unavoidable: they are intrinsic to the story itself. I quote her words of defiance to Tereus immediately after the rape, words that, in Ovid's version, so provoke him that he cuts out her tongue to prevent her from speaking and thus betraying him, as she threatens to do. They are consequently the last words she utters with her human voice:

> si tamen haec superi cernunt, si numina divum
> sunt aliquid, si non perierunt omnia mecum,
> quandocumque mihi poenas dabis. ipsa pudore
> proiecto tua facta loquar; si copia detur,
> in populos veniam; si silvis clausa tenebor,
> implebo silvas et conscia saxa movebo.
> audiet haec aether et si deus ullus in illo est.[1]

[If, however, the gods witness this, if there are such things as divine beings, if everything does not die with me, some day you will pay for my suffering. I myself, casting aside all shame, shall say what you have done; if I am permitted, I shall come before the public; if I am held captive in the woods, I shall fill the woods and move the very rocks in sympathy with my cries. The heavens will hear me, if there is any god up there.]

Philomela's intense desire to break the taboo will, however, not be inhibited by Tereus' further violence. Finding alternative means to represent the crime that has been enacted on her, she will in the end achieve the publicity she seeks on the stage of the world and of history. Her complaint will continue to reverberate, in one language after another: just as the gods grant her an afterlife as a songbird, so too her afterlife in the European tradition will be deeply bound up with poetry and its alternative ways of speaking. At the same time, her use of a visual medium — a tapestry — to disclose Tereus' guilt creates a further strand of engagement with aesthetic representation.

I shall reflect here on three texts. The first two appeared in 1552: the chapter of Rabelais's *Quart Livre* in which Panurge, at the fair on the island of Medamothi, buys a painting depicting the rape of Philomela, and a sonnet from Ronsard's *Amours*. It is all too common to assign the ageing Rabelais and the still youthful Ronsard of this period to two contrasting generations and cultural contexts; they meet here as if by chance at a moment when mythological representations are very much in fashion, whether at Fontainebleau or in the pedagogy of the Collège de Coqueret from which Ronsard was only just emerging.[2] As an epilogue, and to multiply the possibilities of cross-cultural comparison, I shall add a summary reading of the Ovidian story as it is embedded in Shakespeare's early play *Titus Andronicus*.

In the Medamothi episode, the theme of otherness is explicitly present from the outset in the narrative context: this is the first landing of the Pantagrueline fleet on a foreign island.[3] The name of the island is the Greek word for 'Nowhere', and the princes of the country bear names that make them exemplars of a foreignness presented to the tourists' gaze.[4] The theme is at once taken up again in the evocation of the annual fair of Medamothi and of the 'marchandises exotiques et peregrines' [exotic foreign goods] which are on display there. The fact that the word 'exotique' is here used for the first time in the French language is a further sign of Rabelais's effort to make the island the quintessence of otherness.[5] As for the goods themselves, it has often been remarked that Rabelais puts at the front of his stall not only things which are virtually impossible to represent but also the problem of representing them. Whereas he could have begun with the unicorns and the 'tarande', exotic beasts *par excellence*, he chooses first to list a series of pictures the subject of which is unrepresentable to the point of aporia.[6]

Amid the group of five paintings purchased by Pantagruel's companions, the one selected by Panurge occupies a favoured position, as if it were the central panel in a multiple iconographical montage; references to the art of Fontainebleau are indeed included in this passage. It is above all toward this painting, then, that the narrator draws the reader's attention, and it is in this case alone that he allows himself not only to describe the subject but also to add a commentary:

> Panurge achapta un grand tableau painct et transsumpt de l'ouvrage jadis faict à l'aiguille par Philomela exposante et representante à sa sœur Progné, comment son beaufrere Tereus l'avoit depucellée: et sa langue couppée, affin que tel crime ne decelast. Je vous jure par le manche de ce fallot, que c'estoit une painncture gualante et mirifique. Ne pensez, je vous prie, que ce feust le protraict d'un homme couplé sus une fille. Cela est trop sot, et trop lourd. La painncture estoit bien aultre, et plus intelligible. Vous la pourrez veoir en Theleme à main guausche entrans en la haulte guallerie.

Or que les prez, et ore que les fleurs,
De mille et mille et de mille couleurs,
Peignent le sein de la terre si gaye,
    Seul, et pensif, aux rochers plus segretz,
D'un cœur muét je conte mes regretz,
Et par les boys je voys celant ma playe.[12]

[Now that Jupiter, goaded by his seed,
Breathes in great draughts the accustomed fires
And, set alight by the heat of his loins,
Fertilizes Juno's damp womb;
    Now that the sea, now that the vehemence
Of the winds gives way to the great armed ships,
And that the bird amid the thick foliage of the trees
Begins anew her complaint against the Thracian;
    Now that the meadows, and now that the flowers
Paint the bosom of the joyful earth
With thousands upon thousands of colours,
    Alone, and pensive, among the most secret rocks,
I recount my sorrows with a speechless heart,
And pass through the woods, hiding my wound.]

Let us look first at the way the sonnet is constructed. An evocation of cosmic energy (lines 1–11) is placed in sharp contrast to the representation, in the second tercet, of the poet's isolation and exclusion from the sensual and sexual abundance of the natural world. In the first quatrain, Ronsard draws on a passage from Virgil's *Georgics*, which itself echoes a *locus* in Lucretius.[13] The second quatrain reworks lines from one of Horace's odes where one finds the image of warships putting to sea again in the spring coupled with an allusion to the myth of Philomela:

Iam veris comites, quae mare temperant,
impellunt animae lintea Thraciae;
iam nec prata rigent nec fluvii strepunt
    hiberna nive turgidi.

nidum ponit, Ityn flebiliter gemens,
infelix avis et Cecropiae domus
aeternum opprobrium, quod male barbaras
    regum est ulta libidines.[14]

[Already the Thracian breezes, the companions of spring that calm the sea,
drive the ships onward; already the meadows are no longer frozen, no longer
do the rivers thunder, swollen with winter snow.

Piteously bemoaning Itys, the unhappy bird builds her nest, an eternal shame
to the house of Cecrops because she wickedly avenged the barbarous lust of
kings.]

The contrast between the pleasures of spring in the natural world and the poet's pain and isolation also maps on to the *topoi* of Petrarchan poetry: in 'Zefiro torna' (*Rime* 310), in particular, this schema includes a reference to the plaintive cries of Philomela and Procne. It is evident, however, that Ronsard's treatment differs from Petrarch's in that the traditional décor of the forest with its singing birds is infused from the start with sinister and aggressive connotations: the allusion to Philomela is far from being merely, as it is in Petrarch, a graceful ornament. The final tercet of Ronsard's sonnet, for its part, borrows the Petrarchan *topos* 'Solo e pensoso' (*Rime* 35) in order to bring about the reversal from pleasure and abundance to solitude and pain. This poem, then, provides a virtuoso example of the Renaissance technique of *contaminatio* or *imitatio multiplex*: Ronsard conscripts for his own purposes a chorus of foreign voices.[15]

For Marc-Antoine Muret, one of the very first readers of the sonnet, the allusion to Philomela, however fleeting and discreet it may seem, moves into the foreground. Glossing the metonym 'du Thracien' in his commentary, he cites neither Horace nor Petrarch; instead, he offers a long paraphrase of Ovid's version of the story.[16] Any reader of the *Amours* who had consulted Muret's commentary would thus have had the details of the story in mind when reading the sonnet, which would surely have changed the overall perspective. In particular, the second tercet would then lend itself to be read as an appropriation by the poet of the suffering and silence of Philomela herself.[17] It re-stages both her solitude, abandoned as she is in a desolate landscape, and the 'secrecy' this solitude is designed to impose on her: Ronsard here seems to be echoing directly Ovid's 'si silvis clausa tenebor, implebo silvas et conscia saxa movebo.' Her hidden wound and her inability to speak likewise reappear in the phrases 'celant ma playe' and 'd'un cuœur muét', together with the representation of her suffering: 'je *conte* mes regrets.' The representation in this case is obviously not visual: it is poetry that is speaking. Yet the *topos* of poetics according to which poetry is a tapestry, a verbal texture, or indeed a painting ('ut pictura poesis'), allows a reading where Ronsard's sonnet may be assigned a function analogous to that of Philomela's tapestry.

In the light of these remarks, one may propose an alternative way of reading the construction of the poem. The opening scene of a sexual union between Jupiter and Juno that releases cosmic energies is now contrasted with another, namely the crime of Tereus, which has destructive effects, reducing nature to a moral waste land. This opposition structures the sonnet by alternation, since the first tercet takes up the theme of the first quatrain, while the second tercet brings about a transference of Philomela's suffering to the lyric first person. In this way, the form of the sonnet comes to represent — indeed to *frame* — a sexual wounding of which it is almost impossible to speak, but which finally succeeds in making itself public.

It would be hard to argue in this case that the sonnet is merely a youthful Petrarchan exercise where Philomela's pain is reduced to a figure of rhetoric, a cleverly engineered expressive flourish. Even on a first reading, where the play of allusion has not yet been explored, 'Or que Juppin' is a disturbing poem. The extraordinary energy of the opening quatrain, embodied in both theme and rhythm, already becomes aggressive in lines 5–6, where the licence that spring gives to war coincides with an unexpected metrical syncopation and a marked alliteration; sustained by the syntactical anaphora 'Or que', this powerful movement runs headlong towards the final tercet, where its energies are dissipated — or perhaps rather locked up — in expressions of isolation and frustration.

What, then, is one to say about this complex sonnet? First, no doubt, that

Ronsard has not sought to *represent* the rape of Philomela as a narrative, a sexual spectacle. He has clearly grasped the way in which the myth poses, essentially, a problem of expression. On that basis, he has conceived a scenario in which the lyric first person, improvising a path for himself amid fragments of the powerful texts he has inherited, attempts to discern the contours of an alien terrain. He seeks to give voice to a suffering which is uniquely his own, one that is the more capable of defining him because it is also radically foreign to him: the moment the first person singular begins to speak, it speaks of self-alienation. The sonnet thus demonstrates the deepest and most disturbing implications of the humanist doctrine of *imitatio*: in order better to articulate his secret, the first person must appropriate the secret of another.

Neither Rabelais nor Ronsard presents Philomela's story in an ethical — or even a merely sympathetic — perspective. The real suffering of Procne's sister takes place elsewhere, out of their reach. Yet they at least recognize that otherness and inaccessibility; they avoid exploiting it in order to indulge the vicarious sexual pleasure of the voyeur. They use it rather in order to put pressure on the mimetic power of language. In that sense, it may be said that these texts attempt not so much to represent as to *signify* an alien experience.

One possible way of developing this theme would be to explore the analogies between Ronsard's sonnet and Montaigne's chapter 'Sur des vers de Virgile'. Both present the image of a sexual encounter, evoked via powerful ancient texts (Virgil and Lucretius again), which acts as a foil to the awareness in the first-person writer of a lack, or at least a diminution, of his sexual energies. Montaigne, it is true, has no need to borrow a Petrarchan *topos* to tell his readers about his solitary and pensive old age, but he does, as everyone knows, consign his most embarrassing confessions in this chapter to Latin quotations. Rather than pursuing this parallel, which would take us away from the story of Philomela, I shall evoke another text from the late sixteenth century, one where the story (including Ovid's version) does play a central part: Shakespeare's *Titus Andronicus*.

In a particularly repugnant episode, Chiron and Demetrius, the son of Tamora, Queen of the Goths, outdo Tereus himself: having raped Lavinia, they not only cut out her tongue but also cut off her hands, explicitly in order to prevent her from denouncing their crime by writing it down:

> [DEM.]   So, now go tell, and if thy tongue can speak,
>   Who 'twas that cut thy tongue and ravished thee.
> [CHI.]   Write down thy mind, bewray thy meaning so,
>   And if thy stumps will let thee, play the scribe.[18]

Marcus, Lavinia's uncle, who arrives on the scene immediately after, soon guesses that she has suffered a fate even more horrible than Philomela's:

> But sure some Tereus hath deflowered thee
> And, lest thou shouldst detect him, cut thy tongue.
> [...]
> Fair Philomela, why she but lost her tongue,
> And in a tedious sampler sewed her mind;

> But, lovely niece, that mean is cut from thee.
> A craftier Tereus, cousin, hast thou met,
> And he hath cut those pretty fingers off,
> That could have better sewed than Philomel.[19]

One may note in passing that the word 'sampler' in this passage seems to indicate that Shakespeare knew that Philomela had woven letters rather than a picture on her loom: the function of the sampler is to present samples of weaving, often in the form of an ABC.[20] At all events, Marcus' speech indicates that the rapists have read Ovid and learnt from him that it was necessary to go still further than their model in order to reduce their victim to silence.[21]

Although Marcus guesses what has happened, he obviously has no proof, and in this scene he is limited to rhetorical lamentation. It is not until the opening of Act IV that the truth is clearly represented and the movement towards vengeance unleashed. In this scene, Lucius, Lavinia's young nephew, enters pursued by his aunt. He is carrying his school books, and Lavinia finally manages to make it plain that it is these she is interested in, in particular a copy of the *Metamorphoses*. She leafs through it with her stumps and finds the passage recounting the story of Philomela:

> [TITUS]   Lucius, what book is that she tosseth so?
> [BOY]   Grandsire, 'tis Ovid's *Metamorphosis*;
>   My mother gave it me.
> [MARCUS]   For love of her that's gone,
>   Perhaps she culled it from among the rest.
> [TITUS]   Soft, so busily she turns the leaves!
>   What would she find? Lavinia, shall I read?
>   This is the tragic tale of Philomel,
>   And treats of Tereus' treason and his rape —
>   And rape, I fear, was root of thy annoy.
> [MARCUS]   See, brother, see: note how she quotes the leaves.
> [TITUS]   Lavinia, wert thou thus surprised, sweet girl,
>   Ravished and wronged as Philomela was,
>   Forced in the ruthless, vast and gloomy woods?[22]

The play thus cites one of its sources,[23] while at the same time providing the motivation for a denouement where Lavinia's father kills the two rapists and bakes them in a pie which he gives to their mother to eat. The Ovidian imitation is thus extended, with significant modifications, to the end of the play.

In the intertextual contamination that Shakespeare engineers in these scenes, Lavinia's plight exceeds Philomela's in a number of ways. In the first place, she undergoes a double rape. Secondly, while Philomela is eventually transformed into a bird, Marcus' earlier speech compares her to a lopped tree, then to a fountain:

> Speak, gentle niece, what stern ungentle hands
> Have lopped and hewed and made thy body bare
> Of her two branches[.]
> [...]
> Alas, a crimson river of warm blood,
> Like to a bubbling fountain stirred with wind,
> Doth rise and fall between thy rosed lips[.][24]

consulted, the reading of the line in question is unambiguous: Philomela wrote on the tapestry.

21. For a detailed analysis of the Ovidian 'pattern' in *Titus Andronicus*, see Jonathan Bate, *Shakespeare and Ovid* (Oxford: Clarendon Press, 1993), pp. 103–08, 115–17.

22. *Titus Andronicus*, IV.1, lines 41–53 (pp. 213–14).

23. The word 'quotes' in line 50 means 'observes' or 'marks', but the modern sense is also no doubt present in this richly connotative scene; see Bate, *Shakespeare and Ovid*, pp. 103–04.

24. *Titus Andronicus*, II.3, 16–18, 22–24 (p. 188).

25. See Bate, *Shakespeare and Ovid*, pp. 82, 111.

26. In the tragedy *Scédase* by Shakespeare's French contemporary Alexandre Hardy, a double rape, followed by a double murder, apparently takes place on stage.

27. *Titus Andronicus*, ed. by Bate, Introduction, pp. 7–9.

28. See below, pp. 102, 107.

3

The Death of Guillaume Du Bellay:
Rabelais's Biographical Representations[1]

In a sonnet published posthumously, although probably written as early as April 1553,[2] the poet Joachim Du Bellay records a troubled night spent at Saint-Symphorien. His long-dead uncle Guillaume Du Bellay, sieur de Langey, appears to him in a dream, 'plus grand que de coustume' [taller than usual]; waking in fright, he recalls that this was the very place where Langey had died in January 1543. The reference emerges unexpectedly from what appears to be a case of amorous insomnia: Du Bellay is suffering from the 'regret' of leaving both France and the 'beaux yeux' of his mistress.[3] The structure of the sonnet might easily have led the reader to expect a dream image of the beloved; instead, it contrives a deviation into the political world of Du Bellay's family, the world of his more celebrated 'regrets'.

In the poem's concluding lines, Du Bellay evokes Langey's role as a defender of the French monarchy against Charles V; the theme is developed at greater length in a companion sonnet:

> Langé vivant fut à ceux de sa part
> Fosse, tranchee, et muraille et rempart:
> Mais à la fin sa vertu fut contrainte
>
> De nous laisser pour aux astres courir:
> Et en mourant feit encores mourir
> L'espoir François et l'Espagnole crainte.[4]
>
> [Langey when alive was to those of his party
> A moat, a trench, a wall and a rampart;
> But in the end his virtue was compelled
>
> To leave us in order to fly up to the stars;
> And in dying, he also caused the hope of France
> And the fears of Spain to die with him.]

A decade or more after it occurred, Langey's death is still seen as a critical disaster, a turning point in the fortunes of France.[5] The return of the great man's soul to its celestial home is mentioned at the end of both sonnets, yet the return of his dream image to the place where he died is marked by a sense of supernatural horror. The poet is left behind to face the endless political problems that Langey might perhaps have averted had he lived a few years longer.

A similar after-image of Langey is conjured up in two extended and thematically rich episodes of Rabelais's later books: chapter 21 of the *Tiers Livre*, in which Pantagruel proposes that Panurge should consult the dying poet Raminagrobis, and chapters 26 and 27 of the 1552 *Quart Livre*, which form part of the sequence on the isle of the Macraeons. One may assume that Du Bellay had read these chapters; the sonnets quoted above were probably written only a year or so after the publication of the expanded *Quart Livre*, and in the month following Rabelais's own death.[6]

It is not a question here of establishing literary influence. By the end of his life, Rabelais's position as a writer protected by the Du Bellay family was not so different from the one Du Bellay himself was to enjoy; despite the differences between them in age and in cultural formation, they clearly shared many perceptions of the way history was being made in their day, and in particular of the significance of Langey's premature death. The shock of that event must have continued to reverberate within the Du Bellays' milieu long afterwards; like a handful of well-preserved archaeological fragments, the sonnets of Du Bellay and — especially — the passages from Rabelais provide us with a representation of how it was felt, what its imaginative structure might have been.

The analyses of Krailsheimer and Screech go a long way towards clarifying the philosophical and Christian allusions of the two Rabelais passages.[7] They are indispensable to any historical reading of the texts, and I take them for granted as a point of departure. My own approach, however, is intended to be historical in a slightly different sense. It is based on the supposition that belief-systems such as Christian neo-Platonism do not and cannot exhaustively define the mode of thought and perception of any individual; they should rather be understood as enabling structures that provide a coherent frame for the shifting and often conflicting apprehensions of which subjective and even public experience is in practice made. I should like, then, to capture something of the elusive play of a sixteenth-century mind on a traumatic event, to follow the weaving of that event into patterns of reference and image which we would now call 'literary' but which are, again, no less a historical phenomenon than is a certain kind of neo-Platonism.

The reduplication of the reference in Rabelais is, to say the least, striking. If the episodes are considered separately, the evocation of Langey's death in each appears almost accidental; it plays an illustrative role which is clearly subordinate both to the narrative itself and to the themes raised by the narrative. Yet once the parallelism has been noticed, the perspective may well be reversed: it begins to look as if, in two successive books, Rabelais has developed a major episode out of the imaginative material provided by Langey's death. Raminagrobis on the one hand, the Macraeons and their dying Heroes on the other, appear as fictional transpositions of the real but already near-legendary figure of Langey, all the more so when we note that the episode to which the later passage belongs is much longer and composed of many more strands. In retrospect, the Raminagrobis episode has the air of a trial run; or, to put it another way, the *Tiers Livre* raises a ghost that cannot be prevented from returning and having its full say.

In comparing the two references to Langey's death, one may first ask to what extent one is in fact a repetition or reduplication of the other. Most obviously, both are embedded in a sequence of *exempla*, classical *topoi*, adages and analogies. In the *Tiers Livre*, these illustrate the prophetic powers of those approaching death, whereas in the *Quart Livre* the predominant topic is the portents that accompany the death of 'Heroes'; the connection between the two types of supernatural phenomenon is, however, extremely close and is reinforced by the neo-Platonizing provenance of both themes and examples. In terms of *dispositio*, there is again a slight difference overridden by a much deeper similarity. The case of Langey is given a privileged status in the *Tiers Livre*: it is the final and decisive example in Pantagruel's preamble on the divinatory powers of the dying; it is long and detailed; and it emerges from a *praeteritio* which not only shows that Langey's death rightly takes its place alongside the sequence of antique *topoi*, but which also asserts its priority and self-sufficiency: 'Je ne vous allegueray exemples antiques' [I shall not cite for you any ancient examples] — eight examples are then listed — 'seulement vous veulx ramentevoir [...]' [I only wish to recall to your memory [...]].[8] In *Quart Livre* 26, a first brief evocation of Langey's death (cited by Epistemon)[9] follows an extended Platonizing analogy and opens a sequence of examples of disturbances surrounding the death of great men; in chapter 27, Pantagruel develops the same theme through further analogies and examples and finally gives the cue for Epistemon to return to the death of Langey (lines 49–67). This time the narration of the event is longer than in *Tiers Livre* 21 and no less detailed. It also closes the sequence of instances specifically concerning portents: the dialogue moves on to the question whether Heroes die, to the length of their lives, and eventually, in chapter 28, to the celebrated story of the death of Pan. Thus the death of Langey plays a key role in structuring the whole episode: the earlier brief reference may be read as the introduction of a theme which is central to the imagination of the characters, a *memory* to which they cannot help reverting.

The internal similarities between the two accounts of Langey's death are likewise striking. In *Tiers Livre* 21, he is referred to as 'le docte et preux chevalier Guillaume du Bellay, seigneur jadis de Langey' (45–46), in *Quart Livre* 26 as '[le] preux et docte chevalier Guillaume du Bellay' (41–42), and in *Quart Livre* 27 as '[le] docte et preux chevalier de Langey' (50–51). This quasi-formulaic phrase recalls a long tradition of French epic narrative and thus endows Langey with an exemplary status which is significantly different from that of the 'exemples antiques'; it is one of the signs by means of which a shift of temporal and cultural perspective is effected in these passages.

Another is the implied change in the function of first-person pronouns.[10] In introducing learned materials, Pantagruel characteristically uses first-person formulas: 'J'ay [...] souvent ouy dire,' 'Je ne vous allegueray exemples antiques,' 'Je croy que toutes ames intellectives'. He may also use a rhetorical 'nous' to suggest shared experience when adducing comparisons: 'Car comme nous, estans sur le moule [...]'.[11] By contrast, the first-person forms used within the Langey passages denote the presence of the speaker as eyewitness at the great man's death: 'nous praedisant ce que depuis part avons veu [...]', 'Ce que veismes plusieurs jours avant le departement de celle tant illustre, genereuse et heroïque ame', 'Il m'en souvient [...] et encores me frissonne et tremble le cœur [...] quand je pense es prodiges [...] lesquelz veismes apertement'.[12]

This use of deictic, eyewitness pronouns is closely linked to the shift from present to past definite forms of the verb, informing the reader not only that the events narrated are 'historical', like the story of the death of Herod in *Quart Livre* 26, but also that they derive from the living memory of the speaker. A further distinctive feature is the recording of eyewitness *response* to indicate the power and above all the authenticity of the experience narrated: 'combien que pour lors nous semblassent ces propheties aulcunement abhorrentes et estranges' [although at that time his prophecies seemed to us in some way abhorrent and strange] (*Tiers Livre* 21, lines 52–54); and again: 'encores me frissonne et tremble le cœur dedans sa capsule, quand je pense es prodiges tant divers et horrificques lesquelz veismes apertement [...]' [my heart still shudders and trembles in its chamber when I think of all the various horrendous prodigies we clearly saw [...]] (*Quart Livre* 27, lines 52–55). The sense of strangeness, the physical manifestations of horror, are themselves the very proof that these events occurred; this is the rhetoric of the 'true story.'

Even these features, however, are secondary to the central and most visible mark of authenticity. In each case, Rabelais is scrupulously careful to provide a quasi-legal documentation of the event. In the *Tiers Livre* version, he specifies the place of death and then, with almost redundant precision, the date: 'le 10 de Janvier l'an de son aage le climatere et de nostre supputation l'an 1543 en compte Romanicque' [the 10th of January, in the climacteric year of his life and, by our reckoning, the year 1543 according to the Roman calendar] (47–49). Langey may not have died on 10th January, and he wasn't at a 'climacteric' (he was 51, not 49 or 63). But accuracy is here much less important than precision.[13] Rabelais is providing the reader simultaneously with an indication of the symbolic importance of the event and with the proof that it actually happened in recent recorded time. By contrast, even celebrated figures like Isaac, Jacob, Hector, Achilles and Alexander the Great, all cited in the preceding *praeteritio*, seem to belong to a vague, distant, and barely even chronological domain of the past. Even more dramatic is the listing, in *Quart Livre* 27, of sixteen named eyewitnesses, signatories as it were to Epistemon's affidavit; the naming of Rabelais himself among them is of course a special sign for the reader, the ultimate indication that the text has momentarily moved out of the fictional mode into a privileged realm of both private and public experience.

It might be objected that Rabelais is a master of the comic and parodic list, and that the use of his own name might be read as a sign of irony rather than authenticity. Rabelais's writing plays strange tricks with the reader, and these passages are certainly not immune to its habitual complexity; but the massing of effects, the recourse to pathos and a sense of supernatural terror, support the view that Rabelais cannot simply be 'playing' here (whatever that might mean). Nor need the sense be inverted or even undermined by the more-than-legal redundancy. It is more plausible to say that Rabelais's proliferating and deviant language is exploited for a special moment of intensity in honour of Langey and the almost unspeakable charge of meaning carried by his death.

We may now move outwards again towards the integration of these passages into the wider context of the episodes to which they belong. The *Quart Livre* chapters will necessarily predominate here, simply because they supply so many more interconnections; but the complementary relation between the earlier and the later version of Langey's death will be presupposed throughout.

We have seen that the death is presented as both exemplary and actual, and the same double perspective governs Langey's participation in the natural and supernatural realms. In *Tiers Livre* 21, he is said to have reached a symbolic age, a turning point for the world at large as well as for himself; yet he certainly appears primarily as a dying mortal. He is not (as the footnote to the TLF edition has it) himself a Hero: Pantagruel's preceding exposition speaks of Heroes as belonging to the category of quasi-supernatural beings who welcome and console dying men, communicating to them the art of prophecy; Langey is a beneficiary of this gift. Even in the *Quart Livre*, Langey figures in a large and loose category of great men whose death is marked by portents or other perturbations. However, the whole discussion arises here from Macrobe's suggestion that the storm suffered by Pantagruel and his company was a portent associated with the death of a Hero. At the beginning of chapter 27, Pantagruel calls the souls of departed great men 'Heroïques,' and it is the same epithet that he subsequently applies to the soul of Langey. There is thus every reason to suppose that, by 1552, Rabelais had promoted Langey to the rank of Hero, which of course not only adds to his ex-patron's supernatural aura, but also, conversely, makes the category of 'Hero' a more tangible, less theoretical one.

If Langey is both a man who died at a particular, recent moment and a member of the transtemporal class of Heroes, he is by the same token drawn into the imaginative theme which founds the Macraeon episode as a whole: the theme of ageing, which is also that of antiquity and of the loss of some former glory. The ancient ruins and inscriptions the companions find on the island, together with the fact that Macrobe communicates in 'languaige Ionicque,' bespeak a venerable origin (ch. 25, lines 25–36, 46); yet the population of the island is very much reduced, and those who remain are all 'charpentiers et [...] artizans' (19–24). Macrobe subsequently makes the decline explicit:

> Amys peregrins icy est une des isles Sporades jadis riche, frequente, opulente, marchande, populeuse, et subjecte au dominateur de Bretaigne; maintenant, par laps de temps et sus la declination du monde, paouvre et deserte comme voyez. (ch. 26, lines 1–8)

> [Friends and travellers, here is one of the Sporadic Isles, once rich, much-visited, opulent, prosperous in trade, populous, and subject to the ruler of Brittany; now, with the passage of time and the decline of the world, poor and deserted, as you see.]

The temporal pathos of the place is equally embodied in the Daimons and Heroes who inhabit the forest and who have now become old (11–12). Their life guarantees the island's welfare and abundance; when they die, afflictions come (16–22). Thus the history of the island and its civilization is recapitulated in the (admittedly distended) life span of each individual Hero.

Pantagruel and his company arrive at a critical moment, a kind of climacteric portended by the storm they have just endured and embodied in the death of a Hero. As Pantagruel himself says, in reply to Macrobe's explanation of the portents, the passing of these 'ames nobles et insignes' is marked not only by celestial perturbations but also by 'lamentations des peuples, mutations des religions, transpors des Royaulmes, et eversions des Republiques' (ch. 26, lines 31, 37–39). And it is at this point that Epistemon recalls the death of Langey:

> Nous [...] en avons naguieres veu l'experience on decés du preux et docte chevalier Guillaume du Bellay, lequel vivant, France estoit en telle felicité que tout le monde avoit sus elle envie, tout le monde se y rallioit, tout le monde la redoubtoit. Soubdain après son trespas, elle a esté en mespris de tout le monde bien longuement. (40–45)

> [We [...] formerly experienced this as eye-witnesses at the death of the chivalrous and learned knight Guillaume du Bellay, during whose lifetime France enjoyed such prosperity that the whole world envied her, the whole world visited her, the whole world feared her. Ever since his death, she has long been held in contempt by the whole world.]

The imaginative context in which this allusion occurs suggests that Rabelais is attempting to make sense of the critical historical moment in which he lived in terms of wider temporal structures. Whereas in the first two books, a burgeoning and enlightened present was compared with a benighted past, and Utopia (or utopian Thélème) seemed almost within reach, the vision is now reversed: the *translatio imperii et studii* ('transpors des Royaulmes') to France has come and gone, an unfavourable 'mutation de religion' has supervened in so far as the cause of moderate Gallican reform has failed.

Epistemon's later gloss — like Du Bellay's sonnets — represents the passing of Langey as both the cause and the embodiment of this turning point. Witnessing the portents that preceded his death, his friends and servants foresaw 'que de brief seroit France privée d'un tant perfaict et necessaire chevallier à sa gloire et protection' [that France would soon be deprived of a knight so perfect and so necessary to its glory and protection] (64–66). When one juxtaposes this passage with the earlier account, in *Tiers Livre* 21, of Langey's prophecies, a discrepancy appears. Pantagruel claims that Langey spent the last hours before his death

> nous praedisant ce que depuys part avons veu, part attendons advenir: combien que pour lors nous semblassent ces propheties aulcunement abhorrentes et estranges, par ne nous apparoistre cause ne signe aulcun present pronostic de ce qu'il praedisoit. (*Tiers Livre* 21, lines 51–56)

> [predicting to us what we have in part already seen and in part expect to come about, even though at that time these prophecies seemed in some way abhorrent and strange, since no cause or present sign appeared to us that prognosticated what he was predicting.]

Assuming that the 'nous' of this passage is not distinct from the eyewitnesses listed in *Quart Livre* 27, one might think it odd that, after five or six days of portents, Rabelais's friends lacked any 'signe present' to corroborate his prophecies. However, the difficulty is only superficial and is no doubt due to a difference of emphasis. In the earlier version, the theme of prophecy is uppermost; the significant point is that Langey's predictions seemed implausible at the time because nothing then indicated the traumatic changes which were about to take place. In the later passage, the discussion centres on the portents that made the death of Langey seem inevitable; his prophecies are not mentioned. The actual consequences of that calamitous event could only be observed in retrospect, as in the passage in *Quart Livre* 26.

What emerges overall from this configuration of texts is the sense of a very precise, personally experienced historical moment which is also a critical turning point in the affairs of France; the cosmic perturbations that accompany it appear as a projection of the shock and dismay it caused as well as of its quasi-apocalyptic character. Past, present and future are gathered together at a single juncture: the prosperity of a past civilization, the living memory of a great man and his achievements, the present shock of his death, the prophecies that spell out a strange, abhorrent but all too certain future — all these are apprehended in retrospect as a nexus of historical meaning.

It goes (almost) without saying that a central preoccupation here is the correct reading of signs. These may be disconcerting, strange, or unnatural, as when Pantagruel refers to prodigies, portents, monstrous events and other anticipatory signs that contradict the order of nature (*Quart Livre* 27, lines 47–48). They reveal their dark or obscure side to those who witness them, but the signs at issue here are by definition carriers of the truth; they are a divine script. A great deal has been said about the question of signs in Rabelais, particularly in the third and fourth books,[14] and I only propose here to touch on one local aspect of the topic. Pantagruel's account of Langey's prophecies in *Tiers Livre* 21, quoted above, mentions the lack of any 'cause ne signe [...] present pronostic de ce qu'il praedisoit.' His general discourse on portents at the beginning of *Quart Livre* 27 reverts to the same phrasing, while giving the word 'prognostic' a more specific connotation. He embarks on a lengthy simile to explain the function of the heavenly signs that accompany the death of a Hero: 'Et, comme le prudent medicin, voyant par les signes prognostics son malade entrer en decours de mort [...]' [And as the wise doctor, seeing from the prognostic signs that his patient is entering on the process of death] (lines 9–11); the comparison closes as follows: the heavens, before the death of heroes, seem to celebrate with a firework display of 'telz cometes et apparitions meteores, les quelles voulent les cieulx estre aux humains pour prognostic certain et veridicque prediction que, dedans peu de jours, telles venerables ames laisseront leurs corps et la terre' [such comets and meteoric apparitions, which are intended by the heavens as an indubitable presage and truthful prediction for humans that, within a very few days, those venerable souls will leave their bodies and the earth] (22–26). The analogy, then, introduces the figure of a doctor who interprets natural bodily signs to make a prognosis.

The figure can hardly be a mere illustration in this context. The scene evoked in the simile, where the doctor is seen exhorting the family and friends of his patient to come to the deathbed and ensure that everything is left in order after his demise, is precisely relevant to the case in hand — more so, a modern reader might think, than a celestial firework display. Furthermore, the witnesses at Langey's deathbed include one 'maistre Gabriel medicin de Savillan,'[15] and no sixteenth-century reader could have been unaware that Rabelais himself, whose name follows Gabriel's, was a doctor. In consequence, the practice of medicine becomes linked to the art of prognostication and vice versa. Langey's suffering body was studied with a doctor's eye for signs of dissolution; the heavens sent portents which all those present could interpret; and Langey himself uttered prophecies as if reading signs that other mortals could not see. The three levels seem to represent the transition from this world to the next, from natural or physical to supernatural or celestial. Otherworldly signs become more reassuringly tangible, physical signs point towards an event of historic and cosmic significance. And, in a position which is both central and marginal, as a character in a simile, a name in a list, or a displaced first-person pronoun, is represented the doctor whose testimony is here recorded in an act of both homage and interpretation.

Another striking, and crucial, example of a simile whose meaning reaches beyond its immediate context is the comparison in *Tiers Livre* 21 between those who, from the safety of the shore, watch mariners out at sea and pray for their safe arrival in harbour, and supernatural beings (Angels, Heroes, good Daimons) who guide dying humans to their last rest. This simile is of course very close in its structure and purport to the 'doctor' analogy of the *Quart Livre*. What it introduces, however, is not a glimpse at one or more removes of a real deathbed scene, but only, it would seem, a timeworn *topos*: life as a dangerous maritime excursion, death as a safe harbour. In the *Tiers Livre*, this is indeed all it is, apart from the Platonizing references. But in retrospect it may well look like a trailer (or 'signe pronostic'?) for the great storm scenario of the *Quart Livre*, to which the Macraeon episode is intimately linked: the storm is explained as one of the portents accompanying the death of a Hero, and Pantagruel's mouth in that episode is full of references to stormy weather.[16]

The cause of the storm which nearly shipwrecks Pantagruel's company is in fact not unequivocal. The explanation just referred to is given by Macrobe in chapter 26, in reply to Pantagruel's question (ch. 25) as to whether the seas adjacent to this island are particularly subject to tempests. The question might suggest that no other cause than a physical one had ever been implied. This is, however, not the case. At the height of the storm, Frere Jan says of Panurge: 'Ce diable de fol marin est cause de la tempeste' [This devil of a seagoing fool is the cause of the storm] (ch. 20, lines 24–25). The remark is enigmatic: does it simply mean that he is the reason why they have embarked on the voyage (see Pantagruel's remarks, ch. 25, lines 53–57)? That would be an odd reading of the phrase 'est cause de la tempeste'. The only other plausible reading is an allegorical one: the tempest is a manifestation of Panurge's 'folly,' his mental and moral confusion ('Ce diable de fol marin [...]').

A non-literal reading becomes essential, in fact, from the very beginning of this episode, which is arguably the most patently allegorical sequence Rabelais ever wrote. It will be recalled that the company encounters several boatloads of monks and assorted ecclesiastics making their way to the 'concile de Chesil', easily identifiable as the Council of Trent: 'Les voyant, Panurge entra en excès de joye, comme asceuré d'avoir toute bonne fortune pour celluy jour et aultres subsequens en long ordre' [When Panurge saw them, he was beside himself with joy, as if he was now certain of having every kind of good luck on that day and for many days thereafter] (ch. 18, line 7–10). So Panurge makes a favourable prognostication from this sign, throwing in some material donations as an insurance policy. Pantagruel, by contrast, remains 'pensive and melancholic' (17). Frere Jan asks him why, but there is no time for a reply: the wind rises, and the pilot, foreseeing that seriously bad weather is imminent (21–22), puts both crew and passengers on the alert; then a storm of fearful proportions does indeed arise. It is quite clear that Pantagruel's prognostication is the opposite of Panurge's; even though it is the practical pilot (rather like the doctor) who foresees the storm itself, the connections soon become evident. The encounter with the clerics was a sign clear enough for Pantagruel at least to read.

In chapter 18, then, it appears that the monks going to their council are a presage and perhaps even a cause of the storm; in chapter 26, by contrast, Macrobe connects the storm with the death of a Hero. Portents are involved in both cases, but the relations are reversed: in chapter 18, a specific event presages the storm; in chapter 26, the storm portends a specific event (although it is of course also an *effect* of the event). Is this simply an involuntary discrepancy, to be ascribed to the interval between Rabelais's composition of the storm episode for the 1548 edition and his development of the Macraeon episode for the 1552 edition?

The alternative view is that the double explanation creates a relationship between the threatening prospect of Chesil–Trent and the death of a Hero potentially identifiable with Langey. The storm, whether portending or portended, then becomes the allegorical expression of the religious and political crisis of the 1540s, of that turning point in the affairs of France referred to in chapter 26 and of the dire events foretold by Langey on his deathbed. Langey's death was a catastrophe for Rabelais because it deprived France of a major statesman, a man who would not only have championed the French cause against Charles V (as Joachim Du Bellay suggests in his sonnets), but might also have given weight to the moderate faction at Trent and thus prevented a reassertion of hard-line orthodoxy. The allegorical landscape allows the writer to understand and explore a series of events which, in their raw experiential form, are both traumatic and uncontrollable.

This last remark could be extended to the third and fourth books as a whole. In the first two books, problems are raised, the giants and their friends are threatened by hostile forces, but Gargantua and Pantagruel visibly dominate their world, dwarfing and defeating their opponents with gigantic ease. In the third and fourth books, problems become chronically difficult to resolve; the monsters and alien forces of the *Quart Livre* (not least the storm) present serious threats and may prove impossible to evacuate; the safest course, in more than one episode, is evasion. One indicator of this shift is the repeated advocacy, from early in the *Tiers Livre,* of a neo-Stoic disaffection in the face of externals, a *topos* which may perhaps better be regarded as a symptom of disquiet than as a comprehensive philosophical solution. Another is the emergence of the themes of prophecy and portents, largely absent from the earlier books: when the present looks confused and murky, the desire for knowledge of the future becomes critical. Yet another is the reversion to images of old age and decline, already present in the ageing anxious Panurge of the *Tiers Livre.*

Of course there are many other themes and emphases in Rabelais's later books; of course it is a critical commonplace that the tone of these books is more sombre and the role of the giants more subdued, less exuberant. I would argue only for a reading that makes the shock of Langey's death and the quasi-supernatural aura of that 'real' experience central to the renewal of Rabelais's imaginative powers in

§I
Pre-histories: An Introduction[1]

Quand tout ce qui est venu par rapport du passé jusques à nous seroit vray et sçeu par quelqu'un, ce seroit moins que rien au pris de ce qui est ignoré.

[Even if all the reports that have been handed down to us from the past were true and known by someone, they would amount to less than nothing in comparison with what is not known.] (MONTAIGNE, 'Des coches')

A literary text may be classed as a cultural object that bears signs of its provenance. If that is so, then any literary study must necessarily be historical and anthropological. One may, it is true, make a show of considering a given literary object without reference to its temporal dimension, or simply as an *objet d'art* the only function of which is to decorate the drawing room or the mind of its owner. But this suppression of its historical value would only be apparent; or at least, it could never be complete. Both the aesthetic and the economic value of an art object depend on its provenance and on the idea one has of that provenance, even if the idea is erroneous or imaginary. The most aggressively 'modern' production of a play by Sophocles, Shakespeare or Racine has a hidden side, like the dark side of the moon, composed of the half-effaced past to which the public assigns the play in its collective cultural memory.

This memory is no doubt a retrospective construction, and it is liable systematically to suppress everything that is strange and foreign in the past. The *luminous* image that is still persistently projected on to the period called 'the Renaissance' is only the distant reflection of a particularly successful publicity campaign set in motion by the scholars and writers of the period itself.[2] The darkness which is its counterpart is intrinsic not only to the so-called 'Middle Ages' (or their predecessor, the 'Dark Ages') but to the whole of history, since all that remains to us of history is a more or less aleatory set of archaeological and documentary fragments.

This apparently pessimistic way of seeing things may, however, serve as the opening move in a defence of the historical value of literary and para-literary objects. No doubt the survival of literary texts depends for the most part on the economy of the *objet d'art* to which I have already referred; no doubt one should never forget that the scope of these accidental remains as a vehicle of historical knowledge is limited by the fact that they emerge for the most part from a relatively privileged social context. If one wishes to reconstitute the everyday life of a given period in its economic or social aspect, one will draw on archival materials, use statistical methods, explore domains that are anything but literary. It would be wrong, however, to believe that it would be possible in this way to fill the whole space of history, to eliminate its intrinsic darkness. What results from such work (and statistics is here the model) is often simply an assimilation of the particular by the general, as if the particular were *merely* accidental, and thus inauthentic, while the general represented in some sense 'the truth'. Provided we recognize and accept the aleatory aspect of literary objects, we can in fact garner from them valuable information that cannot be delivered by any other historical source.

This is possible in the first place precisely because each literary text is a hapax. Even as it signals its position in relation to a given set of traditions and conventions, it insists on its difference, whereas legal or theological treatises — not to mention the documents piled up in archives — seek primarily to establish an authenticity which can always be transferred and translated. The movement towards difference is made possible above all by the highly complex forms of coding that characterize the literary text. The intensive use of rhetorical and poetic procedures creates a discursive field in which the mutual contamination, overlapping or entanglement of strands belonging to different domains (religious, philosophical, political, ethical, aesthetic, economic, quasi-autobiographical or personal, and so on) is virtually inevitable; this is true even in quite short and uniform texts, *a fortiori* in those vast reservoirs of paradigmatic materials that are the works of Rabelais, Ronsard and Montaigne.

At the aesthetic level, the sixteenth century, instead of censuring such promiscuity, encourages it; it encourages dialogue, multiple or mixed forms, the proliferation of materials and the coexistence of different registers (in short, it encourages *copia*). But the aesthetic domain is here again always inseparable from the historical: the works of the period are profoundly and visibly marked by their immersion in the social, political and religious history that unfolds around them, whether one is thinking of a history of 'events' or of ideas. This relationship of text to context is furthermore not purely passive. Far from being a simple reflection of the world and culture that produced them, literary texts become engaged in it: they enter into history, in the strong sense of the phrase, as one can see from the censorship to which Rabelais's works were subject or from the extraordinary reception history of Montaigne's *Essais* in the early modern period.

In this way, literary texts compose a world which seems at times to be familiar to us, but which is none the less far removed from ours, both in the things it takes for granted, its presuppositions, and in its angle of perception. Like the cultural objects that one finds in a museum of ethnology, they allow us to surmise the existence of an otherness which one can never, without risking the erasure of its very identity, control by means of a formal apparatus of knowledge. All one can do is keep turning the object over, listen to it attentively, trace its coded message deep into its inner recesses.

The studies grouped together in *Pré-histoires* emerge from a poetics that is wholly orientated in this way towards history. One could conceive such a poetics as the mirror image of the highly rigorous theoretical model constructed by Michael Riffaterre, for whom each text carries within it everything one needs to interpret it, including the imprint of the history to which others would like to restore it.[3] In Riffaterre's method, as in mine, the textual object is in some sense *sufficient*; what it signifies is always in excess of the particular glosses with which one can surround it. But the claim that one should therefore not take the glosses into account (unless they happen, conveniently, to form part of the cultural furniture owned by the rather handsomely endowed Riffaterrean critic) is one that I cannot share. More importantly, instead of reading the traces of history inscribed in the cultural object according to the principles of consumer hermeneutics (or of hermeneutic connoisseurship, which amounts to the same thing), the aim of these studies is to elicit from it the fragmentary contours of a lost experience. In order to do this, one needs to determine the precise orientation according to which this precious remnant, like the antenna of some transhistorical receiver, can communicate to us an echo of the voices that surrounded it at the moment when it came into being. Infinitely distant, supremely difficult to hear, let alone translate, they also speak out to us at times with astonishing clarity.[4]

Each of the studies of *Pré-histoires* begins, then, with the particular, the singular even, rather than the general, and does its best not to fill in the blanks — the dark patches — of history. At various points, the metaphor of the archipelago is invoked, as if Rabelais's *Quart Livre* had provided the model of an approach characterized by its irregular landfalls and its detours rather than by the coherence of the mainland or (worse) of some wide-reaching empire.[5] One could equally speak of a diacritical network where what mattered was the nodes and focal points constituted by apparently distinct traces as they intersect or merge with one another.

It is true that questions are sometimes raised in *Pré-histoires* in terms of the now familiar notion of 'grand narratives' ('les grands récits'), which are inevitably instruments of generalization. The heuristic value of this concept is inarguable. It allows one to sidestep the medium-term timescale of positivist history, passing directly from the local to the general; used critically, it also promotes a healthy awareness of the quasi-fictional character of such narratives. I shall return to this point shortly in relation to the notion of a 'pre-history', but for the moment I would simply note that the work of identifying *grands récits* of various kinds (I am thinking here in particular of Foucault's histories) often seems to create a new kind of grand narrative, one in which a long-standing epistemic regime undergoes a crisis and is replaced by another. Certain of the key topics explored in *Pré-histoires* — in particular the emergence of a radical Pyrrhonism in the late sixteenth century and the crystallization of the notion of the self in the same period — stand at the point of intersection of both an older grand narrative (one might mention Burckhardt and Popkin as symbolic figures here) and a newer, 'Foucauldian' one; they are thus subject to enormous interpretative pressures. My purpose has been to use particular cases (particular texts) as a fulcrum by means of which those immense, and immensely powerful, imperializing structures may be displaced, however slightly, and a salutary mobility restored to our sense of the past.

It will be evident that the methodology of *Pré-histoires* was informed in part by the Anglo-American new historicism, which sought to replace the linear narrative and grand syntheses of positivist historiography with a 'thick description' of cultural and historical phenomena, often comparing texts of sharply differentiated character and provenance in order to display the 'circulation of social energy' to which they bear witness.[6] It was also a professed aim of the new historicists to undo textual hierarchies and canons, creating a kind of level playing field where no players were privileged or excluded. Motivated by a radical distrust of all the forms of historical legitimization of European world hegemony and its patriarchal imperialism, they sought to uncover and undo the stifling of female and minority voices which they believed to be inherent in, and even constitutive of, traditional 'Western' historicism. Here, by contrast, literary texts continue to be privileged for the reasons I have already indicated: in fact, the new historicists' supposed radical decanonization was never more than partial, as their persistent preoccupation with Shakespeare shows. As for the ethical questions posed by new historicism, their intrinsic importance for our own culture is in itself sufficient indication that any approach which gives them priority will displace the trajectory of historical enquiry towards unambiguously modern preoccupations. Similarly, in appropriating the new historicists' technique of analysing clusters of contrasted texts, I have endeavoured to ensure that the historical relation between the texts in a given cluster can be rigorously demonstrated. Finally, the work of reconstruction that I have undertaken, in *Pré-histoires* itself and therefore in the studies in this volume that are derived from it, is always to be regarded as partial and provisional; it assumes as a primary requirement an attitude of constant suspicion towards everything that is projected retrospectively on to the traces of the past.

The writing of an 'archipelago history' has necessary consequences for the structure of such a study. Instead of investigating a single phenomenon with the aim of producing a solid block of information and analyses designed as a definitive 'coverage' of the topic, I chose a series of textual instances derived from different domains and genres — the history of ideas, rhetoric, poetics, the novel, the 'essay' — in order to show how and where they meet. Since these nodal points are neither predictable nor symmetrical, the relations between the individual studies and the group as a whole are multi-dimensional. Although the chapters of *Pré-histoires* may no doubt be read separately as studies on specific texts and questions, the reader is — there, as here — invited to reflect on the various ways in which they may interact, opening up new perspectives and new possibilities of enquiry.

These aims may perhaps become clearer if one attends to the sense of the phrase 'textes troublés' ('disturbed texts', 'textual disturbances') which I used as a subtitle for the first of the two volumes of *Pré-histoires*. The objects we call literary are often disturbed or disturbing ones. In the sixteenth century, no less than nowadays or in the days of Plato, they give rise to suspicion and even a degree of contempt or hostility, and they are therefore inclined to surround themselves with apologies, cautions or rectifying glosses.[7] My aim in this perspective was to read a cluster of textual disturbances as the *historical* signs of epistemological uncertainty, or of ontological or axiological anxiety. The detection of a 'disturbance' makes it possible to localize a problematic region of perception, to discover a sort of 'crack' of which the author and his or her contemporaries may not be fully conscious, but which they experience as an unease, a blurred patch on the horizon of thought. The word 'crack' (*fêlure*) was chosen in order to challenge the Foucauldian notion of 'rupture', or at least to reduce the dramatization of history it implies. It may also be considered as a transposition of the term 'fault-line', that seismic metaphor of Californian origin which was very much in vogue among the new historicists. The metaphor is powerful and appealing, since it speaks of a surface sign pointing towards a vast, subterranean phenomenon that is not itself available to our inspection. However, my use of this metaphor again involves a sustained attempt to reduce the drama-tization it implied: the cracks in the surface I attempt to register do not herald some imminent seismic event but at most a local tremor in a series which, in the very long run, may be seen retrospectively to herald a shift in the landscape.

The disturbances explored in *Pré-histoires* may be most easily detected in the more complex and controversial texts of the period, the ones that always seem to escape one's hermeneutic clutches: the problem of belief in Rabelais, Ronsard or Montaigne, for example, may be considered as a function of their writing as such, and thus grasped through the analysis of certain key passages that appear as aporias. These aporias are not constituted solely at the level of literal expression; they are perceptible in the interaction of the literal sense (however problematic that might in itself be) with the rhetoric or poetics of the text in question. Often, at the micro-textual level, the disturbance reveals itself through an inconsistency, an abrupt change of theme or register, a grammatical or syntactical singularity.[8] When these moments of logical or grammatical breakdown occur in a discourse which already in some sense lends itself to suspicion, they have the capacity of showing us the places where the official language of a given period proves inadequate to the task of giving an account of the writer's own experience. At such moments, the text stumbles against a problem that is still unformulated or only partially formulated, and thus disquieting. A ripple of unease runs through the unexpected entrance of Gargantua into the Trouillogan episode of Rabelais's *Tiers Livre*; the intercalation into the 'Apologie de Raimond Sebond' of an aside addressed to an anonymous princess creates a certain turbulence that affects the chapter as a whole; the opening by Ronsard of a parenthesis in the conditional mode in order provisionally to license the worship of the Sun, together with the reopening of the same parenthesis by Montaigne, allows us to glimpse a belief system which is conditionally unsettled.[9] Further examples are provided by the intermittent and unstable intervention of the first person as a character in Rabelais's fictions, or the double narrative of the death of Guillaume Du Bellay in the same author's third and fourth books.

What I am here calling a 'disturbance' may be defined as the textual sign of a psychological response to a phenomenon which, as we see it, is historical. This definition rests on the presupposition that a text does not always mean to say what it says, and vice versa: its intentionality may be in some degree unintentional. It is crucial to emphasize, however, that the approach adopted here is in no sense psychoanalytic, and requires no recourse to Freudian or post-Freudian conceptions of the psyche: it is historically grounded (for example, Montaigne at several points in the *Essais* speaks of the way in which human actions may have motivations that are not present to the agent at the moment the action is performed). Both the instrument and the object of analysis are to that extent strictly historical, as is the purpose of the exercise, namely to use a textual disturbance as a means of access to a history that is not otherwise accessible. It was certainly not my purpose to uncover the putative state of a given writer's psyche as if that writer were the patient of a modern psychoanalyst or psychotherapist.

With those preliminaries in mind, we may now look at the sense of the word 'pre-histories' as I use it, beginning with the complementary word 'threshold' which appears in the sub-title of *Pré-histoires* and in the name of the series ('Seuils de la modernité') to which it belongs. It has become customary — part of an all-embracing 'grand narrative' — to regard the period we are dealing with as the first phase of modern European civilization, the 'early modern' period. The very conception of a Europe composed of independent nations, the secularization of political thought, the first wave of a scepticism that will progressively undermine all of the core beliefs of earlier ages together with the structures of authority that upheld them, the dissemination of an intellectual critique that prepares the way for a scientific revolution, the emergence of a lay self, freed from the constraints imposed by religious and political institutions, the invention of new literary forms (the essay, the autobiography, the novel) — all these historical (or narrative) beginnings are convenient to the extent that they allow us to follow each strand of history back to its supposed source. One cannot in fact deny that analepsis is the necessary condition of any historical narrative. Our advantage over the inhabitants of the distant country of the past consists in our ability to detect, as if we were defamiliarized Voltairean characters such as Candide, L'Ingénu or Micromégas, aspects of their culture that they themselves had difficulty in seeing because they were too close to them. Without that advantage, the method I have sketched out here would be impossible to imagine, since it presupposes the possibility of bringing to light phenomena still embryonic, and thus in some sense hidden, in their own day.

The expression 'seuil de la modernité' was originally proposed by Michel Jeanneret as an equivalent of the English phrase 'early modern period' in the absence of any current translation of the phrase into French. Since the early modern is by definition a broadly-conceived period without precise cut-off points, bypassing value-laden labels such as 'Renaissance', 'Reformation', 'the Baroque', 'the Enlightenment', the notion of a 'threshold of modernity' must be understood in a similar sense. As I use it, the metaphor does not denote a dividing line between an essentialized modernity and what precedes it; nor is it, as we saw earlier, a Foucauldian epistemic rupture; it cannot be identified with any one event, text or agent. In other words, it is essential not to imagine a singular threshold that constitutes a decisive, large-scale turning point, but rather to pluralize the word, as in the series title ('Thresholds of modernity'); when used in the singular, it should be thought of as a hypothetical limit, always mobile and visible primarily from a retrospective viewpoint. Those who were alive at the moment of a supposed threshold can only have had, at most, a vague consciousness of its passing: a disturbed consciousness also, perhaps, to the extent that for them the phenomenon in question was something unfamiliar and difficult to explain in terms of existing explanatory frameworks. Most crucially, they can have had only the dimmest sense of what might follow. The concept is thus above all a heuristic one, a modern tool invented in the hope of tracing the vestiges of a far-off experience rather than imposing on the past an imaginary uniformity and rigidity. Intransigent periodization is only good for those who seek to make history easier to handle, to bring it to heel and control it for other, extra-historical ends.

What, then, is a 'pre-history'? Essentially, it is an account of what precedes a given threshold, of the gradual sedimentation by means of which what appears to us as a threshold is reached. The account must, however, make every effort to avoid analepsis. That might seem virtually impossible, given that we select the strands of the story we want to tell and that we label the threshold as such. But the theoretical impossibility of such an approach cannot be maintained here, since otherwise we would rapidly arrive at a position where we *merely* prioritized our own concerns and ended up by contemplating our own faces in the mirror of history. The ethical arguments advanced in the wake of new historicism for doing just that can surely be inverted by affirming that the ethics of any study (anthropological or other) of human cultures must rest on maintaining our respect, right down to the wire as it were, for what is other in their forms of experience and their modes of expression.

One needs, in other words, to move against the current, in both the methodological and the chronological sense, undoing progressively the narrative that we are inclined to construct. The first step is to abandon entirely the notion of an 'origin', since the origin of a given phenomenon can only be identified by means of analepsis. A threshold is not an origin; it is only the moment when a particular story begins to be definable as such. Before the threshold, there are only (were only) scattered traces, uncertain premonitions of a possible future threshold, but endowed with their own sense in the moment and the context to which they primarily belonged. It is this bundle or cluster of traces[10] — that which was there before there was a history — which I would define as a 'pre-history'.

Among the other strategies one can use in order to decontaminate one's account of these pre-histories is to proceed backwards, against the chronological order. Since a threshold is constituted by what follows rather than by what precedes it, one needs first to see why it is there at all, to make visible the *grand récit* in which it plays a privileged role and then to make the gesture of erasing that narrative and its interpretative burden. In this way one can attempt to drop, piece by piece, the baggage of the future, and as one crosses the threshold, always moving against the flow of time, undo its organizing power. Thus, for example, one needs to evoke the story in which the Cartesian *cogito* heralds the advent of a new age of scientific and philosophical rationality in order to show that it was only one of a series of moments, preceded by others that might have led in a different direction. Once one has reached that point, the writings of Descartes (or of anyone else) no longer appear as one of the founding texts of modernity, in relation to which something called 'Montaigne's scepticism' or the emergence of a lay subject in the *Essais* must necessarily and as if naturally be understood.

This notion of a reversed chronology might sometimes be deployed literally, in the manner of Martin Amis's *Time's Arrow*. More often, however, it remains a heuristic model, a Trojan horse by means of which one can get oneself into the walled citadel of the past. More simply, one can work to take apart the elements of ready-made historical narratives, redefine their value and status in such a way that they begin to sketch the contours of another story, another history whose denouement remains always held in suspense. In every case, the essential objective is to create a virtual zone in which the future that we know has not (yet) happened.

Finally, pre-histories are least vulnerable to the magnetic power of singular thresholds when they, like the thresholds, are plural. This is the sense of the archipelago metaphor, or of the cluster. The fundamental tool in such a method is the microanalysis of a specific textual instance carrying a structured individual perception, be it of a disquieting pattern of ideas or beliefs, a disturbing personal experience, or an unexpected tremor in the political or economic situation of the day. Each of these structured perceptions may open its own window on the history to which it belongs, but in every case it is important to juxtapose it with others, which are usually derived from other genres or other moments in such a way as to create a mutually correcting and mutually defining set of coordinates (subject, once again, to the rule that the relation between the instances chosen must always be beyond reasonable doubt, and not the result of some sophisticated display of hermeneutic acrobatics). The set should be regarded as being capable of indefinite extension: in theory, the more coordinates one has, the more accurate the picture that will emerge. But of course the ultimate goal of producing an adequate representation of the past will always keep receding as we attempt to close with it. 'Relations stop nowhere', as Henry James famously said.[11] Besides, many coordinates have been irreversibly lost; the past is saturated with silence and absence. What has disappeared, what we cannot see, can be neither tamed nor exorcized; it must therefore be treated with respect, for it is always capable of sending from the darkness of historical space a new signal that would contradict our hypotheses and modify the whole picture.

Notes

1. The text translated here was originally a paratext, the introduction to *Pré-histoires*. In this volume, it clearly has a different function: it serves to introduce the set of studies presented in this section, all of which are drawn from *Pré-histoires*, but its broader purpose is to describe the methodology governing the whole of the 1999 book and its sequel. Thus explanations of the structure of the book and some references to sections not reproduced in the present volume have been allowed to stand, displaced into the past tense.

2. In the two volumes of *Pré-histoires*, I avoided the term 'Renaissance', despite the fact that it has been eroded by use to the point where it is almost harmless, in order to suppress the connotations which none the less continue to proliferate around it.

3. This theoretical and methodological principle is maintained with exemplary coherence throughout Riffaterre's writings; see in particular *La Production du texte* (Paris: Seuil, 1979), chs 1–2.

4. This way of conceiving the relationship between history and literature would be sharply contrasted, yet not incompatible, with the conception on which Géralde Nakam's brilliant studies of Montaigne's *Essais* in their historical context are based.

5. I owe this Rabelaisian metaphor to the work of Frank Lestringant, who used it for his title 'L'Insulaire de Rabelais ou la fiction en archipel', in *Écrire le monde à la Renaissance: quinze études sur Rabelais, Postel, Bodin et la littérature géographique* (Caen: Paradigme, 1993), pp. 159–85.

6. The classic statement of this notion is Stephen Greenblatt's *Shakespearean Negotiations* (Oxford: Clarendon Press, 1988), ch. 1.

7. It has become customary nowadays to recall that, in the sixteenth century, the notion of 'literature' did not have the sense it has nowadays (did not cover the same segment of the

textual continuum). Yet it is evident that this constantly renewed suspicion already demarcates a separate or separable category of writing (poetry, fiction, etc.); that the existence of a 'poetics' transmitted from one phase of European culture to another presupposes the existence of a corpus of texts labelled 'poetry' in the broadest sense of the word; and that a parallel tradition of reflection on rhetoric has recognized from its earliest beginnings the extraordinary power of language to move, to persuade, to deceive (in short, to *disturb*) by exploiting its own non-logical or paralogical properties.

8. It is once more Riffaterre who places at the centre of his methodology the pinpointing of an 'agrammaticality' around which the reader is obliged to restructure his or her reading.

9. For this demonstration, see *Pré-histoires*, pp. 51–59.

10. The word 'trace' as I use it in this context is to be understood in its everyday sense ('an indication by means of which one recognizes that something has existed or happened'). It would however be disingenuous not to acknowledge the use of the word by Jacques Derrida and his readers: see in particular the analysis of the term by Marian Hobson (*Jacques Derrida: Opening Lines* (London: Routledge, 1998), especially pp. 13–15), who also cites the work of H. H. Pattee on the problem of designating pre-biological phenomena (the process of biogenesis) without speaking of an 'origin' of life, such an origin being by definition inaccessible to our post-biological instruments of knowledge.

11. Henry James, *Roderick Hudson*, The World's Classics (Oxford: Oxford University Press, 1980), Preface, p. xli.

§2

Imagining Scepticism in the Sixteenth Century

Nous secouons icy les limites et dernieres clotures des sciences, ausquelles l'extremité est vitieuse, comme en la vertu.

[We are shaking here the limits and last fences of the realms of knowledge, where extremity is a vice, as it is with virtue.] (MONTAIGNE, 'Apologie de Raimond Sebond')

This essay explores the ways in which Pyrrhonism is perceived and presented in a small group of sixteenth-century texts. All of these are in some sense paratexts that register a reaction to Pyrrhonism: three are prefaces in Latin to the writings of Sextus Empiricus, while the other two are micro-episodes embedded in a predominantly Pyrrhonist scenario (the debate between Panurge and Trouillogan in Rabelais's *Tiers Livre* and Montaigne's 'address to the princess' in his 'Apologie de Raimond Sebond'). I have deliberately drawn a tight line around texts demonstrably associated with the radical form of scepticism known as Pyrrhonism in order to avoid shading off into vaguer definitions of scepticism. My emphasis will, however, be somewhat different from that of the historians of ideas who have written on Renaissance scepticism.[1] I shall pay particular attention to presentation rather than to content, and the presentation will be considered above all as a symptom of the writer's response to a potentially disturbing mode of thought. My examples will thus be analysed not primarily as explicit philosophical or ideological statements but as complex quasi-literary texts full of narrative devices and figures of speech. It seems to me that these literary elements can neither be taken at face value nor dismissed as marginal, anecdotal, or frivolous. They help us to define the mode of perception, to highlight tensions, hesitations and uncertainties, and that allows us in turn to chart the limits of what it was possible to think in the sixteenth century, as well as the points of tension and friction that indicate the places where the terrain is about to shift and open up new possibilities of thought.

This approach is not an especially novel one these days, but it has not yet been applied in any detail to this body of materials. And yet it would seem obvious that this is a body of materials to which such an approach should above all be applied. This is because scepticism clearly was a question, a matter for unease and controversy, in the sixteenth century; it was one of the prime vehicles of a shift which we think of as the very mark of the early modern. The question of how scepticism was thought before Descartes must be crucial to our understanding of the period, and it cannot be answered by assuming that Pyrrhonist discourse simply means what it says.

Historians of ideas have in fact been very careful to insist that Pyrrhonism was understood by sixteenth-century writers in ways very different from those that are familiar to us, that they did not do with it what later thinkers did. For example, they assimilated it to pre-existing modes of thought that appeared to them to be analogous, such as Cusan mysticism or Augustinian pessimism, and care is needed here in specifying the partners it was assigned to. Catch-all terms such as 'Christian scepticism' erase too many important nuances and should be avoided except perhaps as a reminder that sixteenth-century scepticism always operates within or in relation to a Christian frame of reference. Another crucial defining aspect of the way Pyrrhonism was used in the sixteenth century is its function. What Popkin and Schmitt have exhaustively shown is that its ostensible function was almost always apologetic, and one must again take care here to specify what was being defended — Scripture, revelation, orthodox tradition, reformist theology, counter-reformation theology, the *Theologia naturalis* of Raymond of Sabunde. There are plenty of accidents in the history of Pyrrhonism, but it is certainly not an accident that the text in which the full range of sceptical arguments was first made available in any vernacular was called an 'Apology', nor that Pascal was still using Pyrrhonist strategies for apologetic purposes almost a century later.

However, I want to argue that these express aims cannot tell us everything. They are inadequate — this is visible when one reads the texts — to forestall or neutralize the epistemological disquiet that Pyrrhonism may give rise to. Its exponents present it as in some sense bizarre, even comic; they are apologetic in the other sense, namely defensive. They equivocate. Imagining scepticism is a kind of folly, inviting ironic praise; it also comes to resemble imagining utopia — utopia is a no-place, Pyrrhonism is an anti-philosophy. Most of the texts I consider here are similar in the way they are packaged and presented; they embark on a similar attempt to reorganize mental space, often showing signs of discomfort and unease. What follows is a small contribution to the history of such displacements in the early modern period, and thus to the pre-history of 'modern' scepticism.

Apelles' sponge

In Book I of the *Hypotyposes*, Sextus Empiricus recounts a well-known anecdote in order to illustrate the quasi-accidental discovery by the sceptics of the suspension of judgement (*epochê*) as a means to ataraxia:

> Once, they say, when [Apelles] was painting a horse and wished to represent in the painting the horse's foam, he was so unsuccessful that he gave up the attempt and flung at the picture the sponge on which he used to wipe the paints off his brush, and the mark of the sponge produced the effect of a horse's foam. So, too, the sceptics were in hopes of gaining ataraxia by means of a decision regarding the disparity of the objects of sense and of thought, and being unable to effect this, they suspended judgement; and they found that ataraxia, as if by chance, followed upon their suspension even as a shadow follows the body.[2]

The most characteristic gesture of Pyrrhonism, the *epochê*, emerges here not from a process of philosophical reflection but from a genetic narrative, brief as it is. What is more, its importance becomes evident by chance ('tukhikôs'), as in the story of the discovery of penicillin. It is only when the orthodox philosophical goal of ataraxia is accidentally reached that the accident appears in retrospect as the crucial step, the founding gesture of a philosophy. After this chance *epochê*, the *telos* itself becomes secondary, or rather is suspended. Pyrrhonism will thus be an anti-systematic way of doing philosophy, an always-unfinished enquiry in which unforeseen shifts and reversals are programmatically allowed for.

This fragment of the *Hypotyposes* was certainly known to most if not all of the sixteenth-century writers we shall be considering; one of them explicitly echoes it. However, its function here is not so much to establish a common source for their reflections on Pyrrhonism, but rather to serve as an emblem, if not a paradigm, of certain characteristic themes and procedures within their writings: a story of origins, the theme of chance, and a markedly affective response (exasperation in the case of Apelles; anger, fear, nervous laughter, imaginary fevers, or an abrupt U-turn in his early modern successors). Above all, it presents the Pyrrhonist move as a form or structure (as a 'move') rather than as a collection of arguments. That is how the texts discussed below will be treated.

The generation gap

To begin with the Pyrrhonist episode in Rabelais's third book (1546) is self-evidently to give priority to narrative over philosophical conceptualization. There is strictly no exposition of Pyrrhonism in this episode,[3] and the responses of the fictional audience occupy no less of the foreground than the dialogue between Panurge and the philosopher Trouillogan. Within the narrative sequence, the episode is also introduced accidentally. In chapter 29, Pantagruel decides to invite representatives of the three major disciplines, theology, medicine, and law, to a dinner party to help Panurge decide whether to get married; as an afterthought, to make up the 'Pythagorean tetrad', he adds a philosopher. In the event, Trouillogan will be the last speaker at the symposium; his dialogue with Panurge marks a major crisis at both the epistemological and the narrative levels, the end of the attempt to find reasoned solutions to Panurge's dilemma. An accident thus brings about a critical moment, a turning point.

Initially, there is no indication that Trouillogan is a Pyrrhonist, rather the reverse: 'le Philosophe perfaict, et tel qu'est Trouillogan, respond assertivement de tous doubtes proposez' [the perfect Philosopher, such as Trouillogan is, replies assertively on all uncertainties that may be put forward].[4] His philosophical persuasion is not mentioned until the title of chapter 36, where he is called an 'ephectic and Pyrrhonist philosopher'. This again gives the encounter the character of something unpremeditated, unforeseen; Trouillogan disconcerts his whole audience, and not only Panurge.

Let us now look at the way in which that effect is produced. The episode is divided into two distinct phases by the intervention of Gargantua. The first phase consists of a brief dialogue between Panurge and Trouillogan which is resolved by Gargantua's entrance (chapter 35); there then ensues a longer dialogue, left unresolved by Gargantua's exit (chapter 36). This appearance of Gargantua is yet another surprise: he was supposed to have been translated to the land of the fairies, according to Pantagruel; there are marginal signs of his revival in the *Tiers Livre*, but his entrance here is wholly unprepared and unmotivated.[5] It is brought about with a distinct narrative flourish, the flourish being his dog, a proleptic figure the function of which is to mark the Gargantuan presence as particularly august. When told what has been going on, the aged giant says that he understands Trouillogan's contradictory and perplexing replies and offers a gloss. Pantagruel provides a parallel example and the other experts who are present follow suit, after which the chapter ends with a fully explicit summing-up by Pantagruel. A golden mean or 'harmonization'[6] is achieved which puts a stop to the outbreak of indeterminacy; the voices of wisdom, good sense, and — especially — authority control the situation. Thus the first phase.

In phase two, however, Panurge refuses mediation and hence re-opens the Pandora's box: or, as he puts it, 'je suis descendu on puiz tenebreux onquel disoit Heraclytus estre Verité cachée' [I have gone down into the dark well in which Heraclitus said that Truth was hidden] (p. 248). There follows a re-run of the earlier sequence, leaving Panurge bewildered and exasperated. At this critical point, Gargantua intervenes again, representing himself as an old man who has lived during a period when the world has changed:[7] the figure and his voice are still clearly identifiable to us ('I don't understand what these young chaps are saying nowadays — ephectics, sceptics, Pyrrhonists, Derrideans, post-structuralists, post-modernists, relativists, and the rest. If that's what the world's coming to, I'm glad to be out of it').

The episode thus, in the end, remains unresolved. Whereas, in his famous letter to the young Pantagruel in *Pantagruel*, Gargantua had characterized the generational change in glowingly positive terms as the dawning of a new and more enlightened age, it here appears to be problematic. The representation of Pyrrhonism is attached to a conflict between generations and to an uncertainty about the best way forward; it is also shot through with affect, whether one is thinking of Panurge's anger and exasperation or Gargantua's irritable exit.

When Gargantua leaves, Pantagruel and his friends want to follow him, but he won't let them:[8] nostalgia for a bygone age when truth seemed to be within reach is ruled out, and the protagonists are left in a world of uncertainty, even of epistemological crisis. In retrospect, the resolution proposed at the end of chapter 35 looks like a *morale provisoire*, not at all like the answer to Pyrrhonist doubt.

It is important to stress that the whole discussion in this as in other parts of the *Tiers Livre* takes place under the sanction of Christian faith as mediated by Scripture. Yet that outer ideological framework eliminates neither the problem of Pyrrhonism, nor the anxieties associated with it; the structure of the episode, it seems to me, quite unequivocally reopens the question after an attempt has been made to close it, and leaves it open. Pyrrhonism is also characterized here, by the very presence of the aged Gargantua and not only by his remarks, as a *modern* phenomenon, something novel, disconcerting, a phenomenon both fascinating and repulsive.

We now move back some twenty-five years to 1520 and to the *Examen vanitatis doctrinae gentium, et veritatis Christianae disciplinae* of Gianfrancesco Pico della

Mirandola.[9] The first three books of this work contain the earliest transcription of Pyrrhonist arguments from Sextus Empiricus ever to be printed. Gianfrancesco's project appears to have had no immediate influence, but this does not affect its value as an example of how scepticism was imagined in the earlier sixteenth century.

The explicit argument put forward in the prefaces to the various books of the *Examen* is the one which will characterize later apologetic readings of Sextus Empiricus: the arguments of Pyrrhonism destroy human knowledge, leaving revelation intact. Pagan thought in general is confuted, as the title suggests, but Aristotle is Pico's particular target; the later books are devoted to a demolition of Aristotelian philosophy.[10] Pyrrhonism, Pico argues, is of no interest or value in its own right, but it is useful as a means of countering the arrogance of those who lay claim to certain knowledge. The prefaces thus carefully draw a boundary line round Pyrrhonism; they circumscribe it.

The preface to Book III includes remarks of the kind just quoted, but it also contains an autobiographical account of the genesis of the *Examen*. Gianfrancesco says that his original aim was to write down his thoughts on pagan philosophies (elsewhere he says on more than one occasion that this project was intended as a continuation of the work of his famous uncle).[11] The project was interrupted by a series of political and military events in which the writer was personally involved, and he provides enough detail of these to give a sense of the confusion and unpredictability endemic in war and diplomacy. When he finally had time to take the project up again, he says, he found that his perspective had profoundly changed; he saw philosophy in an entirely different light. Having previously sought to establish the opinions of the ancients on the pursuit of happiness, he now saw that they all disagreed — and that that was the point. There followed further interruptions before he was finally able to compose the second and third books.

Now, this autobiographical fragment is introduced by the anecdote from Sextus Empiricus quoted above. The question then arises, what is the connection between the Apelles story and the autobiographical fragment? The first thing to note is that an *interruption* is followed by a change of view; a break in the sequence of reflection leads to a reorganization of the mental map. Political and military events, as a paradigm of unpredictability, play a role here equivalent to that of Sextus Empiricus' sponge. Secondly, Gianfrancesco's reference to the search for happiness coincides exactly with the point on which the Apelles story bears — happiness is not found by following any of the routes prescribed by philosophy, but through a suspension of judgement, which itself promotes ataraxia.

So far, so good: Gianfrancesco is providing a personal gloss, in the mode of Renaissance *imitatio*, on the Apelles story. Yet it is important to note that he 'corrects' the Apelles story in one significant respect. He insists that it was not chance, as with Apelles and the sponge, that made him change his mind: he was guided by Divine Providence.[12] More importantly, he makes reference neither to the source of the story in Sextus Empiricus, nor even to his own discovery and reading of Sextus. Yet this must have been a major factor in his philosophical volte-face (compare Montaigne's encounter with Pyrrhonism some fifty years later).

To sharpen the point, let us look for a moment at the actual content of the first three books. The first enumerates the general disagreements of philosophers, with special reference to the pursuit of happiness. The second presents central sceptical material such as the Pyrrhonist tropes, and in section 21, where the account of the tropes begins, Gianfrancesco says that he has in the main followed the *Hypotyposes* here, adding relevant material from other authors. Book Three consists of a comprehensive set of attacks on the arts, patently based on the *Adversus mathematicos*. In short, Gianfrancesco's reading of Sextus Empiricus is essential to the composition of this part of the work. So why doesn't he mention it?

The simple answer is that he did not want to credit a pagan with what he means to present as a Christian revelation. However, such an answer cannot in itself smooth away the tensions and discrepancies. All those elaborate precautions can surely not just be intellectual adjustments that enable Pyrrhonism to be tamed and used for limited strategic purposes (the defence of Christian faith), leaving no other trace of their impact. I would suggest that their signification is closely bound up with Gianfrancesco's desire to continue his uncle's project. Pico — the famous Pico, so much more famous than his nephew — was especially well known for attempting to assemble the most ambitiously eclectic philosophical synthesis thinkable at that time, reconciling the major emphases of all known philosophies and religions; also for writing an oration on the dignity of man. It is not for nothing that he has been taken to represent the 'typical Renaissance confidence in man', although he is no doubt better regarded as an extreme, hyperbolic case. Gianfrancesco inevitably had to work in the shadow of his influence. Where, he must have asked himself, does one go from there? The solution will be to reverse Pico's ambition; to empty it out; to add the solvent that makes all the bits of the eclectic synthesis come unstuck and appear as an amorphous mass of irreconcilable fragments; to throw a sponge, in other words, at Uncle Pico. The sponge has now of course become the writings of Sextus Empiricus himself, even though Gianfrancesco doesn't tell us how and when he came across them.

If, then, one reads between the lines of Gianfrancesco's account, one finds another, half-hidden story. That story is familiar to us from studies of Renaissance imitation theory, from the *Querelle des anciens et des modernes*, and so forth; it is also a version of the 'anxiety of influence' *topos*, a tale of generational difference like that enacted in the Trouillogan episode of Rabelais's *Tiers Livre*. It is true that the iconoclastic violence of Gianfrancesco's gesture is masked — or compensated for — by his submission to another, far higher authority: Divine Providence itself. Yet the configuration cannot be reduced simply to the appropriation of Pyrrhonism by Christian apologetics. The Pyrrhonist suspension in this preface begins surreptitiously to show its power, its capacity for producing an intuitive leap into unknown territory, for transforming the mental landscape. The power may then be disguised and contained, but that is precisely because it has been felt; what need would there be otherwise for all those adjustments and precautions, for the displacement of the question to the level of a visibly disturbed autobiography?

A Pyrrhonist fever

We now move on some forty years to Henri Estienne's translation of the *Hypotyposes* into Latin. It is dedicated to Henri de Mesmes, the ideologically liberal patron of an important circle of humanists. The dedicatory epistle immediately invites comparison with the presentation of works like the *Praise of Folly* and *Utopia*: it is playful, full of ironies, disclaimers, self-parody and reversals. It also resembles these texts, and Gianfrancesco's preface to Book III of the *Examen*, in that it provides an autobiographical narrative of the genesis of the work, except that here the instance is quasi-fictional: Estienne describes himself explicitly as 'a character in an invented story' ('fabulae actor'), says that the story is tragi-comic, and offers it to his patron as an allegory for him to interpret.[13]

It tells how 'Henricus' underwent the strange metamorphosis into a sceptic. He had been suffering, he says, from a fever, and the fever had made him hate the study of letters, which he had previously loved. The least thought of books grated on his mind. Then he happened to go into his library, shielding his eyes with his hand in case the sight of the books should make him feel sick. While looking through a lot of old rubbish in a box, he came across some notebooks containing a hasty rendering he had made some time before of some of the arguments of the Pyrrhonist sect. The very sight of them made him laugh (laughter being, of course, already therapeutic); he liked them so much that he got out all the papers, looked for the copy of Sextus in Greek from which he had transcribed these fragments, and finally found it covered in dust. When he had been in good health, he had found the text incoherent, obscure and contradictory, so that he had given up. Now, with renewed strength (despite the fever), he has returned to the task of reading and translation, and finally completed it.[14]

We may note here already that the way the narrative is told implies that there is a complicity between Pyrrhonism and the fever, since the one book he can tolerate in his fever is the *Hypotyposes*, and it is only thanks to the fever that he can complete his work on it. Pyrrhonism is a feverish philosophy or a philosophical fever; it is on the side of the fever in a certain sense; yet it also cures it. It is like a homeopathic medicine.

Having told the story, the narrator asks why there was this strange sympathy between the fever and Pyrrhonism? His own answer is that he had caught the fever because he was working too hard on 'letters', so it was not surprising that he began to hate literary study — it was threatening his life. The merit of Pyrrhonism is, first, that it confutes all the professors of all the arts, thus reinforcing and justifying his hatred of letters; and consequently that it allows him to enjoy the rest of his life, which would otherwise have been spoilt by fruitless study. He has found a reason, in other words, for early retirement.

At this point in the preface, there is a volte-face. Estienne marks the preceding development as playful by using the phrase 'serio loqui' [to speak seriously] for what follows, and he now sets out to circumscribe Pyrrhonism: a classic sixteenth-century gesture, but one which in the context can only make more visible and striking the metaphors of confusion and uncertainty. The humanist (no longer a narrator) now claims that Pyrrhonism has in fact not vindicated his hatred of *litterae*; it has rather reconciled him with them by undermining the assertions of the dogmatists, thus (presumably) releasing him from anxiety in dealing with the problematic texts of the ancients. More importantly, it encourages Christian humility in theological matters: when dogmatists and sceptics are compared on the question of knowledge of God ('Dei notitia'), it is easy to see that the humility of the Pyrrhonists is preferable. In the last part of the preface, Estienne further explains that he has published the book in order to reduce impious dogmatists and their followers to *insania*; or rather to cure them, since there's hope that the illness people contract from the dogmatists will be cured by the force of Pyrrhonist arguments. In other words, Pyrrhonism both makes them mad and cures them of madness: it is a cure by opposites ('contraria contrariorum').[15]

As in the other texts we have looked at, there is thus a final resolution or harmonization of the apparently contradictory nature of Pyrrhonism, deferring to a supernatural principle of authority. Yet it would again be unwise to regard Estienne as merely another 'Christian sceptic'. The playful part of the preface is extensive and elaborate; there is no reason to think that it is less significant than the later part. In fact, it is surely in the autobiographical fiction that the novelty, the strangeness of Pyrrhonism, its capacity to reorient the whole of one's intellectual frame of reference, are most cogently embodied. This is strikingly so in the allegory of the library: a new book is unearthed which displaces all the others, creating almost, but not quite, a *tabula rasa*. We shall return in a moment to an even more striking verbal symptom of Estienne's mental overheating.

Seven years after the publication of Estienne's version of the *Hypotyposes*, the Catholic apologist Gentian Hervet dedicated his translation of the *Adversus mathematicos* to the Cardinal de Lorraine. The Cardinal was a pillar of the orthodox Catholic establishment and a member of the powerful Guise family; it was to him also that Guy de Bruès had dedicated his *Dialogues* on scepticism. Brush describes Hervet's dedicatory epistle as more serious than Estienne's;[16] I would prefer to say that it is more authoritarian. There is little doubt that in this instance the apologetic intention is to appropriate Pyrrhonism in its entirety and so make it subservient to the cause of orthodoxy. Hervet specifically cites Gianfrancesco Pico, who shows, he says, how Sextus Empiricus can be used to defend the dogmas of the Christian religion against the 'externos philosophos' [pagan philosophers]. And he adds that the Pyrrhonist confutation of human arguments may also be used against what he calls the 'new Academics', the heretical proponents of theological novelty.[17] To this, Hervet adds that Pyrrhonist arguments are useful in education, because they provide the best possible training in disputation. They put pupils on their mettle in defending the truth, and make them distinguish the true from the merely probable.[18]

Yet even in this extremely orthodox and strictly policed account, there are indications that Hervet regards Sextus Empiricus' writings as belonging to the category of disconcerting and paradoxical texts. And Hervet too, despite his 'serious' tone, indulges in some autobiographical narrative. He says that he had been in need of recreation after a long period of hard labour translating the commentaries of the

Fathers on Scripture and attacking heresies. Looking for a book to take with him for light reading on a journey, he had gone into the Cardinal de Lorraine's library, where he found the *Adversus mathematicos*. He read it with enormous pleasure, then decided to translate it while recovering his strength for greater things; he now recommends that the Cardinal should read it in his leisure hours.

This version of the 'leisure hours' *topos* is clearly a much paler and less complex version of Henri Estienne's story; the elements are similar, but the balance and emphasis are different. One sees the ideological pressures emerge more strongly: Hervet was well known for his anti-Protestant writings, and should any further guarantee of ideological correctness be required, it is provided by the patronage of the Cardinal de Lorraine. What is more, the Pyrrhonist project of the moderate Protestant humanist Henri Estienne is here conscripted to the Counter-Reformation cause. Estienne's version of the *Hypotyposes*, together with its dedicatory epistle, is printed after the *Adversus mathematicos* in Hervet's edition. This precarious equilibrium is possible, no doubt, because Pyrrhonism is liable to relativize everything it touches. But according to the same logic, the least Pyrrhonist argument would serve to upset the balance once again, allowing the *epoché* further licence to demonstrate its powers. This is what happens — as we shall see below — with Montaigne, who in the course of the following decade will read the *Hypotyposes* in at least one of these editions.

A detour: antiperistasis

All of the texts we have considered so far set in motion, by means of the various narrative and rhetorical devices they deploy, a kind of boomerang effect: the centrifugal energy of Pyrrhonism, when it encounters the resistance of censorship or prudent orthodoxy, rebounds towards intellectual and moral safety. In Pico and Hervet, the rebound appears rapidly to negate the initial outward movement; even there, however, as we have seen, the imposition of closure is accompanied by signs of disturbance at both the epistemological and the psychological level. Rabelais's staging of the encounter with Pyrrhonism is more complex, comprising as it does a double reactive movement. In the first phase, the strategies of Pyrrhonist philosophy, presented as a possible solution to Panurge's problem, instead disconcert and annoy him. The disturbance is provisionally brought under control by the intervention of Gargantua, but it then returns in an increasingly alarming form, and closure is only brought about by another peremptory edict from 'above'. This example shows how the relative force (or inadequacy) of the movement of counter-reaction serves to measure the energy that Pyrrhonism threatens to release; all the more so because the episode finishes not with an affirmation of orthodoxy but with a mere gesture of irritation.

In Estienne's preface, equally, Pyrrhonist folly or fever on the hand and theological caution on the other are in unstable equilibrium; each serves to reinforce the power and the value of the other. The process is even more clearly visible here, given that the humanist both acts out the comedy of his intellectual changes of direction and at the same time supplies his own commentary. In order to find an adequate term to describe the phenomenon, he draws on his vast multilingual vocabulary, making use of it in particular at the critical volte-face mentioned above, the point where he shifts from the ludic to the serious register:

> Verum ut tandem aliquando serio loqui incipiam, tantum abest ut Sceptice animum meum in illo adversus literas odio obfirmaverit, ut potius per quandam ἀντιπερίστασιν cum illis me reconciliaverit. (p. 5)

> [But in fact, to speak seriously at last, far from reinforcing my mind in its hatred for letters, sceptical thought rather reconciled me with them by a kind of antiperistasis.]

Towards the end of the preface, the word reappears in order to characterize the process by which the truth emerges after a rigorous stripping away of all forms of error and falsehood:

> Quinetiam tantum est abest ut veritas oppugnata expugnari, vel eius lux mendaciis obrui possit, ut, perinde ac manus ex contrectatione nivis per ἀντιπερίστασιν calorem paulo post acquirit: ita etiam veritas, offusa illi mendacii caligine, haud multo post nova quadam luce aucta videatur. (p.8)

> [There is no question of the truth being defeated when it is attacked, or its light being obscured by falsehoods: for just as the hand, when it comes into contact with snow, becomes warm by antiperistasis, so too the truth, shrouded in a fog of lies, reappears soon after with increased brilliance.]

The recourse to this obscure Greek word could be regarded as a mere philological flourish. However, its strangely appropriate appearance on the scene in order to describe a complex and disconcerting effect demands further commentary. In Budé's *Lexicon* and in Estienne's own *Thesaurus*, where the definition is clearly indebted to the earlier compilation, 'antiperistasis' is given a not inconsiderable amount of space. Budé defines it as a 'mutua cohibitio, compressio undique circunfusa' [a mutual constraint, a compression applied from all sides].[19] In order to explain the definition, he cites Theophrastus: in the human body, antiperistasis occurs when heat is produced in one part of the body by an excess of cold in another part; in winter, the exhaustion trees suffer, their expenditure of humours in producing leaves and fruit, itself sets in train by antiperistasis the restoration of their vital energies.

Estienne cites in addition several further *loci* from Aristotle and Theophrastus where the principle of antiperistasis is invoked in order to explain a range of effects from the meteorological via the seismic to the biological.[20] Modern commentators on these ancient texts often have difficulties in translating the word: the phenomenon it designates is all the more disconcerting and paradoxical to us because it is only imaginable in terms of a physics that is now entirely defunct. By contrast, sixteenth-century humanists, for whom Aristotelian physics was still very much alive, seem to have been able to assimilate it without too much difficulty. Ambroise Paré uses it, for example, to explain why one is hungrier in wintertime:

> L'Hyver [...] est froid et humide de son temperament: à cette cause il augmente nostre chaleur naturelle, l'appetit, et le phlegme: la chaleur par antiperistase, qu'on appelle, c'est à dire, par contrarieté de l'air voisin, qui estant froid, retient,

et par ce moyen augmente et fortifie la chaleur interne au dedans: mais le phlegme, parce qu'augmentant l'appetit, il rend les hommes plus voraces, dont s'ensuit crudité.[21]

[The winter [...] is cold and wet by temperament: for that reason it increases our natural heat, the appetite, and the phlegm. It increases heat by antiperistasis, as it is called, that is to say by the contrary action of the surrounding air, which, being cold, retains and thus increases and fortifies our warmth on the inside. But phlegm is increased because the cold enhances our appetite, making men more voracious, from which follows indigestion.]

This passage presupposes the traditional analogy between the seasonal cycle and the human somatic cycle. More revealing, no doubt, is the fact that Paré takes the trouble to define antiperistasis as a technical term, unfamiliar to his lay readers.

It is true that, in a vernacular treatise, some such explanation would seem to be indispensable. Paré's use of the French form of the word is however not exceptional, in so far as it seems to have enjoyed a modest success in France in the early modern period.[22] Maurice Scève uses it in the *Délie* to provide an erudite variant of the Petrarchan commonplace whereby the lover simultaneously burns and freezes: 'Il me suffit pour elle en froit, et chault / Souffrir heureux doulx antiperistase' [I am content to suffer happily for her, in cold and heat, a sweet antiperistasis].[23] One might argue that this instance is rhetorical rather than scientific and that 'antiperistasis' here comes to means something like 'paradox' in the modern sense (a contradiction in terms) or 'oxymoron'; on the other hand, given the cosmic frame of reference within which the love-experience of the Délie cycle is acted out, one could equally well argue that Scève is renewing a commonplace Petrarchan oxymoron ('I burn, I freeze') by means of an eroticized physics of thermodynamic antiperistasis.

The term is also often used in the vernacular to designate physical effects on the cosmic scale. It occurs, for example, in a passage of Du Bartas' *Sepmaine* describing the meteorological interaction of heat and cold, which is immediately followed by an explanation, reminiscent of Paré's, of why appetite is increased in winter and in cold regions.[24] But Du Bartas' poetic habit of mind leads him also to elaborate an epic simile in order to bring out the sense of the word, which in consequence acquires a psychological connotation (it is transferred here to a conflict of beliefs): antiperistasis is analogous, he claims, to the surge of courage and motivation experienced by Christian soldiers when they are particularly hard pressed by their Turkish adversaries (pp. 58–59, lines 417–38).

Du Bartas also follows Paré in adding a parenthesis to justify his use of a foreign word:

> Ceste antiperistase (il n'y a point danger
> De naturalizer quelque mot estranger,
> Et mesme en ces discours, où la Gauloise phrase
> N'en a point de son crû qui soient de telle emphase)
> Est celle qui nous faict beaucoup plus chaud trouver
> Le tison flamboyant sur le cœur de l'hiver,
> Qu'aux plus chaus jours d'esté. (lines 439–45)

[This antiperistasis (there is no danger in naturalizing a foreign word, especially on these topics, where Gallic phrasing has none of its own growth which are so high-flown) is what makes us find a blazing coal to be much hotter in the depths of winter than in the hottest days of summer.]

The naturalization of the term seems, however, to be more or less a fait accompli in this period. When Cotgrave composes his French–English dictionary in 1611, he includes 'antipéristase' as if it were a standard French word, giving a definition that echoes Budé's and Estienne's while adding a supplementary gloss:

> A mutuall, or generall cohibition, compression, or repulsion of humors, &c., whereby they become the stronger, and the more strongly possesse the parties they are in.[25]

Here again, the mention of humours shows that users of late sixteenth-century French automatically associated the term with physics and medicine. This remains the case, it seems, nearly a century later, albeit with a dramatic change of cultural style. Littré provides this amusing example from one of Madame de Sévigné's letters about the danger of eating ice and chocolate together:

> je veux [...] vous demander si vos entrailles n'en sont point offensées, et si elles ne vous font point de bonnes coliques, pour vous apprendre à leur donner de telles antipéristases: voilà un grand mot.[26]

> [I would like [...] to ask you whether your intestines are not offended by them, and whether they do not give you a good dose of colic, to teach you to give them such antiperistases: there's a fine word for you.]

From this set of examples, one may draw two conclusions about the way Henri Estienne uses the word 'antiperistasis'. In the first place, as a skilled lexicographer, he has taken care to choose a term that describes a process that is at once natural (it occurs in nature) and disconcerting; at the same time, the function he assigns to it is primarily metaphorical, with the result that in his preface the word has the character of a figure of thought (*figura sententiae*). This figurative transference, which could also be regarded as a catachresis, turns antiperistasis into the name for an unfamiliar epistemological and psychological phenomenon; like the Pyrrhonist *epochê* in the story of Apelles' sponge, it designates a sort of allopathic therapy which consists of obliging the mind to undergo a phase of epistemological disturbance so that it may subsequently reach a state of ataraxia.

In this sense, antiperistasis may be regarded as a heuristic and thus cognitive instrument. Situated at the frontier between an intellectual reflection and a psychological reaction, its logic is shadowed by a corresponding unease. It is also, above all, a *movement*: the figure we are dealing with here is fundamentally unstable, representing the effort of the mind to grasp as a whole the elements of a thought that is in its essence both troubling and disparate.

With the help of this complex figure, we shall now read a key passage from Montaigne's 'Apologie de Raimond Sebond'. It will be argued here that the dynamics of antiperistasis allows us better to understand the ways in which Pyrrhonism was rewritten in the sixteenth century, and in particular to understand this huge, unstable chapter which is often used to characterize Montaigne's thought as a whole. It enables us to avoid, on the one hand, reducing Montaigne's 'position' to a supposed Christian scepticism, and, on the other, anachronistically attributing to the writers of this period a radical, 'modern' Pyrrhonism.[27] The transfer of the term 'antiperistasis' to the context of the *Essais*, where it does not in fact appear, may be justified both by the assumption that Montaigne must have known Estienne's preface, no doubt in the 1562 edition of the *Hypotyposes*, and more broadly by the fact that he inhabited a culture (more specifically, a high culture) in which the term already 'made sense'. Nothing, indeed, could be less anachronistic than the strategy of drawing on the lexis and the intellectual problems of the 1560s in order to explicate a text of the 1570s, one which takes up again, in its own way, that same set of problems.

The logic of antiperistasis in Montaigne's 'Apologie'

In the passage in question, Montaigne pauses in mid-flow to evaluate the function and use of Pyrrhonist arguments.[28] It is thus an implied preface, the equivalent within the 'Apologie' of Gianfrancesco's preface or Estienne's dedication. Like Estienne's preface, it is also a kind of dedicatory epistle, since it is addressed to the anonymous princess who apparently commissioned the defence of Sabunde and who is usually identified as Marguerite de Navarre, the wife of the future Henri IV, who in the 1570s was a Catholic princess in a Protestant court.

Read as a 'preface', however, its position is to say the least eccentric. It occurs at an almost random point about two-thirds of the way through this exceptionally long chapter, interrupting the meandering exposition of the deficiencies of dogmatic philosophical systems and arguments and of the potential merits of Pyrrhonism as an anti-dogmatic mode of thought. It thus has the character of a parenthesis, although in this case the parentheses could also be turned the other way, so that they bracket and delimit the whole of the Pyrrhonist discourse that constitutes the greater part of the chapter.[29] That is certainly what the function of this passage would have been if it had been printed separately in the usual paratextual position, that is to say as a dedicatory preface. As it is, it creates a curious turn or twist in the text, after which the sceptical arguments proceed with renewed vigour.

From the outset, the 'long body' of the chapter is marked as extraordinary ('Vous, pour qui j'ai pris la peine d'estendre un si long corps contre ma coustume' [You, for whom I have taken the trouble to stretch out such a long body contrary to my habits]) — extraordinary for the writer himself, deviant, extravagant. In this way, Montaigne's 'Apologie' appears on the wrong side of a lexical antithesis that pervades the address. On the one hand, one finds a lexis of order, authority, limits, restraint, measure, moderation, temperance; on the other, of extravagance, novelty, strangeness, rashness, instability, danger, volubility, dissolution, vanity, diversity, deformity, licence. This lexical antithesis is supported by a series of metaphors: of self-destructive aggression (fencing, combat, war, the 'outrageous sword' of Pyrrhonism); of potentially transgressed outer limits or borders;[30] of bridled and unbridled licence (the image of a runaway horse, a recurrent one in Montaigne's writing, is visible here between the lines); of familiar paths contrasted with 'vagabondage'.

At the end of the passage, a final double metaphor, of plague and poison, provides a suitably controlled and cautious exit from the rhetoric of admonition. The plague or poison is the 'novelty' of heterodox religion, promoted by doctors (of theology) who show off their intellectual ingenuity in the princess's presence. If the plague is seen to become dangerously infectious, Pyrrhonism is itself licensed to be used as a 'limit', a prophylactic that will either prevent the plague or void it. Since Pyrrhonism is connected with instability throughout the passage up to this point, it consequently appears on both sides of the antithesis: it is both a dangerous flux and a cordial against the flux of novelty; it is both the disease and the cure, a homeopathic medicine.[31]

The first movement of antiperistasis set in motion by this passage is thus a reflex of reaction: the epistemological discourse that precedes it is replaced by a contrary discourse in which control and censorship are dominant. By the same token, the level at which it operates has also changed, shifting from the reflective world of the writer surveying and exploring different kinds of philosophy to the domain of practical, political and ideological concerns. A voice of authority, couched in the quasi-oral mode of the second person, has taken over the text — provisionally, as it will prove, but drawing on the rhetoric of prudence, constraint and moral severity with an intensity unusual in the *Essais*. This voice or persona is at least partially determined by the status and position of the addressee. Like a latter-day Gargantua (or a Polonius), Montaigne is speaking here as a kind of elder statesman to a younger woman of the highest rank who wants him to supply apologetic arguments. This is the most obvious reason why he uses the rhetoric of caution. It is his public duty, so to speak, to give a strictly limited licence to Pyrrhonist arguments.

The question immediately arises whether the stance adopted in this passage is merely for show, a gesture of what Montaigne elsewhere pejoratively calls 'ceremony'. In the first place, it should be recalled that Pyrrhonism itself creates a separation between the realm of philosophical reflection and the public, practical domain, where existing laws and customs should be respected because no alternative can be adequately defended. Secondly, it is easy to show that the fluctuation between a discourse of licence and a discourse of moderation (an abiding dislike, for example, of 'novelty', especially in the religious domain) is intrinsic to the *Essais* as a whole; when Montaigne says 'toutes les voyes extravagantes me faschent' [all deviant paths annoy me], the reader has little difficulty in situating the first-person pronoun by reference to other utterances of the same kind. Finally, as we have seen, the first sentence of the passage from the outset already admits the *excess* of this chapter, its tendency to extension and its deviation from Montaigne's 'custom': it is undeniably Montaigne's Pyrrhonist exercise which itself seems to escape all limits, provoking a counter-movement of restraint. In this passage, then, censure and censorship become internalized, seeking to bridle with their own redundant rhetoric the apparently unstoppable flow of writing and epistemological reflection that the chapter had unleashed. Consequently, the volte-face we are looking at here operates at the psychological as well as the ideological level, those two levels being simply complementary aspects of the same process.

Described in this way, Montaigne's 'address to the princess' looks remarkably similar to Estienne's preface, enacting much the same movement of antiperistasis. Yet the Pyrrhonist arguments deployed in the 'Apologie' are not a body of materials translated into Latin from a little-known Greek author, but a reader-friendly vernacular discourse inserted into a book which will rapidly become a best-seller, not only in France but throughout Europe.

Besides, as we have seen, the passage is not a preface but a parenthesis, and one with unstable edges at that. One may immediately test this effect by reading the sentence that follows it, which unleashes a further ricochet in the argument:

> La liberté donq et gaillardise de ces esprits anciens produisoit en la philosophie et sciences humaines plusieurs sectes d'opinions differentes, chacun entreprenant de juger et de choisir pour prendre party.

> [Thus the liberty and liveliness of those ancient minds produced in philosophy and the humane disciplines various sects holding different opinions, each one undertaking to judge and choose in order to adopt its standpoint.]

'La liberté *donq*'? What is the logical connection here? 'Liberty', it is true, is a near-synonym of the 'licence' that was the theme of the address to the princess, but it reverses the pejorative associations of its twin, and is now associated with the joyful freedom of choice of the philosophers of antiquity. Evidently, the 'donc' stands outside the parenthesis: it refers us back to the series of philosophical opinions Montaigne had examined immediately before the cautionary passage. More generally, it recalls the preliminary classification of philosophical schools into three groups — dogmatics, Academics and Pyrrhonists — which Montaigne had borrowed from Cicero much earlier in the chapter; the reprise is in fact subsequently confirmed in a passage where Montaigne cites in succession the Aristotelian Theophrastus, the Academics and the Pyrrhonists on the question of plausible opinions.[32] This broader level is no doubt the more relevant, given that the opinions of the various philosophical sects on the nature of the soul are cited in a markedly negative, quasi-satirical register in order to demonstrate their inanity. Here, by contrast, as we have seen, the multiplicity of views that arises from the liberty of the individual judgement appears in a positive light.

This happy freedom is evidently seen to characterize classical antiquity as a whole. Montaigne has at least temporarily dropped his Augustinian cross-examination of the human mind and its capacity for knowledge in order to indulge in a bout of humanist nostalgia, reinforced by an opposition between the ancient and the modern schools:

> Mais à présent [C] que les hommes vont tous un train, *qui certis quibusdam destinatisque sententiis addicti et consecrati sunt, ut etiam quae non probant, cogantur defendere*, et [A] que nous recevons les arts par civile authorité et ordonnance, [C] si que les escholes n'ont qu'un patron et pareille institution et discipline circonscrite, [A] on ne regarde plus ce que les monnoyes poisent et valent, mais chacun à son tour les reçoit selon le pris que l'approbation commune et le cours leur donne. On ne plaide pas de l'alloy, mais de l'usage: ainsi se mettent égallement toutes choses. (pp. 559–60)

> [But nowadays, when [C] everyone follows the same line, 'being attached and bound by oath to certain definite and prescribed opinions, so that they are

had become deeply attached, 'Montaigne's scepticism', as it is usually known? The figure of antiperistasis perhaps offers a way of escaping from this impasse.

Once again, antiperistasis is not a simple contrast, self-contradiction, paradox (always in the modern sense) or *coincidentia oppositorum*, but a movement of transvaluation that allows one to hold successively, in the same trajectory of thought, two or more radically different attitudes. It is the sign of a profound malaise in the intellectual world of the late sixteenth century, recording as it does an unstable movement between two poles: on the one hand, a religious ideology, a system of censorship, an official education programme, and on the other a strange and disconcerting epistemological strategy that resists attempts to tame it.

Using antiperistasis as an indicator, one could say, then, that Montaigne belongs in broad terms to the intellectual climate that produced the responses to Pyrrhonist thought of Gianfrancesco Pico, Estienne, Hervet and (not least) Rabelais, yet at the same time one sees the balance already shifting: the boundaries are placed further out and are more permeable. Pyrrhonism is now transposed into the vernacular in a secular work which represents neither official scholarship nor official apologetics, and this transposition gives it more imaginative scope, allowing it to be read differently, even if the new readers it seems to invite will not materialize immediately. This explains what one might call the 'deferred action' of the 'Apologie', a text which will later — notoriously — be read as the very epitome of free-thinking scepticism.

The movement of antiperistasis which all these texts share to a varying degree is, I believe, a much more sensitive indicator of the changing historical import of Pyrrhonism in the early modern period than are the officially resolved positions the writers put forward. What these prefatory responses imply is neither a commitment to those positions as such, nor some thinly veiled profession of radical Pyrrhonism, but an unstable balance between the two. It is also important to emphasize that the official positions are in no sense hypocritical. They don't just pay lip service to authority, but rather record the extent to which the individual writer is conditioned by (has internalized) the orthodox ideologies of his day.

This interpretation is designed to give a fuller account of sixteenth-century Pyrrhonism than orthodox histories of ideas can give. Such histories, concerned as they are above all with argument, are inclined to undervalue the complex forms in which early modern writers envelop their responses. Even their efforts to avoid the anachronism of representing sixteenth-century writers on Pyrrhonism as modern sceptics are liable to cause distortion, since they frequently end up reasserting the structures of power and authority which are visible in these texts at the expense of the counter-movements we have examined here. They thus risk glossing over those very disturbances, those shakings of the boundary fence, that enable us to define with some precision the scope and limitations of what it is possible to think in the sixteenth century.

Notes

1. See Richard H. Popkin, *The History of Scepticism from Savonarola to Bayle* (New York and Oxford: Oxford University Press, 2003), and Popkin's article on scepticism in *The Cambridge History of Renaissance Philosophy*, ed. by Charles B. Schmitt, Eckhardt Kessler and Quentin Skinner (Cambridge: Cambridge University Press, 1988), pp. 678–84; Craig B. Brush, *Montaigne and Bayle* (The Hague: Nijhoff, 1966); Charles Schmitt, *Gianfrancesco Pico della Mirandola (1469–1533) and his Critique of Aristotle* (The Hague: Nijhoff, 1967), also *Cicero Scepticus: A Study of the Influence of the 'Academica' in the Renaissance* (The Hague: Nijhoff, 1972). Important contributions have also been made by Elaine Limbrick in a series of articles on scepticism in France and in the introduction and notes to Francisco Sanches, *That Nothing is Known (Quod nihil scitur)*, trans. by Douglas F. S. Thomson (Cambridge: Cambridge University Press, 1988) (see the bibliography of this translation for a review of the field as a whole, including details of Limbrick's articles). As indicated above, this study will be limited in the main to writers demonstrably familiar with the works of Sextus Empiricus as the most technically elaborate exposition of Pyrrhonism. Sextus Empiricus' writings pose the problem of the reception of sceptical ideas with particular clarity. A broader study would of course take into account the presentation of sceptical and quasi-sceptical materials by writers such as Agrippa von Nettesheim, Guy de Bruès and Sanches, whose works bear no clear trace of the influence of Sextus Empiricus.
2. Sextus Empiricus, *Outlines of Pyrrhonism*, trans. by R. O. Bury (vol. 1 of the works of Sextus Empiricus in the Loeb Classical Library) (Cambridge, MA: Harvard University Press; London: Heinemann, 1976; first edn 1933), pp. 19–21 (l.xii.28–29). I have slightly modified the translation.
3. On the sources Rabelais is likely to have drawn on for this episode, see Emmanuel Naya, 'Ne scepticque ne dogmatique, et tous les deux ensemble', *Études rabelaisiennes*, 35 (1998), 81–129. For a recent study of the sense of the episode, see Tournon, *'En sens agile'*, pp. 90–94.
4. Rabelais, *Tiers Livre*, in *Œuvres complètes*, ed. by Huchon, pp. 444–45.
5. For earlier references to Gargantua in the *Tiers Livre*, see *Œuvres complètes*, ch. 9 (p. 379) and ch. 13 (p. 390).
6. For a reading of this episode that makes the 'harmonization' central, see Screech, *Rabelais*, pp. 328–34.
7. He is presumably referring to the sudden surge of interest in scepticism (based largely although not exclusively on Cicero's *Academica*) in the Paris of the 1540s, which will culminate in 1548 in Omer Talon's *Academica*.
8. See Carla Freccero, *Father Figures: Genealogy and Narrative Structure in Rabelais* (Ithaca, NY: Cornell University Press, 1991), pp. 153–58.
9. I refer in this section to the first edition of this work, printed at Mirandola by Giovanni Mazzocchi (Bodleian Library, Oxford, Byw. F. 3. 6). For the proemium to Book Three, see fols. lxxv–vi. Here as elsewhere, I use section numbers rather than page numbers and identify prefaces by the book in which they appear. See also the commentary by Schmitt, *Gianfrancesco Pico*, especially pp. 45–50.
10. The conflict between scepticism and the highly systematic and dogmatic philosophy of Aristotle and his followers is a recurrent feature of sixteenth-century texts. It recurs, for example, in the circle of Ramus and Talon (see above, note 7) and in the *Dialogues* of Guy de Bruès (1559).
11. For reference to Gianfrancesco's uncle, see *Examen*, I.2 and IV.2; see also Schmitt, *Gianfrancesco Pico*, pp. 47–48, 61–62.
12. *Examen*, fol. lxxvi^r.
13. *Sexti Empirici philosophi Pyrrhoniarum hypotypôseôn libri III [...]; graece nunquam, latine nunc primum editi* ([Geneva]: Estienne, 1562) dedicatory epistle (pp. 2–8). No further page references will be provided for this text.
14. I have paraphrased the story at some length both for the benefit of readers who may not have access to the original and because Brush's retelling of the story (*Montaigne and Bayle*, p. 31) abbreviates it drastically and thus deprives it of much of its intrinsic force and interest.
15. Similar tropes continue to the end of the preface: for example, Pyrrhonism is itself characterized

as a madness, as something absurd and fantastic; anyone who believes in it must be deranged ('toto caelo errare existimabo').

16. Brush, *Montaigne and Bayle*, p. 32.

17. *Sexti Empirici viri longe doctissimi adversus mathematicos, Hoc est, adversus eos quo profitentur disciplinas, Opus eruditissimum* (Paris: Le Jeune, 1569), dedicatory epistle (fols. a2–a3); the epistle is dated 1567. The transposition of what in antiquity had been a philosophical debate to a theological context is common enough in the sixteenth century, but the references here to the pernicious novelty of the Reformers anticipate a key sentence in Montaigne's 'address to the princess' (see above, p. 122).

18. This defence of Pyrrhonism as a pedagogical tool, which is repeated in Hervet's preface to the reader, had also been used by Estienne. It illustrates another of the ways in which Pyrrhonism was assimilated to established forms of argument, in this case the *pro et contra* method.

19. Guillaume Budé, *Lexicon graeco-latinum* ([Geneva]: Jean Crespin, 1554), fol. [n vi]ᵛ.

20. Among the many references to antiperistasis in the works of Aristotle, see for example *Meteorologica* 347.b.6 (the formation of dew), 348.b.2 (the formation of hail), 382.b.10 (the manner in which cold can 'burn'); *Physica* 215.a.15, 267.a.16; *Problemata* 867.b.32, 962.a.2. For references in Theophrastus, see *De causis plantarum* I.12.3, I.13.5, II.6.1, II.8.1, II.9.8, VI.7.8, VI.8.8, VI.18.11–12. Plutarch uses the term in *De placitis philosophorum* III.15 (896.c) and IV.1 (898.b), and in *Platonicae quaestiones* 7 (1004.d).

21. Ambroise Paré, *Les Œuvres* (Lyon: Claude Prost, 1641), p. 10 (Livre I, ch. vii).

22. For further examples, see Huguet, *Dictionnaire de la langue française au XVIe siècle*, art. 'antipéristase', where an example is cited from the *Cresme philosophale* attributed to Rabelais (*Œuvres complètes*, p. 918), another from François de Sales's *Amour de Dieu* II.5.

23. Scève, *Délie*, ed. by I. D. MacFarlane (Cambridge: Cambridge University Press, 1966), p. 278, *dizain* 293.

24. Guillaume Salluste Du Bartas, *La Sepmaine*, ed. by Y. Bellenger (Paris: Nizet, 1981), pp. 59–60 ('Le Second Jour', lines 439–56).

25. Randle Cotgrave, *A Dictionarie of the French and English Tongues* (London: Adam Islip, 1611; facsimile edn, Columbia, SC: University of South Carolina Press, 1950), fol. [E iv]ʳ.

26. Letter of 28 October 1671.

27. The bibliography of commentary on the 'Apologie' is too extensive to be reviewed here. In addition to Popkin's classic (but now dated) account, the following are especially relevant to the present discussion: Brush, *Montaigne and Bayle*, ch. 4, esp. pp. 71–76; Blum (ed.), *Montaigne: Apologie de Raimond Sebond* (Paris: Champion, 1990); Tournon, *La Glose et l'essai*, pp. 228–56, and '*Route par ailleurs': le 'nouveau langage' des 'Essais'* (Paris: Champion, 2006), especially pp. 15–31, 87–89; Limbrick, 'Was Montaigne really a Pyrrhonian?', *Bibliothèque d'Humanisme et Renaissance*, 39 (1977), 67–80; Marie-Luce Demonet and Alain Legros (eds), *L'Écriture du scepticisme chez Montaigne* (Geneva: Droz, 2004).

28. Montaigne, *Essais*, pp. 557–59; this reference covers all of the ensuing quotations from this part of the chapter.

29. This reading is reinforced by the apologetic preamble to the chapter, which gives licence to Pyrrhonist arguments as a provisional strategy only; see in particular the often-quoted sentence: 'Considerons donq *pour cette heure* l'homme seul, sans secours estranger, armé seulement de ses armes, et despourvu de la grace et cognoissance divine, qui est tout son honneur, sa force et le fondement de son estre' (p. 449; my italics).

30. Perhaps the most powerful of these metaphors is the one quoted as an epigraph at the beginning of this essay (above, p. 109).

31. Cf. the well-known Pyrrhonist comparison of sceptical thought with rhubarb, which stimulates bowel movements and is thus itself voided as a result (cited by Montaigne, p. 527); and see John O'Brien, 'Question(s) d'équilibre', in *Lire les 'Essais' de Montaigne: perspectives critiques*, ed. by Noël Peacock and J. J. Supple (Paris: Champion, 1998), pp. 107–22.

32. For the initial classification, see pp. 502–07; for the reprise, see pp. 560–62.

33. Montaigne's quotation is from Cicero, *Tusculan Disputations* II.ii.

34. It is striking that the post-1588 additions to this passage greatly increase this effect, as if Montaigne no longer felt the need for the caution he had built into his text in the 1570s.

35. This passage should be juxtaposed with another development some twenty pages earlier in the chapter which resembles it closely not only in argument but also in phrasing (pp. 538–39, especially the passages 'les opinions des hommes [...] et en mensonge' and 'Vrayement c'estoit bien raison [...] aux escholes et aux arts').

36. For a further exploration of this rich passage, and in particular of the second-level linking elements and antiperistases it contains, see *Pré-histoires*, pp. 45–48.

3

Fragments of a Future Self:
From Pascal to Montaigne

There is no necessary relationship between the appearance of a new linguistic phenomenon and an evolution, still less an abrupt shift, in the conceptual domain. The same concept may be expressed by a different word, as it is when one translates from one language into another. Inversely, a word or expression may survive for hundreds of years in the vocabulary of a language, little noticed until the moment when a shift in the conceptual field assigns it a central role. It is none the less evident that, in such instances, the linguistic item will always be inflected towards a new meaning, however slightly, by this very change; likewise, the invention of a linguistic tool may crystallize preoccupations that had up to then remained virtual, and thus open up new ways of thinking.

The history of the word *moi* provides an exemplary illustration of such processes. As we shall see, the possibility of assigning a substantival function to the pronoun only begins to emerge in France in the later sixteenth century; by the mid-seventeenth century, it has become an established feature. At the same moment, the English word 'self' broadens its grammatical and semantic range.[1] This parallel evolution seems to confirm a well-established historical, literary and philosophical *grand récit* according to which the modern notion of personal identity is said to begin to form around the end of the sixteenth century.[2] It must however be conceded that other languages had long before used a personal pronoun as a noun: the Latin expressions *alter ego* and *alter idem* are attested in Cicero;[3] Aristotle calls a friend 'another self' (*heteros autos*);[4] in Sanskrit, the word *âtman* is both a reflexive pronoun and a widely used noun that plays a key role in the Hindu conception of the soul and the human person.[5] There is however a distinction to be made here. In the French expression, *le moi*, it is the disjunctive form of the first person singular, rather than an impersonal form such as the Greek *autos*, the Latin *idem* or the English 'self', which is transformed into a noun.[6] It is true that Cicero's *alter ego* is an exception, but the texts in which it appears have to do with social relations rather than with philosophical or other forms of introspection.

Where the topic of the self is concerned, it is particularly important to avoid generalization and historical dramatization, since the *grand récit* in question is one that plays a dominant, even invasive role in current cultural historiography. Historians of philosophy and literature are broadly in agreement in situating a decisive evolution in the notion of personal identity in the early modern period. Whether one is thinking of a Foucauldian archaeology or a genealogical history analogous to George Eliot's, Goethe repeats and re-energizes the painful story of the abused foundling, even while relegating it to the margins of his Enlightenment allegory, with a consequence that he could not possibly have foreseen: it will be Mignon and her story, far more than Wilhelm and his, that will obsess nineteenth-century European culture.

It is perhaps because of this unsettling *agon* at the heart of both novels that they have a further feature in common: their endings prove to be only the threshold to an unguessable future. The traditional recognition plot deals in closure, in homecomings or irreversible disasters. Of course, homecomings may not always be synonymous with stasis, and even Oedipus turns out to have a future; besides, recognitions, as I have argued elsewhere, are often problem moments rather than full resolutions.[31] Yet a distinction needs to be made between cases where the overwhelming direction of the narrative is towards full closure and others where the knot is palpably left untied or even untieable. The *Bildungsroman* ends by its very nature on a threshold: the protagonist's apprenticeship is meant to be a prelude to a new life.

Goethe's experimental continuation of *The Magic Flute* shows that already at this stage of his career he was scornful of the easy certainties of the opera's recognition scenes: life after recognition continues to be uncertain, turbulent, often painful.[32] Similarly, many years later, he will lead Wilhelm into an unfinished purgatorial journey, undertaken under the sign of renunciation ('Entsagung'). Only after this, it is suggested, will he be fit to enter on his marital life with Natalie; but that consummation continues to be relegated into an uncertain future.[33]

The *Wanderjahre* is a disjointed, indeed fragmentary text, combining narrative with moral discourse and concluding with a collection of maxims. Taken as a whole, it has none of the features of a recognition plot, quite the reverse. But it includes in its earlier stages an extended episode set in the area where Mignon was born and spent her childhood. Already with the arrival of the Marchese, in the final book of the *Lehrjahre*, Mignon's home in Italy had become a real and reachable place rather than merely a nostalgic fantasm. Indeed, the Marchese offers his sister's (i.e. Mignon's mother's) inheritance to Wilhelm as a reward for his rescue and protection of the abducted child.[34] A journey to Italy and a visit to the scenes of Mignon's childhood are thus envisaged. In this sense, too, Mignon's story is displaced or taken over by Wilhelm's. But in the *Wanderjahre*, her image comes back to revisit him.

This is a strange episode. Together with his three companions (none of whom figures in the *Lehrjahre*), Wilhelm enjoys several days of luxury tourism on Lake Maggiore, their way made smooth by an expert guide. Picnics on the lake alternate with brief landfalls. An artist whom Wilhelm has conveniently met just before this episode begins, and who devotes himself almost obsessively to painting the scenes evoked in 'Kennst du das Land?', also turns out to be an accomplished singer. He borrows a stringed instrument similar to the one Mignon herself had played on, but at first he carefully avoids the songs of the *Lehrjahre*.[35] On the last night, however, carried away by the atmosphere, he launches into 'Kennst du'. The response is immediate. The character known as the 'beautiful widow' stops him and the women turn aside; the pain is too much for them to bear. The idyll is broken, the members of the party go their separate ways, and the rule of renunciation is reimposed.[36] There is thus, in this narrative fragment written a quarter of a century after the *Lehrjahre*, an *anagnorisis* of the pain of Mignon's story.[37] It comes too late for Mignon herself, but it more than suffices to acknowledge the story's imaginative and psychological reach.

The denouement of *Daniel Deronda* is less unsettled than that of *Wilhelm Meisters Lehrjahre*. As I suggested earlier, George Eliot lavished great care on tying up the threads that Goethe had left loose. Yet her ending is also only a prelude: for Daniel and Mirah, who sail off into a future more problematic than any George Eliot can possibly have imagined; and for Gwendolen, who has only now begun to see what a life might be like that is not lived solely for personal happiness. One can imagine Daniel's *Wanderjahre*, and Gwendolen's, and one knows that they could not conceivably include a romance ending. Gwendolen's future, and no doubt Daniel's too, is likely to unfold under the sign of renunciation, the theme of the *Wanderjahre*, in the sense that renunciation is non-fulfilment: it means giving up the expectation of any final closure other than death.

In the case of *Wilhelm Meister*, it is not difficult to read structural dissonance as a symptom of a tectonic shift in the history of the novel. The loose weave of Goethe's *Bildungsroman* joins several of the available narrative modes — the picaresque, the allegorical, the ancient foundling plot — in order finally to evacuate them and leave the ground clear for an individual story that belongs to none of the *grands récits*. What emerges is a secular narrative without a predetermined goal. *Daniel Deronda*, for its part, revives the overarching *grand récit* of recognition, only to leave it behind according to the same rule, that of the *Bildungsroman*.

In their different ways, too, both novels rewrite the relation of narrative to history. While Goethe was working on the definitive version of the *Lehrjahre* in the 1790s, Europe was in turmoil, with all its social and political presuppositions potentially called in question. We may recall here Schlegel's famous remark of 1797/98: 'Die französische Revolution, Fichtes Wissenschaftslehre und Goethes "Meister" sind die größten Tendenzen des Zeitalters' [The French Revolution, Fichte's philosophy of knowledge and Goethe's 'Meister' are the most significant trends of our age].[38] In that context, for the well-off bourgeois Wilhelm *simply* to marry a noblewoman and settle down to a comfortably moral life would have been unthinkable for a writer of Goethe's intellectual range and insight. Although George Eliot lived most of her life, by contrast, at a time of high Victorian assertiveness, she was able both to write from inside that frame and to perceive and judge it from the outside, that is to say from a European and even a global perspective. The microcosmic social life is there, with all its prejudices, its self-preoccupation and self-protectedness, but it is shown to be inadequate: the personal recognitions are engulfed in the recognition of world-historical narratives and destinies.

Anagnorisis, as the word itself implies, is a looking back, a recovery of the path that led to the place where the here and now coincide with the eternal. *Wilhelm Meisters Lehrjahre* and *Daniel Deronda* trace that path, in complex and sometimes baffling patterns; yet they are both also turned, in their final pages, towards the future, inviting the reader to move outwards into a troubled world where the old certainties no longer apply.

Angela Carter's *Nights at the Circus* extends the sense of a historical shift across the imaginary borderline between the nineteenth and twentieth centuries and completes the link with our own age. It is set in the last months of 1899, on 'the cusp of the modern age', in 'those last, bewildering days before history, that is, history as we know it, that is, white history, that is, European history, that is Yanqui history — in that final little breathing space before history *as such* extended its tentacles to grasp the entire globe'.[39] Furthermore, its narrative is prescient of 'historical' events now familiar to us: the Russian Revolution, economic and cultural globalization, the coming of age of the women's rights movement and of gender equality. It writes a 'pre-history', a glimpse of the apparently impossible freedoms which will begin to be realized in the characters' future.[40] Even Gwendolen, suddenly and vertiginously seeing the world opening up far beyond her parochial imagination, could not have begun to grasp the reach of the changes that Fevvers and her companions intuit, still less Carter's notion of history itself as a time-bound and culture-bound phenomenon.

What, then, becomes of *anagnorisis* in such a world? Is history itself, or the epiphany of the modern, the object of an ultimate recognition? Does the recognition that the stories of both Narrative and History are finite absorb and empty out all other local recognitions by forestalling any possibility of closure? Or is it rather that the recognition scene, now that the troubling equivocations of fictional *anagnorisis* are finally brought out into the open, can play out its intensities, its longing for wholeness, without incurring the charge of bad faith? Carter's novel gives some clues as to how these questions might be answered.

It should be said at once that *Nights at the Circus* is not, in its overall structure, a recognition novel. It is a classic postmodern narrative of flight and dispersal, with no final resolving scene. The question with which the reader — like the reader's surrogate, the journalist Walser — is teased from the outset, the question whether Fevvers' wings are real, appears to be answered, but in a way that delivers no explanation.[41] Her parentage remains unknown, her relation to her foster mother Lizzie uncertain.[42] This is in keeping with the rule of magic realism: elements of the 'marvellous', such as Fevvers' escape from the Russian Grand Duke or the crypto-human behaviour of the circus monkeys, are left untouched by rationalizing frames of reference.

It is characteristic of the postmodern novel, however, that it should be conscious of its own evasions. When Fevvers and Lizzie, in the final chapter, are on their way to find Walser in the Siberian village where he has become a budding shaman, Lizzie reminds Fevvers that she risks finding herself committed to the conventional comic closure of marriage; this makes Fevvers pause for thought, but her reply goes beyond the traditional assumptions on which that comic convention depends.[43] Asserting the freedom which is proper to her essential self, she gives herself the right to the infectiously joyful sexual consummation that ends the narrative.

This primary narrative structure holds within it a number of secondary narratives, as is appropriate in the picaresque genre. Of these, the story of Mignon has a central function, not only because of its position (it emerges at the very heart of the novel and continues to reverberate to the end) but also because of its powerful

> They were just the same height, both little things, frail, one as fair as the other was dark, twinned opposites. And both possessed that quality of exile, of apartness from us, although the Princess had chosen her exile amongst the beasts, while Mignon's exile had been thrust upon her.[53]

At the same time she finds a lover and discovers her true sexual orientation. When the song ends, the Princess and Mignon kiss; Fevvers and Lizzie 'let out great breaths of relief and likewise kissed each other': they have saved Mignon from 'the cruel sex'.[54] The feminist point carries the more weight here because it is handled with a light touch.

Like a musical motif, this transcendental scene is reprised in the following chapter, where this time Mignon herself dances with a tiger while a somewhat worse-for-wear Walser waltzes with the tiger's jealous mate. Mignon's personal and sexual liberation, confirmed by her dazzling appearance in a romantic ballgown and by the image of a caged bird set free, ripples outwards to include the tigers, who dance themselves for a brief moment into a world without bars and without conflict: 'All the tigers were on their hind legs, now, waltzing as in a magic ballroom in the country where the lemon trees grow.'[55] But for them, the moment is indeed brief. The tigress, deserted by Walser, will soon attack Mignon in a fit of jealousy and have to be shot. And as the circus, already disintegrating internally, subsequently travels out into the open landscape of Siberia, the train is blown up and the tigers are reduced to their reflections in fragments of broken glass, a kind of ideal aesthetic captivity.

Yet it is only at the price of such a disaster, breaking the magic circle of the circus and its economic coercions, that an authentic liberation is possible.[56] At the Transbaikalian Academy, Mignon sings again, differently because she herself is transformed (here it is the last song of Schubert's *Winterreise*):

> When we first heard her sing, in the Hotel de l'Europe, it sounded as if the song sang itself, as if the song had nothing to do with Mignon and she was only a kind of fleshy phonograph, made to transmit music of which she had no consciousness. That was before she became a woman. Now she seized hold of the song in the supple lassoo of her voice and mated it with her new-found soul, so the song was transformed yet its essence did not change, in the same way a familiar face changes yet stays the same when it is freshly visited by love.[57]

The song itself is a negative mirror image of Mignon's yearning for a magic lost land of the south: the young man wanders off forlornly into the snow, accompanied only by a halting, out-of-tune hurdy-gurdy. When the bearded and decrepit old musician who lives in the Academy recognizes the song, he begins to pick out the accompaniment, which makes him a reincarnation of Goethe's Harpist.

Here, however, these memories of iterated pain are summoned up in redemptive mode. The Princess regains her speaking voice and fixes the old man's piano, setting the scene for a reversal, a modulation from minor to major. Mignon sings her signature tune, and the narrator now provides an upbeat interpretation: 'She does not ask you if you know that land of which she sings because she herself is uncertain it exists — she knows, oh! how well she knows it lies somewhere, elsewhere, beyond the absence of flowers.'[58] The company might well say 'Look!

we've come through!' — through the bars, out of the circus, past the invisible walls of a post-Mallarméan ideal,[59] into an utterly strange and beautiful landscape that exists in a way for which the fake, exploitative world of the circus is only a figure, seen as through a glass darkly. And now the myth of Orpheus is played out once more with tigers, this time superbly and untameably wild ones:

> We saw the house was roofed with tigers. Authentic, fearfully symmetrical tigers burning as brightly as those who had been lost. These were the native tigers of the place, who had never known either confinement or coercion; they had not come to the Princess for any taming, as far as I could see, although they stretched out across the tiles like abandoned greatcoats, laid low by pleasure, and you could see how the tails that dropped down over the eaves like icicles of fur were throbbing with marvellous sympathy. Their eyes, gold as the background to a holy picture, had summoned up the sun that glazed their pelts until they looked unutterably precious […]
>   I thought to myself: when those tigers get up on their hind legs, they will make up their own dances — they wouldn't be content with the ones she'd teach them. And the girls will have to invent new, unprecedented tunes for them to dance to. There will be an altogether new kind of music to which they will dance of their own free will.[60]

In this way, the Orphic moment of Mignon's earlier rendering of 'Kennst du das Land?' is reaffirmed as an epiphany at a higher and more inclusive level. In *Wilhelm Meister*, Mignon's story has its epiphanic moments, but they are relegated to the margins of the central allegory of enlightenment. There, Mignon has to die; there is no other way out for her, and — as the episode in the Italian lakes in the *Wanderjahre* showed — her memory necessarily becomes a memory of unbearable pain and severance. Carter uses the same plot structure in the sense that her Mignon too appears almost accidentally, and thereafter comes and goes with her songs intermittently; nor does she bring full closure to Fevvers' story itself. But the discovery of Mignon and of what she brings with her is clearly indispensable to the outcome. It is Fevvers as narrator who witnesses and comments on the final scene of singing with tigers, and immediately after she will follow Walser's trail to the remote village where her own desires and her own freedom will be consummated. Mignon has once more been rescued by a novelist who understands both the history and the poetics of her story.

   It remains to show how conscious, how intended, that rescue is. The plurally generic character of *Nights at the Circus* is in fact openly signalled at various points in the novel. Just before this last episode begins, Fevvers, reflecting on her apparently endless journeyings, remarks: 'Young as I am, it's been a picaresque life', and asks herself ironically whether her fate will be to be 'a female Quixote, with Liz as my Sancho Panza'; Lizzie says that the old musician at the Transbaikalian Academy is behaving like a character from one of Shakespeare's late comedies, except that he's found two daughters rather than one.[61] Just before the denouement, as we saw earlier, there is a joking reference to comedies ending in marriage. But at the beginning of the same chapter, Lizzie expounds an interpretation of their story as at once a picaresque adventure and an allegory:

> Don't you remember what a motley crew we were when we first set out from

England? [...] a gaggle of strangers drawn from many diverse countries. Why, you might have said we constituted a microcosm of humanity, that we were an emblematic company, each signifying a different proposition in the great syllogism of life. The hazards of the journey reduced us to a little band of pilgrims abandoned in the wilderness upon whom the wilderness acted like a moral magnifying glass, exaggerating the blemishes of some and bringing out the finer points in those we thought had none. Those of us who learned the lessons of experience have ended their journeys already. Some who'll never learn are tumbling back to civilisation as fast as they can as blissfully unenlightened as they ever were. But as for you, Sophie, you seem to have adopted the motto: to travel hopefully is better than to arrive.[62]

We thus return to the generic mix with which we began, the gene pool out of which *Wilhelm Meister* and the *Bildungsroman* were born. In this passage, Carter unambiguously declares her novel to be a story of enlightenment, of characters with different learning curves, some of whom — Walser, Samson the Strong Man, the circus monkeys, the Princess and of course Mignon — find new and better selves, while others fall back into their old ways and their old illusions. Fevvers herself, despite Lizzie's parting shot, has not travelled in vain. After all, her given name is Sophie: as the embodiment of a special kind of wisdom, she presides over the whole bundle of stories. *Nights at the Circus* is thus (among many other things[63]) an extraordinary reconstruction of *Wilhelm Meister*, with the circus as metaphor replacing the theatre and with an entirely new theme, a new suite of characters, and a new perspective on historical change. At the centre, as a visible sign of the connection, Mignon returns to sing her song again and help remake the world through recognition.

Notes

1. I discuss these transformations at various points in *Recognitions*; see especially I.2–4 and II.1–5.
2. *Télémaque* also flaunts its lineage as a narrative of epic wanderings, with a double *anagnorisis* in the final chapter. Although these recognitions do not in any sense structure the plot as such, it is clear that they have an allegorical value, marking the culmination of the hero's initiation into the secrets of Minerva.
3. See Rosemarie Haas, *Die Turmgesellschaft in 'Wilhelm Meisters Lehrjahren'. Zur Geschichte des Geheimbundromans und der Romantheorie im 18. Jahrhundert* (Frankfurt am Main: Peter Lang; Bern: Herbert Lang, 1975).
4. Goethe was working on this libretto in 1795, not long before he completed *Wilhelm Meisters Lehrjahre*. See below, p. 175 and note 32.
5. See Schlegel's remark quoted below, p. 176.
6. See, once again, Kermode's classic study *The Sense of an Ending*. See also above, pp. 164–66.
7. See *Wilhelm Meisters Lehrjahre* (henceforth abbreviated for the purposes of reference as *WML*), in *Johann Wolfgang von Goethe: Werke Kommentare und Register*, ed. by Erich Truntz, vol. VII (Munich: Beck, 1981), in particular Book 1, ch. 17, Book 2, ch. 9, and Book 3, ch. 9. I develop this theme at greater length in my essay 'The Afterlife of the *Poetics*', in *Making Sense of Aristotle: Essays in Poetics*, ed. by Øivind Andersen and Jon Haarberg (London: Duckworth, 2001), pp. 197–214 (pp. 207–08).
8. *WML*, Book 6.
9. See Schiller's letter of 2 July 1796 and Goethe's letters of 5 and 7 July in reply (reproduced in *WML*, pp. 632, 639); cf. Wilhelm von Humboldt's letter to Goethe of 24 November 1896 (*WML*, p. 659).

10. See for example Schiller's letter to Goethe of 28 June 1796 (*WML*, p. 628), and the letter of 2 July (pp. 632–33); also Friedrich Schlegel's essay, where the appearance of the 'holy child' (Mignon) is said to give rise to 'even sweeter shudders [than the figure of the Harpist] and as it were a beautiful sense of horror', suddenly releasing 'the innermost spring of this strange work' (reproduced in *WML*, p. 664). The early critical reception of *Wilhelm Meister* was indeed unanimously enthusiastic about the Mignon strand: see Dorothea Flashar, *Bedeutung, Entwicklung und literarische Nachwirkung von Goethes Mignongestalt* (Berlin: Emil Ebering, 1929), p. 112.

11. See the fragment reproduced in *WML*, p. 685.

12. See in particular the story of the Princess and the young man (ch. 3), the figure of the exiled and abused Saracen woman (ch. 4), who is especially reminiscent of Mignon, and the symbolic role of the poet Klingsohr and his daughter Mathilde. See also Schlegel's remark that in Mignon's and the Harpist's 'romantic songs', 'poetry is revealed to be the natural language and music of beautiful souls' (*WML*, p. 666).

13. *WML*, Book 8, ch. 2, pp. 512–13.

14. *WML*, pp. 240–41. I discuss the double narrative motivation of this song in a somewhat different context in my article 'The Afterlife of the *Poetics*'.

15. See Rosemary Ashton, *The German Idea: Four English Writers and the Reception of German Thought, 1800–1850* (Cambridge: Cambridge University Press, 1980), the same author's 'Mixed and Erring Humanity: George Eliot, George Henry Lewes and Goethe', *George Eliot — George Henry Lewes Studies*, 24/25 (1993), 93–117, and Elinor Shaffer, 'George Eliot and Goethe: "Hearing the grass grow"', *Publications of the English Goethe Society*, 66 (1997), 3–22.

16. See the laconic but graphic entry in George Eliot's diary for 2 December 1870: 'I am reading Wolf's Prolegomena to Homer. In the evening aloud, Wilhelm Meister again!' (*The Journals of George Eliot*, ed. by Margaret Harris and Judith Johnston (Cambridge: Cambridge University Press, 1998), p. 141).

17. See, among other studies, Susan Fraiman, '*The Mill on the Floss*, the Critics and the Bildungsroman', *PMLA*, 108 (1993), 136–50.

18. The most thorough recent study is the final chapter of Gerlinda Röder-Bolton's *George Eliot and Goethe* (Amsterdam and Atlanta, GA: Rodopi, 1998).

19. Röder-Bolton mentions it briefly and then discards it as superficial (*George Eliot and Goethe*, pp. 190–91). For further remarks on this critical silence, see my article 'Mignon's Afterlife in the Fiction of George Eliot', *Rivista di letterature moderne e comparate*, 56 (2003), 173–74.

20. What follows is an abridged version of my account of the rescue scene in 'Mignon's Afterlife', pp. 174–77.

21. '"Do you belong to the theatre?" "No, I have nothing to do with the theatre," said Deronda, in a decided tone' (*Daniel Deronda*, ed. by Terence Cave, Penguin Classics (Harmondsworth: Penguin Books, 1995), p. 191; subsequent page numbers refer to this edition, abbreviated as *DD*).

22. In fact, Mignon learns that she has actually been bought by actors and offers to repay them by becoming their servant (*WML*, p.106). Mirah wants at all costs to escape from theatrical circles, with their moral corruption and economic pressures.

23. *DD*, p.192. See also the following exchange: '"You are English? You must be — speaking English so perfectly." [...] "You want to know if I am English?" [...] "I want to know nothing except what you like to tell me [...] Perhaps it is not good for you to talk." "Yes, I will tell you. I am English-born. But I am a Jewess [...] I am come a long way — from abroad. I ran away: but I cannot tell you — I cannot speak of it. I thought I might find my mother again [...]"' (*DD*, p. 193).

24. Her well-known essay 'The Morality of *Wilhelm Meister*', first published in the *Westminster Review*, offers a defence of that morality at the level of the depiction of sexual mores, but has nothing to say on finer ethical points of the kind we have been considering. At all events, twenty years later George Eliot will make sure that her version of the plot will need no apology.

25. *DD*, pp. 190–91.

26. *DD*, pp. 367–68.

27. See below, n. 37.

28. *DD*, p. 559.

29. On the connections between Mignon and child acrobats and street-performers in England in the

nineteenth century, see Carolyn Steedman's *Strange Dislocations: Childhood and the Idea of Human Interiority, 1780–1930* (London: Virago, 1995).

30. In *La Gitanilla*, the 'gypsy girl' proves to be the daughter of a noble family and can thus marry her noble lover; in *The Spanish Gypsy*, the young noblewoman discovers that she is the daughter of a gypsy and finally renounces her noble lover.

31. *Recognitions*, p. 489 and *passim*.

32. In Goethe's account, Tamino and Pamina, now married, lose their child and are obliged to embark on a new series of purgatorial ordeals. For a comprehensive study of *anagnorisis* in Mozart's operas, see Jessica Waldoff, *Recognition in Mozart's Operas* (New York: Oxford University Press, 2006).

33. It seems to be no accident that the narrative poem *Alexis und Dora*, written in the year *Wilhelm Meisters Lehrjahre* was first published, features a couple who, after a passionate moment of anagnorisis, are flung apart.

34. See *WML*, p. 594.

35. *Wilhelm Meisters Wanderjahre*, in *Werke*, vol. VIII, p. 232.

36. Ibid., pp. 239–40.

37. Cf. Piero Boitani's essay 'Recognition: The Pain and Joy of Compassion', in *Recognition: The Poetics of Narrative. Interdisciplinary Studies on Anagnorisis*, ed. by Philip F. Kennedy and Marilyn Lawrence (Oxford: Peter Lang, 2009), pp. 213–26, on pain as a sign of authenticity in recognition scenes, and also on the epiphany of both recognition and pain in song, as in the Homeric scene of Odysseus at the palace of Alcinoüs. The same conjunction, drawing this time on texts from Aeschylus via Virgil to Dante (see Boitani, 'Recognition', p. 220), reappears in *Daniel Deronda* in the scene where Daniel rescues Mirah: their first contact is made when she hears him singing Rossini's setting of Dante's version of this topos.

38. Cited in *WML*, p. 661.

39. Angela Carter, *Nights at the Circus* (London: Vintage, 2003), p. 265 (references to *Nights at the Circus* will henceforth be in the form *NC*). The historical setting in fact provides an explicit frame for the novel: see for example p. 11 ('For we are at the fag-end, the smouldering cigar-butt, of a nineteenth century which is just about to be ground out in the ashtray of history. [...] And Fevvers has all the *éclat* of a new era about to take off') and p. 86 ('we do believe her [the Sleeping Beauty's] dream will be the coming century').

40. When the novel was first published in 1984, the author and her readers could not have guessed that they were about to witness yet another series of transformations: the fall of the Berlin wall and the collapse of communist regimes in Eastern Europe; the demise of apartheid and of white rule in South Africa; the domestication of computer technology and the invention of the internet. On the notion of 'pre-history', see above, pp. 100–08.

41. See p. 294, where Fevvers admits that she 'fooled' Walser by claiming that she was the 'only fully-feathered intacta in the history of the world'. Since the preceding description suggests that she really does have feathers, presumably it is the 'intacta' claim which was false, but the question and its answer are engulfed in the great wave of Fevvers' laughter on which the novel ends.

42. The question whether Lizzie was her real mother remains suspended, despite references to Fevvers as Lizzie's 'daughter' (see for example p. 286), since these may be read as meaning 'foster daughter'.

43. *NC*, pp. 280–81.

44. As far as I have been able to detect, there is no specific allusion to *Daniel Deronda* in *Nights at the Circus*.

45. *NC*, pp. 133–38; cf. *WML*, pp. 514–16 (the episode that features the song 'So laßt mich scheinen').

46. *NC*, p. 132.

47. The choice of a popular song rather than an art song for this first manifestation of Mignon's mesmeric powers as a singer echoes George Du Maurier's *Trilby*, where the sentimental American ballad 'Ben Bolt' becomes Trilby's 'signature tune'.

48. This also has its parallel in *Trilby*: see the scene where Gecko improvises on the theme of 'Ben Bolt' to Svengali's accompaniment, and in particular the climactic scene of the Paris concert (George Du Maurier, *Trilby*, ed. by Elaine Showalter, Oxford World's Classics (Oxford: Oxford

University Press, 1999), pp. 21–23 and 210–20 respectively). *Nights at the Circus* contains an explicit allusion to *Trilby* (NC, p. 28).

49. *NC*, p.154.

50. The narrator refrains from naming the exact version; the English student had 'hesitated deliciously between Liszt's setting and Schubert's' (p. 154). Since there are many nineteenth-century settings of 'Kennst du das Land?', it is difficult to know whether these two are chosen at random (why not Beethoven's, or Schumann's, or Wolf's?) or whether they should be taken to represent two contrasted ways of perceiving the Mignon of Carter's novel: Schubert's version is forthright and deliberately naïve, Liszt's is a high romantic setting with an elaborate piano accompaniment and an almost operatic vocal line. At all events, if Mignon is to get her recognition, the Princess (or her piano) must have chosen the right one, the one the student chose, while the reader is left suspended, held at one remove from the *anagnorisis* itself (although a later reference seems to suggest that it was Schubert's version: see p. 268).

51. *NC*, p.155.

52. The 'otherness' of the mythical vision afforded by the scene is enhanced by the insistent separation of music from speech. The Princess never speaks, she plays the piano; Mignon doesn't understand the words of the songs she sings, even when they are in German. 'To sing is not to speak', says Fevvers; and a page later, the narrator rephrases: 'To speak is one thing. To sing is quite another' (pp. 153, 154).

53. *NC*, pp. 153–54.

54. *NC*, p. 155.

55. *NC*, pp. 164–65.

56. This critical moment is figured in the narrative, intercalated at precisely this point, of the female Siberian prison, which echoes other societies of enslaved women in the novel (Ma Nelson's whore-house, the women held captive by Madame Schreck in the Gothic mansion), while culminating in liberation and a 'republic of free women'.

57. *NC*, p.247.

58. *NC*, p.249. The narrator at this point is Fevvers herself.

59. I refer here to the phrase 'beyond the absence of flowers', which shows that Carter is entirely familiar with Mallarmé's reflections on language and music. Perhaps the circus tigers became trapped in a purely aesthetic ideal constructed only out of negation.

60. *NC*, p. 250. The paragraph I have omitted here evokes an Orphic awakening of the whole landscape. Equally important, however, is the consciously relativistic character of Carter's vision, her awareness that she is playing on a specifically European ('Western') set of cultural allusions: the same scene is viewed uncomprehendingly, a few pages later, by the 'forest-dwellers' who have adopted Walser and who 'were deaf to the mythic resonances, since these awoke no echoes in their own mythology [...] they scarcely recognized the Schubert *lied* as music' (p. 268).

61. *NC*, p. 245; p. 272.

62. *NC*, p. 279.

63. Not least, of course, a rewriting of the *Arabian Nights*, with its framing narrative of a story told by a woman to expand the time of night indefinitely and thus liberate herself, and with its multiple plots full of wanderings, deceits, near-magic events, fabulous jewels and the like (including a dervish turned into a monkey with a talent for calligraphy; see the Second Dervish's Tale from the Porter and Three Ladies Cycle, and *NC*, pp. 107–09, 169, etc.). I am grateful to Philip Kennedy for providing me with this reference.

SELECT BIBLIOGRAPHY

Note: only works or editions referred to more than once in the volume are listed below. The full bibliographical details of all works not listed below will be found where reference is made in the text.

Primary Works

AMYOT, JACQUES, see under Heliodorus

BOCCACCIO, GIOVANNI, *Genealogie deorum gentilium libri*, Scrittori d'Italia, 200, 2 vols (Bari: G. Laterza, 1951)

CARTER, ANGELA, *Nights at the Circus* (London: Vintage, 2003)

DU BELLAY, JOACHIM, *Œuvres poétiques*, II: *Recueils de sonnets*, ed. by Henri Chamard, (Paris: Comély, 1910)

—— *Deffence et illustration de la langue françoyse*, ed. by H. Chamard (Paris: Didier, 1948)

DU MAURIER, GEORGE, *Trilby*, ed. by Elaine Showalter, Oxford World's Classics (Oxford: Oxford University Press, 1999)

ELIOT, GEORGE, *Daniel Deronda*, ed. by Terence Cave, Penguin Classics (Harmondsworth: Penguin Books, 1995)

ESTIENNE, HENRI, see under Sextus Empiricus

FICINO, MARSILIO, *Commentaire sur le Banquet de Platon*, ed. by R. Marcel (Paris: Les Belles Lettres, 1956)

GOETHE, JOHANN WOLFGANG VON, *Wilhelm Meisters Lehrjahre*, in Goethe, *Werke Kommentare und Register*, ed. by Erich Truntz, VII (Munich: Beck, 1981)

HELIODORUS, *L'Histoire aethiopique de Heliodorus [...] Nouvellement traduite du grec en francoys*, trans. by Jacques Amyot (Paris: Estienne Grouleau, 1547)

HERVET, GENTIAN, see under Sextus Empiricus

LEMAIRE DE BELGES, JEAN, *Œuvres*, ed. by Jeanne Stecher, 4 vols (Louvain: J. Lefever, 1882)

MAGNY, OLIVIER DE, *Les Odes*, ed. by E. Courbet, 2 vols (Paris: A. Lemerre, 1876)

MARULLUS, MICHAEL, *Michaelis Marulli Carmina*, ed. by A. Perosa (Turin: Thesaurus mundi, 1951)

MONTAIGNE, MICHEL DE, *Les Essais: édition conforme au texte de l'Exemplaire de Bordeaux*, ed. by Pierre Villey and V.-L. Saulnier, 3 vols (Paris: PUF, 1965)

Ovide moralisé, ed. by C. de Boer, in 'Verhandelingen der Koninklijke Nederlandse Akademie van Wetenschappen, Afdeeling Letterkunde', *Nieuwe Reeks*, 61.2 (Amsterdam: North-Holland, 1954)

PASCAL, BLAISE, *Œuvres complètes*, ed. by Louis Lafuma (Paris: Seuil, 1963)

PICO DELLA MIRANDOLA, GIANFRANCESCO, *Examen [...] vanitatis doctrinae gentium, et veritatis Christianae disciplinae* (Mirandola: Giovanni Mazzocchi, 1520)

RABELAIS, FRANÇOIS, *Œuvres complètes*, ed. by Mireille Huchon, Bibliothèque de la Pléiade (Paris: Gallimard, 1994)

—— *Le Tiers Livre*, ed. by M. A. Screech, Textes Littéraires Français (Geneva: Droz; Paris: Minard, 1964)

—— *Le Quart Livre*, ed. by Robert Marichal, Textes Littéraires Français (Geneva: Droz, 1947)

RONSARD, PIERRE DE, *Œuvres complètes*, ed. by Paul Laumonier and others (Paris: Hachette/ STFM, 1914–75)

SEXTUS EMPIRICUS, *Sexti philosophi Pyrrhoniarum hypotypôseôn libri III [...] Graecè nunquam, latinè nunc primùm editi, interprete Henrico Stephano* ([Geneva]: Henri Estienne, 1562)

—— *Sexti Empirici viri longe doctissimi adversus mathematicos, Hoc est, adversus eos quo profitentur disciplinas, Opus eruditissimum*, trans. by Gentian Hervet (Paris: Le Jeune, 1569)

SHAKESPEARE, WILLIAM, *Titus Andronicus*, ed. by Jonathan Bate, The Arden Shakespeare (London: Routledge, 1995)

TYARD, PONTUS DE, *Solitaire premier*, ed. by S. F. Baridon (Geneva: Droz, 1950)

—— *Œuvres poétiques complètes*, ed. by J. C. Lapp (Paris: Didier, 1966)

VIDA, MARCO GIROLAMO, *L'Arte poetica*, ed. by R. Girardi (Bari: Adriatica, 1982)

Secondary Works

BATE, JONATHAN, *Shakespeare and Ovid* (Oxford: Clarendon Press, 1993)

BRUSH, CRAIG B., *Montaigne and Bayle* (The Hague: Nijhoff, 1966)

CASTOR, GRAHAME, *Pléiade Poetics* (Cambridge: Cambridge University Press, 1964)

CAVE, TERENCE, see 'Publications by Terence Cave' below

CHARLES, MICHEL, *Rhétorique de la lecture* (Paris: Seuil, 1977)

COLEMAN, DOROTHY GABE, *The Gallo-Roman Muse* (Cambridge: Cambridge University Press, 1979)

COMPAGNON, ANTOINE, *La Seconde Main, ou le travail de la citation* (Paris: Seuil, 1979)

FUMAROLI, MARC, *L'Âge de l'éloquence: rhétorique et 'res literaria' de la Renaissance au seuil de l'époque classique* (Geneva: Droz, 1980)

GREENE, THOMAS M., *The Light in Troy: Imitation and Discovery in Renaissance Poetry* (New Haven and London: Yale University Press, 1982)

HUGUET, E., *Dictionnaire de la langue française du seizième siècle* (Paris: Champion, 1925–67)

KERMODE, FRANK, *The Sense of an Ending: Studies in the Theory of Fiction* (London and New York: Oxford University Press, 1966)

KRAILSHEIMER, A. J., *Rabelais and the Franciscans* (Oxford: Clarendon Press, 1963)

LESTRINGANT, FRANK, *Écrire le monde à la Renaissance: quinze études sur Rabelais, Postel, Bodin et la littérature géographique* (Caen: Paradigme, 1993)

McKINLEY, MARY B., *Words in a Corner: Studies in Montaigne's Latin Quotations* (Lexington, KY: French Forum, 1981)

MERRILL, R. V. and R. J. CLEMENTS, *Platonism in French Renaissance Poetry* (New York: New York University Press, 1957)

MORGAN, BEN, 'Developing the Modern Concept of the Self: The Trial of Meister Eckhart', *Telos*, 116 (1999), 56–80

MOSS, ANN, *Printed Commonplace-Books and the Structuring of Renaissance Thought* (Oxford: Clarendon Press, 1996)

ONG, WALTER J., 'Commonplace Rhapsody: Ravisius Textor, Zwinger and Shakespeare', in *Classical Influences on European Culture AD 1500–1700*, ed. by R. R. Bolgar (Cambridge: Cambridge University Press, 1976), pp. 91–126

POPKIN, RICHARD H., *The History of Scepticism from Savonarola to Bayle* (New York and Oxford: Oxford University Press, 2003)

RIFFATERRE, M., *La Production du texte* (Paris: Seuil, 1979)

RÖDER-BOLTON, GERLINDA, *George Eliot and Goethe* (Amsterdam and Atlanta, GA: Rodopi, 1998)

SAYCE, RICHARD, *The Essays of Montaigne: A Critical Exploration* (London: Weidenfeld and Nicholson, 1972)

SCHMITT, CHARLES B., *Gianfrancesco Pico della Mirandola (1469–1533) and his Critique of Aristotle* (The Hague: Nijhoff, 1967)

SCREECH, M. A., *Rabelais* (London: Duckworth, 1979)

SEZNEC, JEAN, *The Survival of the Pagan Gods: The Mythological Tradition and its Place in Renaissance Humanism and Art*, trans. by B. F. Sessions (New York: Pantheon, 1953; French original, London: Warburg Institute, 1940)

SMITH, PAUL J., *Voyage et écriture: étude sur le Quart Livre de Rabelais* (Geneva: Droz, 1987)

STEEDMAN, CAROLYN, *Strange Dislocations: Childhood and the Idea of Human Interiority, 1780–1930* (London: Virago, 1995)

TOURNON, ANDRÉ, *'En sens agile': les acrobaties de l'esprit selon Rabelais* (Paris: Champion, 1995)

—— *Montaigne: la glose et l'essai*, rev. edn (Paris: Champion, 2000 [1983])

WILSON, DUDLEY, *Ronsard: Poet of Nature* (Manchester: Manchester University Press, 1961)

WIND, EDGAR, *Pagan Mysteries in the Renaissance* (London: Faber and Faber, 1958)

PUBLICATIONS BY TERENCE CAVE

Note: asterisked items have been incorporated in *Retrospectives* in partial, revised and/or translated form.

Books

Devotional Poetry in France, c.1570–1613 (Cambridge: Cambridge University Press, 1969)

The Cornucopian Text: Problems of Writing in the French Renaissance (Oxford: Clarendon Press, 1979); trans. by Ginette Morel as *Cornucopia. Figures de l'abondance au XVIe siècle: Érasme, Rabelais, Ronsard, Montaigne* (Paris: Macula, 1997)

Recognitions: A Study in Poetics (Oxford: Clarendon Press, 1988)

Pré-histoires: textes troublés au seuil de la modernité (Geneva: Droz, 1999). [The 'Introduction', ch. 4, and parts of ch. 5 (pp. 129–38) and of ch. 6 (pp. 143–55) have been incorporated in *Retrospectives* in revised and translated form.]

Pré-histoires II: langues étrangères et troubles économiques au XVIe siècle (Geneva: Droz, 2001)

How to Read Montaigne (London: Granta, 2007)

Co-Authored Books

Sarah Kay, Terence Cave and Malcolm Bowie, *A Short History of French Literature* (Oxford: Oxford University Press, 2003)

Edited Books

Ronsard the Poet, ed. by Terence Cave (London: Methuen, 1973)

Neo-Latin and the Vernacular in Renaissance France, ed. by Grahame Castor and Terence Cave (Oxford: Clarendon Press, 1984). The volume is a tribute to I. D. McFarlane.

Thomas More's 'Utopia' in Early Modern Europe: Paratexts and Contexts (Manchester: Manchester University Press, 2008)

Articles and Essays

'The Love Sonnets of Jean de Sponde: A Reconsideration', *Forum for Modern Language Studies*, 3.1 (1967), 49–60

'The Protestant Devotional Tradition: Simon Goulart's *Trente tableaux de la mort*', *French Studies*, 21.1 (1967), 1–15

'Peinture et émotion dans la poésie religieuse de César de Nostradame', *Gazette des Beaux-Arts*, 75 (1970), 57–62

*'The Triumph of Bacchus and its Interpretation in the French Renaissance: Ronsard's *Hinne de Bacus*', in *Humanism in France*, ed. by A. H. T. Levi (Manchester: Manchester University Press, 1970), pp. 249–70

*'Ronsard's Bacchic Poetry: From the *Bacchanales* to the *Hymne de l'Automne*', *L'Esprit Créateur*, 10 (1970), 104–16

'L'Univers mythologique de Ronsard', in *Ronsard aujourd'hui*, ed. by Gilbert Gadoffre (Loches: Institut Collégial Européen, 1972), pp. 9–13

'Ronsard's Mythological Universe', in *Ronsard the Poet*, ed. by Terence Cave (London: Methuen, 1973), pp. 159–208

'Ronsard as Apollo: Myth, Poetry and Experience in a Renaissance Sonnet-Cycle', *Yale French Studies*, 47 (1972), 76–89. Reprinted in *French Poetry: The Renaissance through 1915*, ed. by Harold Bloom (New York and Philadelphia: Chelsea House, 1990), pp. 99–108

'Mythes de l'abondance et de la privation chez Ronsard', *Cahiers de l'Association Internationale des Études Françaises*, 25 (1973), 247–60

'Copia and cornucopia', in *French Renaissance Studies, 1540–70: Humanism and the Encyclopedia*, ed. by Peter Sharratt (Edinburgh: Edinburgh University Press, 1976), pp. 52–69

'*Enargeia*: Erasmus and the Rhetoric of Presence in the Sixteenth Century', *L'Esprit Créateur*, 16.4 (1976), 5–19

'Recognition and the Reader', *Comparative Criticism*, 2 (1980), 49–69

'Desportes and Maynard: Two Studies in the Poetry of Wit', in *The Equilibrium of Wit: Essays for Odette de Mourgues*, ed. by Peter Bayley and Dorothy Gabe Coleman (Lexington, KY: French Forum, 1982), pp. 86–94

★'The Mimesis of Reading in the Renaissance', in *Mimesis: From Mirror to Method, Augustine to Descartes*, ed. by John D. Lyons and Stephen G. Nichols (Hanover, NH, and London: University Press of New England, for Dartmouth College, 1982), pp. 149–65

'Panurge and Odysseus', in *Myth and Legend in French Literature*, ed. by Keith Aspley, David Bellos, and Peter Sharratt (London: Modern Humanities Research Association, 1982), pp. 47–59

★'Problems of Reading in the *Essais*', in *Montaigne: Essays in Memory of Richard Sayce*, ed. by I. D. McFarlane and Ian Maclean (Oxford: Clarendon Press, 1982), pp. 133–66

'Scève's *Délie*: Correcting Petrarch's Errors', in *Pre-Pléiade Poetry*, ed. Jerry C. Nash (Lexington, KY: French Forum, 1985), pp. 111–24

'Reading Rabelais: Variations on the Rock of Virtue', in *Literary Theory / Renaissance Texts*, ed. by Patricia Parker and David Quint (Baltimore and London: Johns Hopkins University Press, 1986), pp. 78–95

'La Contamination des intertextes: le sonnet "Or que Juppin"', in *Ronsard: Colloque de Neuchâtel*, ed. by André Gendre (Geneva: Droz, 1987), pp. 65–73

'La Muse publicitaire dans les *Odes* de 1550', in *Ronsard en son IVe centenaire: Ronsard hier et aujourd'hui*, ed. by Yvonne Bellenger, Jean Céard, Daniel Ménager and Michel Simonin (Geneva: Droz, 1988), pp. 9–16

'Transformations d'un *topos* utopique: Gaster et le rocher de Vertu', in *Rabelais en son demi-millénaire: Actes du Colloque International de Tours (24–29 septembre 1984)*, ed. by J. Céard and J.-C. Margolin, Études Rabelaisiennes, 21 (Geneva: Droz, 1988), pp. 317–25

'Corneille, Oedipus, Racine', in *Convergences: Rhetoric and Poetic in 17th-Century France. Essays for Hugh M. Davidson*, ed. by D. Rubin and M. McKinley (Columbus: Ohio State University Press, 1989), pp. 82–100

'"*Suspendere animos*": pour une histoire de la notion de suspens', in *Les Commentaires et la naissance de la critique littéraire, France/Italie (XIVe–XVIe siècles)*, ed. by Gisèle Mathieu-Castellani and Michel Plaisance (Paris: Aux Amateurs de Livres, 1990), pp. 211–18.

'Panurge, Pathelin and Other Polyglots', in *Lapidary Inscriptions: Renaissance Essays for Donald A. Stone, Jr.*, ed. by Barbara C. Bowen and Jerry C. Nash (Lexington, KY: French Forum, 1991), pp. 171–82

★'Imagining Scepticism in the Sixteenth Century', *Journal of the Institute of Romance Studies*, 1 (1992), 193–205

'Keeping up with the Doxa: An Unofficial Reply to John Holyoake', *French Studies Bulletin*, 44 (1992), 17–19. (Cf. J. Holyoake, '"Montaigne is Meaningless" — Official', *French Studies Bulletin*, 41 (1991/92), 3–5)

★'The Death of Guillaume Du Bellay: Rabelais's Biographical Representations', in *Writing the Renaissance: Essays on Sixteenth-Century French Literature in Honor of Floyd Gray*, ed. by Raymond C. La Charité (Lexington, KY: French Forum, 1992), pp. 43–55

'Au cœur de l'*Apologie*: la logique de l'antipéristase', in *Le Lecteur, l'auteur et l'écrivain: Montaigne 1492–1592–1992*, ed. by Ilana Zinguer (Paris: Champion, 1993), pp. 1–15

'L'Économie de Panurge: "moutons à la grande laine"', *Réforme, Humanisme, Renaissance*, 37 (1993), 7–24

'"Or donné par don': échanges métaphoriques et matériels chez Rabelais', in *Or, monnaie, échange dans la culture de la Renaissance: Actes du 9e Colloque International de l'Association Renaissance, Humanisme, Réforme, Lyon 1991*, ed. by André Tournon and G.-A. Pérouse (Saint-Étienne: Publications de l'Université de Saint-Étienne, 1994), pp. 107–17

'Psyché et Clio: le cas Montaigne', in *Carrefour Montaigne*, ed. by Fausta Garavini (Pisa, ETS; Geneva, Slatkine: 1994), pp. 95–116

'Travelers and Others: Cultural Connections in the Works of Rabelais', in *François Rabelais: Critical Assessments*, ed. by Jean-Claude Carron (Baltimore: Johns Hopkins University Press, 1995), pp. 39–56, 197–200

'Le Récit montaignien: un voyage sans repentir', in *Montaigne: espace, voyage, écriture*, ed. by Zoé Samaras (Paris: Champion, 1995), pp. 125–35

'Le Clair et l'obscur dans la littérature française de la Renaissance', in *Renaissances européennes et Renaissance française*, ed. by Gilbert Gadoffre (Montpellier: Espaces 34, 1995), pp. 211–21

'Fictional Identities', in *Identity: Essays based on Herbert Spencer Lectures given in the University of Oxford*, ed. by Henry Harris (Oxford: Clarendon Press, 1995), pp. 99–127

'"Je pareillement": instances de la première personne chez Rabelais', *Cahiers Textuel*, 15 (1996), 9–18

'*Le Voyage des princes fortunez*: un cas particulier de l'*ordo artificialis*', in *Béroalde de Verville 1556–1626*, Cahiers V.-L. Saulnier, 13 (Paris: Presses de l'École Normale Supérieure, 1996), 157–67

★'Suspense and the Pre-History of the Novel', *Revue de Littérature Comparée*, 4 (1996), 509–16

'"Si je n'avois une certaine foy": Montaigne lecteur de Ronsard', in *Lire les 'Essais' de Montaigne*, ed. by Noël Peacock and James J. Supple (Paris: Champion, 1998), pp. 183–94

'A "Deep though Broken Wisdom": George Eliot, Pascal, and *Middlemarch*', *Rivista di letterature moderne e comparate*, 51.3 (1998), 305–19

'Joseph Conrad: The Revenge of the Unknown', in *Joseph Conrad*, ed. by Andrew Roberts (New York: Longman, 1998), pp. 47–70

'Ancients and Moderns: France', in *The Cambridge History of Literary Criticism*, III: *The Renaissance*, ed. by Glyn P. Norton (Cambridge: Cambridge University Press, 1999), pp. 417–25

'Fragments d'un moi futur: Pascal, Montaigne, Rabelais', in *'D'une fantastique bigarrure': le texte composite à la Renaissance. Études offertes à André Tournon*, ed. by J.-R. Fanlo (Paris: Champion, 2000), pp. 105–18

'Rime et structure du dizain dans la *Délie* de Maurice Scève', in *Les Fruits de la saison: mélanges de littérature des XVIe et XVIIe siècles offerts au professeur André Gendre*, ed. by Philippe Terrier, Loris Petris, and Marie-Jeanne Liengme Bessire (Geneva: Droz, 2000), pp. 49–57

'The Afterlife of the *Poetics*', in *Making Sense of Aristotle: Essays in Poetics*, ed. by Øivind Andersen and Jon Haarberg (London: Duckworth, 2001), pp. 197–214

'"Outre l'erreur de nostre discours": l'analyse des passions chez Montaigne', in *La Poétique des passions à la Renaissance: mélanges offerts à Françoise Charpentier*, ed. by François Lecercle and Simone Perrier (Paris: Champion, 2001), pp. 389–406

'Mignon's Afterlife in the Fiction of George Eliot', *Rivista di letterature moderne e comparate*, 56 (2003), 165–82

'Polygraphie et polyphonie: écritures plurielles de la Renaissance à l'époque classique', *Littératures classiques*, 49 (2003), 385–400

★'Thinking with Commonplaces: The Example of Rabelais', in *(Re)inventing the Past: Essays on French Early Modern Culture, Literature and Thought in Honour of Ann Moss*, ed. by Gary Ferguson and Catherine Hampton (Durham: Durham Modern Languages Series, 2003), pp. 34–50

★'Comment représenter l'altérité: le mythe de Philomèle chez Rabelais, Ronsard et Shakespeare', in *Self and Other in Sixteenth-Century France: Proceedings of the Seventh Cambridge French Renaissance Colloquium, 7–9 July 2001*, ed. by Kathryn Banks and Philip Ford (Cambridge: Cambridge French Colloquia, 2004), pp. 93–105

'Written on the Scroll: Diderot, Goethe and Blixen', *Oxford German Studies*, 33 (2004), 51–69

'Master-Mind Lecture: Montaigne', *Proceedings of the British Academy*, 131 (2005), 183–203

'Modest and Mignon: Balzac Rewrites Goethe', *French Studies*, 59.3 (2005), 311–25

'Locating the Early Modern', *Paragraph*, 29 (2006), 12–26

'Locking the Citadel: Ducksburg, Augsburg, Utopia', in *Urban Preoccupations: Mental and Material Landscapes*, ed. by Per Sivefors (Pisa and Rome: Fabrizio Serra, 2007), pp. 33–44

★'Singing with Tigers: Recognition in *Wilhelm Meister*, *Daniel Deronda* and *Nights at the Circus*', in *Recognition: The Poetics of Narrative. Interdisciplinary Studies on Anagnorisis*, ed. by Philip F. Kennedy and Marilyn Lawrence (Oxford: Peter Lang, 2009), pp. 115–34

'Lapin ou canard? Essai sur les binômes littéraires', in *Au corps du texte: hommage à Georges Molinié*, ed. by Delphine Denis, Mireille Huchon, Anna Jaubert, Michael Rinn, and Olivier Soutet (Paris: Champion, forthcoming 2010)

Co-Authored Essays

With Michel Jeanneret and François Rigolot, 'Sur la prétendue transparence de Rabelais', *Revue d'Histoire Littéraire de la France*, 86.4 (1986), 709–16

With Kirsti Sellevold, ' "Or, ces exemples me semblent plus à propos": une phrase inaugurale dans les *Essais* de Montaigne', in *'Éveils': Mélanges offerts à J.-Y. Pouilloux*, ed. by Valérie Fasseur, Olivier Guerrier, Laurent Jenny, André Tournon (Paris: Garnier, forthcoming)

Prefaces, Forewords, and Epilogues

'Epilogue', in *Philosophical Fictions and the French Renaissance*, ed. by Neil Kenny, Warburg Institute Surveys and Texts, 19 (London: The Warburg Institute, 1991), pp. 127–32

'Epilogue', in *Logique et littérature à la Renaissance: Actes du Colloque de la Baume-les-Aix, Université de Provence 16–18 septembre 1991*, ed. by Marie-Luce Demonet-Launay and André Tournon (Paris: Champion, 1994), pp. 235–37

'Afterwords: Philomela's Tapestry', in *(Ré)interprétations: études sur le seizième siècle*, ed. by John O'Brien, Michigan Romance Studies, 15 (Michigan: University of Michigan, 1995), pp. 271–78

'Conclusions', in *Amour sacré, amour mondain: Poésie 1574–1610. Hommage à Jacques Bailbé* (Paris: École Normale Supérieure, 1995), pp. 141–46

'Préface', in Geneviève Demerson, *Joachim Du Bellay et la belle romaine* (Orleans: Paradigme, 1996), pp. 5–8

'Préface', in Perrine Galand-Hallyn, *Poétiques de la Renaissance: le modèle italien, le monde franco-bourguignon et leur héritage en France au XVIe siècle* (Geneva: Droz, 2001), pp. ix–xiv

'Epilogue: Time's Arrow', in *Pre-Histories and Afterlives: Studies in Critical Method*, ed. by Anna Holland and Richard Scholar (Oxford: Legenda, 2008), pp. 135–46

'Epilogue: The Prehistories of Plagiarism', in *Borrowed Feathers: Plagiarism and the Limits of Imitation in Early Modern Europe*, ed. by Hall Bjørnstad (Oslo: Unipub, 2008), pp. 235–43

'Foreword', in an issue of *Paragraph* in memory of Malcolm Bowie, ed. by Diana Knight and Judith Still, forthcoming in July 2009

Critical Editions

George Eliot, *Daniel Deronda*, ed. with an Introduction by Terence Cave, Penguin Classics (Harmondsworth: Penguin, 1995)

——*Silas Marner*, ed. with an Introduction by Terence Cave, Oxford World's Classics (Oxford: Oxford University Press, 1996)

Métamorphoses spirituelles: anthologie de la poésie religieuse française, 1570–1630, ed. by Terence Cave and Michel Jeanneret (Paris: José Corti, 1972). Rev. edn: *La Muse sacrée: anthologie de la poésie spirituelle française*, ed. by Cave and Jeanneret (Paris: José Corti, 2007)

Pierre de Ronsard, *I: Poems of Love* (1975) and *II: Odes, Hymns and Other Poems* (1977), selected and ed. by Grahame Castor and Terence Cave (Manchester: Manchester University Press)

Introductions to Translations

Gargantua and Pantagruel, trans. by Sir Thomas Urquhart and Pierre Le Motteux, with an Introduction by Terence Cave, Everyman's Library (London: David Campbell, 1994).

Gustave Flaubert, *Madame Bovary: Life in a Country Town*, trans. by Gerard Hopkins, with an Introduction by Terence Cave, and notes by Mark Overstall, Oxford World's Classics (Oxford: Oxford University Press, 1998)

Translations

Madame de Lafayette, *The Princesse de Clèves, The Princesse de Montpensier, The Comtesse de Tende*, trans. and ed. by Terence Cave, Oxford World's Classics (Oxford: Oxford University Press, 1992)

Henriette-Julie de Murat (attrib.), 'Starlight' and 'Bearskin', trans. by Terence Cave, in *Wonder Tales: Six Tales of Enchantment*, ed. by Marina Warner (London: Chatto and Windus; New York: Farrar, Straus and Giroux, 1994; repr. New York: Oxford University Press, 2004)

Biographical Memoir

'Ian Dalrymple McFarlane, 1915–2002', *Proceedings of the British Academy*, 124 (2004) 182–203

Book Reviews and Review Articles

Artscribe   B. Vickers, *In Defence of Rhetoric* (Nov.–Dec. 1983, pp. 93–95)

Comparative Criticism   Erasmus, *Collected Works*, vols 23 and 24: *Literary and Educational Writings*, ed. by C. R. Thompson; R. L. DeMolen (ed.), *Essays on the Works of Erasmus*; M. A. Screech, *Rabelais* ('Translating the Humanists: Erasmus and Rabelais', 3 (1981), 279–93)

Comparative Literature   T. Reiss, *Tragedy and Truth* (34 (1982), 276–77); L. Jardine, *Erasmus, Man of Letters* (48 (1996), 381–83); D. Quint, *Montaigne and the Quality of Mercy* (52 (2000), 182–84)

XVIIe Siècle   H. Lafay, *La Poésie française du premier XVIIe siècle (1598–1630)* (124 (1979), 313–14)

French Studies   François de Sales, *St Francis de Sales: A Testimony by St Chantal*, ed. by E. Stopp (22 (1968), 152–53); R. Ortali, *Un poète de la mort: Jean-Baptiste Chassignet* (24 (1970), 170–71); Jean-Antoine de Baïf, *Poems*, selected and ed. by M. Quainton (26 (1972), 447–48); P. Smith, *Clément Marot, Poet of the Renaissance* (27 (1973), 53–55); Charles Fontaine, *Un poeta della preriforma: Charles Fontaine. Epistres, Chantz royaulx, Ballades, Rondeaux et Dixains [...]*, ed. by R. Scalamandrè (28 (1974), 61–62); M. Yardeni, *La Conscience nationale en France pendant les guerres de religion (1559–1598)* (28 (1974), 62–63); G. Demerson, *La Mythologie classique dans l'œuvre lyrique de la 'Pléiade'* (30 (1976), 442–44); Marie de Romieu, *Les Premières Œuvres poétiques*, ed. by A. Winandy (30 (1976), 450); Jehan Thenaud, *La Lignée de Saturne*, ed. by G. Mallary Masters (32 (1978), 311); A. Boase, *Vie de Sponde* (32 (1978), 317); Jean de Sponde, *Œuvres littéraires*, ed. by A. Boase (33 (1979), 439–41); Jacques Bereau, *Les Églogues*, ed. by M. Gautier (33 (1979), 637–38); B. Braunrot, *L'Imagination poétique chez Du Bartas* and L. Keller, *Palingène–Ronsard–Du Bartas* (33 (1979), 641–43); F. A. Yates, *Astraea: The Imperial Theme in the Sixteenth Century* (33 (1979), 662–64); Le Chevalier de Berquin, *La Complainte de la paix (1525)*, ed. by É. V. Telle (34 (1980), 66–67); R. Arbour, *L'Ère baroque en France (1585–1643)*, Parts I and II (34 (1980), 328–29); P. Bayley, *French Pulpit Oratory 1598–1650* (35 (1981), 70–71); Antoine de Chandieu, *Octonaires sur la vanité et inconstance du monde*, ed. by F. Bonali-Fiquet (35 (1981), 190–91; Du Bartas, *La Sepmaine*, ed. by Y. Bellenger (36 (1982), 324); P. Bayley (ed.), *Selected Sermons of the French Baroque (1600–1650)* (38 (1984), 456–67); M. Greenberg, *Classicism and the Ruses of Symmetry* (42 (1988), 468); P. Ford and G. Jondorf (ed.), *Ronsard in Cambridge* (43 (1989), 80–81); C. Blum, *La Représentation de la mort dans la littérature française de la Renaissance* (47 (1993), 65–66); Ronsard, *Œuvres complètes*, ed. by J. Céard, D. Ménager, and M. Simonin (51 (1997), 67)

Modern Language Review   *Saga-Book, Vol. XV, Parts 1–2* (58 (1963), 146–47); *The Poetic Edda*, trans. and ed. by L. M. Hollander (58 (1963), 614–17); *The Saga of Gisli*, trans. by G. Johnston, ed. by P. Foote (59 (1964), 686); F. Simone, *Umanesimo, Rinascimento, Barocco in Francia* (66 (1971), 183–84); J. Sacré, *Un sang maniériste* (74 (1979), 457); G. Gadoffre, *Du Bellay et le sacré* (75 (1980), 190–91); I. Silver, *Three Ronsard Studies* (75 (1980), 653–54); M. Gutwirth, *Montaigne ou le pari de l'exemplarité* (75 (1980), 885–86); *Textes et intertextes: études pour Alfred Glauser* (76 (1981), 694–96); D. G. Coleman, *The Gallo-Roman Muse* (76 (1981), 461–62); G. Defaux, *Le Curieux, le glorieux, et la sagesse du monde dans la première moitié du XVIe siècle* (79 (1984), 449–51)

Notes and Queries   Anne d'Urfé, *Œuvres morales et spirituelles inédites*, ed. by Y. Le Hir (24 (1977), 570–71); S. Sturm-Maddox, *Ronsard, Petrarch, and the 'Amours'* (48 (2001), 326–27)

Oxford Magazine   P. Horden (ed.), *Freud and the Humanities* (12 (1986), 14–15)

Paragraph   C. Prendergast, *The Order of Mimesis* ('New Representations for Old', 11 (1988), 99–105)

Renaissance Quarterly   I. Silver, *Ronsard and the Hellenic Renaissance in France*, II: *Ronsard and the Grecian Lyre, Part II* (40 (1987), 357–58) and *Part II* (43, (1990), 42)

Revue d'Histoire Littéraire de la France   R. C. La Charité, *Recreation, Reflection and Re-Creation: Perspectives on Rabelais's 'Pantagruel'* (82 (1982), 453); G. S. Hanisch, *Love Elegies of the Renaissance: Marot, Louise Labé and Ronsard* (82 (1982), 647)

Rhetorica   A. Moss, *Printed Commonplace-Books and the Structuring of Renaissance Thought* (15 (1997), 337–40)

Studi francesi   J. H. Matthews, *An Anthology of French Surrealist Poetry* (31 (1967), 183)

The Times Literary Supplement   P. A. Chilton, *The Poetry of Jean de La Ceppède* (13 Oct. 1978, p. 1184); G. Pocock, *Boileau and the Nature of Neoclassicism* (3 Oct. 1980, p. 1085); M. Fumaroli, *L'Âge de l'éloquence: rhétorique et 'res litteraria' de la Renaissance à l'époque classique* (27 Feb. 1981, p. 236); A. Compagnon, *Nous, Michel de Montaigne* (15 May 1981, p. 540);

G. Mathieu-Castellani, *Mythes de l'éros baroque* and D. L. Rubin, *The Knot of Artifice: A Poetic of the French Lyric in the Early Seventeenth Century* (26 Feb. 1982, p. 226); T. Greene, *The Light in Troy: Imitation and Discovery in Renaissance Poetry* (4 March 1983, p. 211); M. Chaillou, *Domestique chez Montaigne* and J. Starobinski, *Montaigne en mouvement* (3 June 1983, p. 579); F. Rigolot, *Le Texte de la Renaissance: des Rhétoriqueurs à Montaigne* (14 Oct. 1983, p. 1123); M. Riffaterre, *Text Production*, trans. by T. Lyons (16 March 1984, p. 278); Marguerite de Navarre, *The Heptameron*, trans. by P. A. Chilton (27 July 1984, p. 830); P. Brooks, *Reading for the Plot: Design and Intention in Narrative* (4 Jan. 1985, p. 14); A. Moss, *Poetry and Fable: Studies in Mythological Narrative in Sixteenth-Century France* and G. P. Norton, *The Ideology and Language of Translation in Renaissance France and their Humanist Antecedents* (18 Jan. 1985, p. 66); M. Charles, *L'Arbre et la source* (18 April 1986, p. 429); P. Gillet, *Le Goût et les mots: littérature et gastronomie, XIVe–XXe siècle* and M. Jeanneret, *Des mets et des mots: banquets et propos de table à la Renaissance* (8–14 July 1988, p. 762); L. Marin, *Food for Thought*, trans. by M. Hjort (5–11 Jan. 1990, p. 21); J. D. Lyons, *Exemplum: The Rhetoric of Example in Early Modern France and Italy* (15 March 1991, p. 20); P. Sturgess, *Narrativity* (5 March 1993, p. 23); W. Iser, *The Fictive and the Imaginary: Charting Literary Anthropology* (24 Dec. 1993, p. 18); A. Compagnon, *Chat en poche: Montaigne et l'allégorie*, P. Desan, *Les Commerces de Montaigne: le discours économique des 'Essais'*, and P. Desan, *L'Imaginaire économique de la Renaissance* (25 Feb. 1994, p. 24); M. Fumaroli, *L'Âge de l'éloquence* (see above), 2nd edn, and M. Fumaroli, *La Diplomatie de l'esprit: de Montaigne à La Fontaine* (28 Oct. 1994, p. 26); Antoine Compagnon, *Le Démon de la théorie: littérature et sens commun* (15 Jan. 1999, p. 25)

Yearbook of English Studies   E. Kern, *The Absolute Comic* (1984, pp. 300–01)

INDEX

PART IV

Afterlives

§1

Towards a Pre-history of Suspense

The form taken by a narrative is a way of thinking. This is true even if one can easily show that certain narrative procedures recur from one culture and historical period to another without any very evident signs of transformation, prompting theorists ancient and modern to feel justified in reducing narrative form to a set of fundamental, atemporal principles. Such enduring structures might be regarded as basic skills which are available to be adapted to local cultural habits, assumptions and needs. Shifts in use, or in modes of description and prescription (poetics), may thus give us a particular insight into changing habits of thought in a given period and culture. One such shift is the development of a theory of suspense in the sixteenth century, together with corresponding developments in practice, even if the practice does not always map neatly on to the theory.

It should be acknowledged from the outset that to use the word 'suspense' to designate a particular narrative and dramatic device is anachronistic. In early modern Latin, Italian and French, the verbal form of the word and its past participle (*suspendere, suspensus, suspendu, sospeso*) were in use; the French phrase *en suspens* was also current at the time, but is not to be found in treatises on poetics or the prefaces of fictional works. No equivalent term seems to have existed in classical antiquity. Aristotle speaks of ways of making the plot more coherent and gripping by abandoning the historical sequence of events; he speaks of surprise and wonder as aspects of audience response, and of a denouement that counters the expectations of the characters or the spectators; his analysis of *peripeteia* and *anagnorisis* presuppose something equivalent to suspense as a feature of dramatic plots; but the feature itself is not singled out and labelled. As for Horace, the highly elliptical lines that he devotes to narrative sequence rehearse the Aristotelian opposition between history and epic ('nec gemino bellum Troianum orditur ab ovo' [nor is the Trojan war traced from the twin egg]) and add two further precepts: first, that the exordium should not provide a summary of the entire story (the poet must lead the reader 'from the smoke to the fire'); and secondly, that the narrative should begin 'in medias res'.[1] Horace is clearly concerned with engaging and sustaining the reader's (or listener's) interest, but he says nothing even of expectation or surprise, let alone suspense.

Despite this absence, classical Latin authors did have at their disposal expressions such as *suspendere animos, tenere animos suspensos* to indicate the way in which a state of anxious expectation may be created in the listener's mind. The most relevant example is provided by Quintilian, who speaks of a technique that may be used by the orator to hold the attention of the judges ('cum diu *suspendisset* iudicum animos'). According to Quintilian, this is what Celsus called *sustentatio* [suspension].[2] However, 'suspense' is presented here as a figure of rhetoric rather than as an aspect of narrative *dispositio*. Latin literary criticism seems not to have made use of such expressions to designate a narrative effect or develop a model of narrative structure.[3]

A humanist theory of suspense: Girolamo Vida

It is therefore all the more remarkable that, in the second book of Marco Girolamo Vida's *Ars poetica* of 1527, the verb *suspendere* is used four times in the space of some seventy lines. The passage in question is a discussion of narrative *dispositio* grafted, like an extended commentary, on to the Horatian *locus* we have already looked at: the phrase 'in medias res' occurs at the very beginning of this development, and later one finds a variant of 'nec gemino [...] orditur ab ovo'.[4] The standard commentaries on Horace's *De arte poetica* that were printed in the early sixteenth century make no mention of suspense; in Vida's treatise, by contrast, the Horatian *topoi* are integrated from the outset into a theory of reading as a desire for the unexpected and the novel. Vida arrives at the 'in medias res' principle precisely by way of suspense. The poets, he says, take care to confront their readers with the unexpected, to keep their minds suspended by feeding them new materials ('suspensosque animos novitate tenere'), and to develop the plot by digressions ('ambages') (lines 56–58). The *locus* is completed by the recommendation that the poet, having begun directly and bewilderingly in the centre of the action, should compensate by providing a detailed exposition of the incidents leading up to that moment so that the reader does not remain in the dark (lines 64–65).

This first passage thus proposes a balance between ignorance and knowledge, between the art of making the reader wait and the art of fulfilling expectations. The technique of digression allows the poet to dangle in front of the reader a narrative end that appears close while at the same time systematically removing it, and Vida here uses the classic epic metaphor of a sea voyage indefinitely prolonged (lines 69–73). What results from this set of themes and images is the idea of a process, a movement of progressive narrative transformation, whereas the poetics of classical antiquity had given priority to the overall nature of the narrative and its effect.

After citing various passages from Virgil and Homer in order to illustrate these techniques, Vida comes back to the question of suspense while, it seems, changing the recommended order. The example of the canonical poets is now used to insist that the narration of epic actions be deferred until the circumstances from which those actions arose have been enumerated. Yet the prime recommendation is still that the reader should long be kept 'suspended' and uncertain of the outcome ('tenuisse legentem / *suspensum* incertumque diu, qui denique rerum eventus maneant'; lines 98–100). The apparent discrepancy reveals all the more clearly that the fundamental principle for Vida is less the 'in medias res' than the structure of expectation, in other words the psychology of the reader.

It is once again the mind of the reader that provides the central reference point in the gloss that follows: 'Lectores cupidi expectant durantque volentes, / nec perferre negant superest quodcunque laborum' [Readers avidly await the outcome and willingly sustain their attention, / nor do they refuse to see it through to the end, no matter what torments they have to suffer] (lines 104–05). The desire to read on must overcome even the most urgent physical needs, be it sleep or hunger; the poet must therefore contrive to stimulate this desire, turn the readers' minds this way and that, 'suspend' them, and thus torment them ('*suspendit*que diu miseros torquetque legentes'). What matters to Vida is the power relation between author and reader and the anxiety that the reader should be made to feel. According to his model, reading becomes a kind of masochistic pleasure.[5]

Vida subsequently continues to explain his theory of narrative organization without using the word *suspendere*, but adding further metaphors and examples. The poet is to provide clues ('indicia') that allow the reader to glimpse, as through clouds and darkness, an eventual enlightenment: that is the function, for example, of prophecies (lines 124 ff.).[6] The same notion returns a little later, where Vida prescribes that the denouement must be anticipated by the reader, but in a confused and obscure manner (lines 148–49). The reader will thus be in the same position as travellers who, believing that they can see walls on distant hills, continue their journey more energetically than they would if all they could see was an interminable extension of their own obscure trajectory (lines 150–55).

Vida returns to this metaphorical frame of reference repeatedly in the course of his analysis of narrative organization, but the essential model is in fact already there at the outset:

> Protinus illectas succende cupidine mentes
> et studium lectorum animis innecte legendi.
> Iam vero cum rem propones, nomine nunquam
> prodere conveniet manifesto; semper opertis
> indiciis longe et verborum ambage petita
> significant umbraque obducunt. (lines 38–43)

[Without delay, seduce the minds of your readers, set them alight with desire and infuse in them the urge to read. It is important that when you narrate an event, you never do so too explicitly; poets always indicate the way the story is going a long way ahead by means of hidden clues and verbal detours, wrapping it in obscurity.]

The sub-text here is once again Horace's remarks about the exordium.[7] Vida, however, introduces his account of how an epic poem should begin by way of figural notions such as metaphor, periphrasis, displacement of the proper term. The detours ('ambages') of narrative originate in his account — literally, as Vida is talking of narrative beginnings — in a periphrasis ('ambage').

These lines make it clear how far the *Ars poetica*, like many other treatises on poetics in this period, is dependent on the rhetorical tradition. Vida must, one assumes, have been familiar with the *locus* where Quintilian presents the art of *sustentatio* as a figure of discourse. The theory of suspense in the early sixteenth century thus seems to arise from a drafting of figural theory into Horatian poetics.

This fusion of poetics and rhetoric must have been facilitated, in part at least, by the continuing popularity in early modern Europe of practices of allegorical narrative, allegory being defined since classical antiquity as perpetual metaphor. All these analyses in Vida's treatise of a narrative where knowledge is at once hidden and progressively revealed recall, in fact, the medieval theory of allegorical reading, but with one crucial reservation: Vida's theory is unambiguously humanist and secular; it carries no trace of any religious or moral teleology.

Amyot's Heliodorus and the triumph of *ordo artificialis*

By any standards, Jacques Amyot's translation into French of Heliodorus' *Aethiopica* (1547) was a major event. As his celebrated version of Plutarch would later show, Amyot was a superb translator, and his preface to the *Aethiopica* openly seeks to sell the merits of the Greek novel to a generation of readers brought up on chivalric romances. Heliodorus outdoes his ancient and modern rivals, he says, by a spectacular structural device: like the epic poems of antiquity, the *Aethiopica* begins *in medias res*, but it uses this standard technique in a novel way. The opening scene presents a situation wholly incomprehensible to the reader, provoking 'great amazement' ('un grand esbahissement') and

> un passionné desir d'entendre le commencement [i.e. the events that precede and motivate this scene] et toutefois il les tire si bien par l'ingenieuse liaison de son conte, que l'on n'est point resolu de ce que l'on trouve tout au commencement du premier livre jusques à ce que l'on ayt lu la fin du cinquiesme. Et quand on est là venu, encore a l'on plus grande envie de voir la fin, que l'on n'avoit auparavant d'en voir le commencement: De sorte que tousjours l'entendement demeure suspendu, jusques à ce que l'on vienne à la conclusion, laquelle laisse le lecteur satisfait, de la sorte que le sont ceux, qui à la fin viennent à jouyr d'un bien ardemment desiré, et longuement atendu.[8]

> [a passionate desire to hear the beginning, and yet he leads them on so successfully by the clever sequence of his narrative that you don't get the explanation of what you encounter at the very beginning of the first book until you have read the end of the fifth. And when you have got to that point, you have an even greater desire to see the end of the novel than you previously had to understand its beginning. By this means, your mind remains suspended until you come to the conclusion, which leaves the reader satisfied in the same way as someone is satisfied when they at last reach the consummation of an ardently desired and long awaited pleasure.]

In the language of Renaissance poetics, the *Aethiopica* is an exemplary instance of *ordo artificialis*, as opposed to the *ordo naturalis* appropriate to historical narrative.[9] The device was imitated in France within a few years in Barthélemy Aneau's strange unfinished novel *Alector* (Lyon, 1560),[10] and by the beginning of the seventeenth century it had become a standard and even distinctive feature of the baroque novel, exploited notably by Honoré d'Urfé in the *Astrée*.[11]

We may well ask, then, what is going on here. Does the re-emergence of the Greek novel on the European scene represent a new way of thinking about narrative? Does it impose new ways of reading narrative? Does it contribute significantly to the pre-history of what we call 'the novel', that is to say the form that extended prose fiction took in the nineteenth century? Or is it only a variant of an earlier form usually known as 'romance'?

We may note first that Amyot brings out above all the obsessive character of the type of reading this structural technique is meant to generate. He draws on the language of desire, the psychology of the lover, so that the suspense he speaks of takes on an unmistakably erotic character. It is true that he subsequently devalues the novel precisely because it seems to be designed for pleasure alone, then saves it by evoking its utility as a vehicle of 'beaux discours' [fine speeches], 'sentences' [moral maxims] and the like; but by expressing these reservations, he in fact demonstrates that the novelty of the work consists in its virtuoso construction and in its manipulation of the reader rather than in any moral utility that might be derived from it. This kind of fiction is thus entirely different from allegorical narrative, including allegorizations of canonical works such as the *Odyssey*. Amyot is here sketching out, one might say, a purely secular economy of the novel.

It is difficult to believe that Amyot was ignorant of Vida's poetics. Both focus on the way in which the reader's expectations can be exacerbated and frustrated, and the phrase 'l'entendement demeure *suspendu*' seems directly to echo the terms of Vida's analysis. Yet Vida refers exclusively to the epic *poems* of antiquity; there is nothing to suggest that his theory was derived from a reading of Heliodorus, which was first printed in Greek in Basle in 1534. Suspense and the *Aethiopica* are linked for the first time in Amyot's preface. It is important to recall here that the *Odyssey* and the *Aeneid* were also regarded as instances of *ordo artificialis*, since they both introduce flashbacks retracing the earlier history of the characters and thus supplying the reader with the information that had been excluded by an opening *in medias res*. However, that further information is not strictly essential to an understanding of the earlier parts of the poem, and there is no enigmatic opening scene as there is in the *Aethiopica*. In consequence, the narrative structure engineered by Heliodorus is far tighter, and seems more systematically designed to create in the reader psychological dependence of the kind so graphically defined by Amyot.

Seen from that viewpoint, Vida's lengthy exposition of the virtues of suspense may seem somewhat puzzling. Unless we are to suppose that this was a random mutation of narrative theory which accidentally found a fertile application only a few years later, a conjectural explanation must be sought in Vida's cultural conditioning. His narrative reading habits must have been formed in part at least by the romance tradition, particularly by its Renaissance variants, the romances of Boiardo and Ariosto, and these were structured according to a principle of constantly renewed suspense. Developing the 'interlace' composition of their medieval predecessors, they proceed by means of a technique of controlled interruption. The narrative thread is cut off in the middle of an episode, leaving the reader in a state of uncertainty; another thread is then picked up and developed until it is cut off in its turn; eventually the earlier thread returns, provisional answers are given to some questions, but others remain open and new ones are always being raised.

One might well imagine, then, that it was in terms of these reading habits that Vida understood the structure of ancient epic and its theorization in Horace. Suspense becomes a focal aspect of the reading experience, but it is a local suspense, operating from episode to episode. The reader may vaguely wonder how the whole thing may end, but that ultimate resolution remains in a constantly deferred limbo of expectation. It is no doubt that context above all that gives meaning to Vida's metaphor of a journey whose end is always distant and difficult to make out.

Further evidence for this hypothesis is provided by the mid-sixteenth century Italian theorists of the romance. Using Aristotelian rather than Horatian terminology, Pigna, for instance, defines the denouement as the resolution of a plot that had held the reader in suspense ('La sciorre è, ogni volta che un intrico, che sospeso tenea il lettore, si sviluppi').[12] Although the model is theatrical in origin, Pigna is applying it here to the reading of a narrative, as is clear from his reference to the reader. The phrase 'ogni volta' [every time] seems to imply, furthermore, that he is considering the denouement as a recurrent feature of a lengthy sequence rather than as a single event in an individual narrative.[13] Scaliger, too, even though he cites the *Aethiopica* as the best model for the epic poet who wishes to create suspense,[14] speaks primarily of techniques for beginning a narrative and for maintaining interest thereafter.

In this respect, then, Amyot appears to stand alone. Distinguishing between two major phases in the construction of a narrative written according to the *ordo artificialis*, he imagines a primary suspense which is carried through the whole of the first five books, then a second-wave suspense which is not resolved until the end of the novel. One might think of this as a 'synoptic' mode of suspense (and thus of overall construction and consumption), as opposed to the local or intermittent suspense that characterizes the romance model.

This analytic difference is accompanied by a crucial difference in the mode of presentation. Vida writes in Latin verse, addressing himself to a humanist audience and to would-be epic poets. Scaliger's *Poetics* is likewise a massive learned work in Latin, again using a rhetoric of prescription ('Do not begin your narrative with the origins of the story'). Even Pigna and his teacher and colleague Giraldi, although they use the vernacular and defend the 'modern' genre of the romance, adopt the style of post-Aristotelian theorists. Whatever traces of everyday vernacular consumption they may carry or presuppose are hidden amid the panoply of erudite culture. Amyot, by contrast, writes a brief and non-technical French preface to market what is in effect, for the sixteenth century, a new product. He refers to Horace and to other poets of antiquity in order to give authority to his enterprise, but brings them into direct contact with popular reading materials such as the chivalric romance. Far from being a work of theory citing Heliodorus as an example, the preface has the function of affording direct access to the novel which it accompanies. It is part of a *practice* — a practice of reading, not of humanist rewriting.

If we are to consider Amyot's Heliodorus as a symptom of potential change in ways of reading narrative, it is thus tempting to focus on the shift from local and continuous suspense to synoptic or end-directed suspense as an anticipation of the later evolution of the novel. One factor here must presumably be the impact on reading habits of the printed book and its wide availability, by the mid-sixteenth century, to readers of moderate means and culture. Once the story is fixed in print, in multiple copies, readers know that their book contains a single whole narrative whose ending is always there waiting for them, unchangeable, in the final printed pages. Earlier manuscript traditions are notorious for allowing the indefinite modification of a narrative cluster from version to version; in this sense, manuscript narrative remains much closer to oral narrative and its consumption by groups of readers in constantly shifting contexts.[15] With the *Aethiopica* in Amyot's version, the age of the individual reader, the individual purchaser of discrete fictions, seems to have arrived. It is marked by a secular conception of narrative in which the purpose of narrators is to capture their readers, make them become as it were sexually obsessed with the story, so that they will continue to read in a state of continuous arousal until the moment of consummation at the end.

Yet there are clearly problems with this view, and precisely in the sense that Amyot remains an *exception*. The model of group oral consumption so visible in Chaucer and Boccaccio is still operative in Marguerite de Navarre's *Heptaméron*, which is almost exactly contemporary with Amyot's Heliodorus. Similarly, the assumption by Ariosto that his tale is being read aloud and listened to by a group of aristocratic customers will be no less valid in the social conditions of seventeenth-century France: the *Astrée* and many other novels of its day lend themselves perfectly to *salon* discussions of questions of love and ethics. Of course these novels and collections of stories, once printed, were available to be read by single readers; for these, the sense of participating in an aristocratic pastime must have been a seductive fantasy, a powerful incentive for buying the book in the first place. The fact remains that, if there is a change, it is a very slow and gradual one, accommodating itself within an existing framework rather than replacing it.

One particularly striking symptom of the persistence of such earlier habits of reading is the publication of so many unfinished narratives. The perpetually unresolved interlace of the *Orlando* narratives continues to attract many readers well into the seventeenth century; in France, the replacement of the standard sixteenth-century translation of the romance by François de Rosset's new version in 1615 shows that there was still a vigorous market for this type of narrative structure. Even fictions that exploit the technique of *ordo artificialis* according to the model of Greek romance often remain unfinished: this is true of Aneau's *Alector*, Béroalde de Verville's *Voyage des Princes Fortunez* (1610), and above all the *Astrée* itself (for which a conclusion was provided by another author after d'Urfé had died in 1625). It seems indeed that, despite the remarkable impact of the *Aethiopica* and of other Greek novels, in France and elsewhere in Europe, and despite the fashion for spectacular uses of *ordo artificialis* that went with it, the message of Amyot's synoptic analysis of narrative structure was not assimilated by many seventeenth-century novelists. The earlier seventeenth-century novel is characteristically episodic; if there is an opening mystery, it is designed to ensure that the reader is firmly hooked, not to anticipate an eventual denouement.

Novel futures

These fragments of the pre-history of the novel are only part of the story. It is not difficult to see, however, that the popularity of picaresque and burlesque narratives in the seventeenth and eighteenth centuries points in the same direction. Even the epistolary novel, with its radically internalized and relativized point of view, draws on a paradigm of open-ended social exchange. Models of collective consumption of narrative, together with a taste for episodic and indefinitely prolonged modes of suspense, show increasing signs of strain, but persist long after the possibility emerges of an alternative model.

Such phenomena are of course themselves only local symptoms of more wide-ranging changes of social and political organization, sensibility, and epistemology. For example, it seems reasonable to suppose that the desire for a determinate ending which resolves all of the preceding narrative strands (the 'detective novel' model) increases in proportion as the belief in a transcendental order — religious, political, social — declines: the ultimate destiny of romance heroes is in a sense predictable (apotheosis, marriage, restitution to the social order), whereas the mediate and particular destiny of nineteenth-century characters demands a mediate and particular end.[16]

This shift can be pinpointed with some precision in George Eliot's *Daniel Deronda*, a novel which makes as striking a use of *ordo artificialis* as if Eliot had had Amyot's preface in mind. Its plot often echoes romance, and evokes vast historical perspectives stretching away into the past and the future; yet it is articulated by the accidental embroilments of strictly human and secular characters; it answers all of the narrative questions it poses, while leaving the protagonists with a future which is still unpredictable. Furthermore, certain of its epigraphs explicitly evoke the tradition of Aristotelian poetics in order to reflect on narrative uncertainty. The one that prefaces the opening chapter reinterprets the 'in medias res' *topos* in relation to a conception of ultimately indefinite beginnings and endings:

> Men can do nothing without the make-believe of a beginning. Even Science, the strict measurer, is obliged to start with a make-believe unit, and must fix on a point in the stars' unceasing journey when his sidereal clock shall pretend that time is at Nought. His less accurate grandmother Poetry has always been understood to start in the middle; but on reflection it appears that her proceeding is not very different from his; since Science, too, reckons backwards as well as forwards, divides his unit into billions, and with his clock-finger at Nought really sets off *in medias res*. No retrospect will take us to the true beginning; and whether our prologue be in heaven or in earth, it is but a fraction of that all-presupposing fact with which our story sets out.[17]

The epistemological and narratological shift to which examples like this bear witness is accompanied by a mutation in reading habits so profound that most modern readers find it impossible to enjoy the narratives that early modern readers consumed obsessively. This phenomenon seems to suggest that the nineteenth-century novel has only a residual pre-history, and was not the consequence of a strictly cumulative development. Amyot's preface is perhaps best considered, in the long historical perspective, as an exceptional variant within a context of sixteenth-century reflections on reading.

This view should however be distinguished from a value judgement whereby 'the novel' is reified and cordoned off from supposedly inferior and false antecedents.[18] It should also be attenuated in the light of strong evidence that alternative ways of consuming narrative continued throughout and *beyond* the very period when the novel held sway. Serial storytelling remained popular in the nineteenth century; radio and television have shown in our own age how powerful the open serial mode can be, with its local suspense and its endlessly renewed interlace; and the electronic media have created the possibility of further modes such as virtual and interactive narrative. Not only is the nineteenth-century novel itself irreducibly diverse; it is also just another way of packaging and selling stories, a highly successful one in an age of mass print culture, but having no claim to absolute priority over others. The only thing that remains constant is the desire for narrative.

Notes

1. Horace, *De arte poetica*, lines 136–50 (this reference includes all the points listed).
2. Quintilian, *Institutio oratoria* IX.2.22; Cornelius Celsus was an encyclopaedist of the first century CE. See also IX.2.16 on prolepsis; and cf. the pseudo-Longinus, *Treatise on the Sublime* 22.4, on hyperbaton (the Greek word *anakremasas*, the equivalent of the Latin *suspensus*, is used here).
3. The Greek commentators on the *Odyssey* (particularly Eustathius) analyse the way in which the recognition of Odysseus is deferred, but without using metaphorical expressions equivalent to the Latin *suspendere animos*. The only exception I have been able to find occurs in Demetrius' *On Style* (IV.216): in speaking of a story of which the denouement is deliberately deferred in order to 'keep the listener is suspense', Demetrius uses the phrase *kremnônta ton akrotêri* (the verb has the same root as the one used by Longinus in the passage cited above, previous note).
4. Vida, *L'Arte poetica*, ed. by R. Girardi (Bari: Adriatica, 1982), p. 118, lines 59–61, 74–76 (references will henceforth be confined to line numbers provided according to the cited edition; where I provide no translation for quotations, their sense is paraphrased in the surrounding argument).
5. See also line 115: 'exspectare avidum saevaque cupidine captum'. As an example of this model of coercion of the reader by the author, Vida mentions the passage from the *Odyssey* where Penelope herself 'keeps minds in suspense' by deferring the moment when she brings out Odysseus' bow. In this case, it is a fictional character who demonstrates the technique of suspense on behalf of the author.
6. The use of the word 'indicia' evokes an epistemological 'deep structure' that stretches from the archetypal model of the hunt to the modern detective novel; see my *Recognitions*, especially pp. 250–54.
7. See also Vida, lines 30 ff.; Horace, *De arte poetica*, lines 14 and 136 ff. On the exordium of the *Odyssey* as a model, compare Horace, lines 141–42 and Vida, lines 47–49.
8. Jacques Amyot, *L'Histoire aethiopique de Heliodorus [...] Nouvellement traduite du grec en francoys* (Paris: Estienne Grouleau, 1547), 'Proësme du translateur', fol. A iii^r.
9. See Giorgetto Giorgi, *Antichità classica e seicento francese* (Rome: Bulzoni, 1987), pp. 13–57, and 'Due fonti del romanzo barocco francese: Apuleio e Eliodoro', in *Il seicento francese oggi: situazione e prospettiva della ricerca*, ed. by G. Dottoli (Bari: Adriatica; Paris, Nizet, 1994), pp. 87–99.
10. See Marie Madeleine Fontaine (ed.), *Alector* (Geneva: Droz, 1996), also M. M. Fontaine, '*Alector* de Barthélemy Aneau: la rencontre des ambitions philosophiques et pédagogiques avec la fiction romanesque en 1560', in *Philosophical Fictions and the French Renaissance*, ed. by N. Kenny (London: The Warburg Institute, 1991), p. 39.
11. See Georges Molinié, *Du roman grec au roman baroque: un art majeur du genre narratif en France sous Louis XIII* (Toulouse: Publications de l'Université de Toulouse–Le Mirail, 1982), pp. 57–65; G. Giorgi, *L'Astrée' di Honoré d'Urfé tra barocco e classicismo* (Florence: La Nuova Italia, 1974), pp. 17–28; also my chapter, 'Béroalde de Verville: le sujet au pays de l'anamorphose', in *Pré-histoires*, pp. 155–64. Amyot's translation of the *Aethiopica* remained popular until new translations began to appear in the seventeenth century (especially J. de Montlyard's 1623 version), attesting to the continued enthusiasm of readers for the novel itself; in addition, Alexandre Hardy dramatized it in the form of eight consecutive plays (1623).
12. Giovanni Battista Pigna, *I romanzi* (Venice: Vincenzo Valgrisi, 1554), p. 38.
13. Cf. the use of the plural in the remark which immediately follows 'this [i.e. the denouement] is most powerfully brought about by means of Recognitions' ('e cio fassi massimamente per le Agnitione').

14. Julius Caesar Scaliger, *Poetices libri septem* (Lyon: Antoine Vincent, 1561), III.xcvi (p. 144). He also gives suspense itself the highest priority in epic construction, defining it as the art of keeping the listener captive: 'ea sane vel unica vel praecipua virtus, auditorem quasi captivum detinere'.

15. On reading as a group activity, performed orally, see also above, pp. 11–12.

16. Frank Kermode's *The Sense of an Ending: Studies in the Theory of Fiction* (London and New York: Oxford University Press, 1966) remains the most persuasive account of this question.

17. *Daniel Deronda*, ed. by Terence Cave, Penguin Classics (Harmondsworth: Penguin Books, 1995), p. 7. The notion of the 'two infinities' in this passage may well be indebted to Pascal, whom Eliot greatly admired; but it also clearly presupposes a post-Newtonian universe. See also the epigraphs to chapters 16, 21 and 41 (where the *Poetics* is specifically quoted) and the introduction to the edition cited above, pp. xxiv–xxxii. An extended variant of Eliot's reflection is provided by Thomas Mann's prologue to his 'Joseph' novels, although the similarity is presumably accidental.

18. Such a view is implied in Ian Watt's *The Rise of the Novel* (London: Chatto and Windus, 1957), which has itself become virtually a canonical work. Watt seeks to dismiss the claims of Greek and chivalric romance to anticipate the true (nineteenth-century) novel, which for him was born in England in the eighteenth century.

§2

Singing with Tigers:
Recognition in *Wilhelm Meister*,
Daniel Deronda and *Nights at the Circus*

The recognition plot gives retrospective shape to a life, often to several lives in their connectedness. The shape may be social, moral, spiritual, psychological, or some combination of these, but it always embodies knowledge, an attempt to make cognitive sense of human agency in the face of the contingent world. In the early modern period, the pressures exerted on such plots by rapidly changing epistemological and cognitive frames of reference are discernible in the emergence of new modalities of recognition and the mutation of older ones.[1] In the novel, especially its picaresque versions, the threads which make up a destiny are often tenuous and intermittent, the recognition itself indefinitely deferred. In Scarron's unfinished *Roman comique*, for example, the reader is led by the quasi-allegorical names of the leading figures, Le Destin and L'Estoile, to suppose that these two actors may turn out to be of noble origins and eventually recover their inheritance. Yet perhaps their names are only actors' names, and their destinies only illusory ones, a mirage created by the theatre of the world. Likewise, the reader never discovers whether Marianne, in Marivaux's *La Vie de Marianne*, was in fact the child of the apparently well-born couple who are murdered by highwaymen in the opening scene; the possibility of an ultimate recognition scene seems to hover over the narrative, but it fails to materialize.

This type of plot was quite common in the seventeenth and eighteenth centuries; but at the same time, another very different kind of plot flourished alongside it. The ancient principle of allegorical reading, which could turn virtually any plot — including the picaresque, as the example of the *Roman comique* already shows — into a transcendental drama of recognition, persisted in new narrative forms, of which the novel of the protagonist's education or enlightenment is the most prominent. Some of Voltaire's best-known *Contes* are a satirical picaresque inversion of this type of plot, while Françoise de Graffigny's *Lettres d'une Péruvienne* gives another twist to the narrative of enlightenment through experience of a European society in which corruption is endemic. Fénelon's *Télémaque*, known and imitated throughout Europe, provides an alternative model for fictions of the hero's education,[2] and the German forerunners of *Wilhelm Meisters Lehrjahre* belong to this broad generic category,[3] as indeed does *The Magic Flute*, an opera which Goethe admired but whose message he set out to complicate in his own unfinished sequel, *Der Zauberflöte zweiter Teil*.[4]

Wilhelm Meister itself combines the picaresque adventures of a wandering troupe of actors (as in *Le Roman comique*) with the early modern allegory of the world as theatre; at the same time, it is generally claimed to be the model and forerunner of the nineteenth-century realist *Bildungsroman*. It occupies a position at the very cusp of change, and not only in the world of literary forms: this is also the historical moment when European and American political systems were in the process of radical and irreversible transformation.[5] The decline of the *grands récits* of religion and philosophy, with their supernatural explanations of human destiny and agency, is likewise palpable in the ways all kinds of narrative are constructed, from fable via the *conte* and the novel to historiography.[6] The status of *Wilhelm Meisters Lehrjahre* as a major event in the history of the novel hinges to a large extent on this development. The text includes intermittent discussions by the characters of the theme of chance and fate, and these discussions propose a radical revision of the 'plot of destiny':[7] events in the world, it appears, are governed by chance, not by an end-directed fate or providence (as in romance), although they may be read retrospectively by the subject as shaping elements within his or her individual life. Similarly, the representation of religion and of religious belief, in characters such as the 'Abbé', in the episode entitled *Bekenntnisse einer schönen Seele* and in Mignon's funeral, has a powerfully demystifying function. And the novel ends with the central character's future still unresolved: it looks as if he will marry Natalie, but the conclusion is notoriously rapid, and we know at least that the marriage is likely to be deferred for some considerable time.

Despite these uncertainties, Goethe chose to stage, in the last two books of the novel, one of the most elaborate non-parodic recognition sequences of modern times. Most of the recognition scenes, as might be expected, revolve around Wilhelm, throwing light on mysterious episodes in the preceding narrative and helping to clarify his emergence into adulthood and social responsibility: he discovers that he is the father of Felix, he recognizes his grandfather's collection of *objets d'art* in Natalie's château, and he finds and recognizes Natalie herself, not to mention other members of the so-called *Turmgesellschaft* whom he had met during his travels. The allegorical schema and its focus on the inner life remain dominant here. There is never any doubt about Wilhelm's genealogical identity or his social provenance; his recognitions mark the unfolding of a moral and social *anagnorisis*. Wilhelm's wish to become a great writer and actor is an illusion which he must abandon in order to fashion a new and more pragmatic set of relations and responsibilities. To this one may add that the women Wilhelm meets in his wanderings are for the most part figures of the moral choices he eventually has to make, the paths he might follow. Mariane, Philine and Aurelie variously embody the life of theatrical illusion, while the mysterious 'Amazon' becomes the ideal representation of the elevated moral and social life towards which he is gradually conducted. With the single exception of the *Bekenntnisse einer schönen Seele*,[8] which is written in the first person by a woman character in a time earlier than that of the novel as a whole, everything revolves around Wilhelm himself, his ambitions, his amorous inclinations, his discomforts, his dilemmas, his mistakes and finally his passage from the status of apprentice to that of 'Meister'. The romance elements of the plot thus seem to be secondary and contingent; suspense is not an overriding feature at any point, and there is little of the surprise brought about by spectacular recognitions that reorganize all the elements of the story into a new pattern.

However, this account omits one important strand in the novel's narrative construction. The story of Mignon and the Harpist, which begins in the second book, when Wilhelm has only just set out on his travels, continues intermittently until the final book. From the outset, it raises questions. Who is the Harpist, and why is he melancholy to the point of madness? What are Mignon's origins, which are alluded to in her famous song 'Kennst du das Land?' [Do you know the land?] (the phrase 'Kennst du [...]' that opens each stanza of the song is of course itself one of the most archetypal of recognition questions, with its insistence on knowledge and on a place of origin). Why is she so unwilling to speak of her past? These questions are fully resolved in Book 8, after the death of both characters, when an Italian nobleman arrives who, as Mignon lies in her coffin, recognizes her by a birthmark. It turns out that Mignon is the daughter of the Harpist and his sister: not only are their destinies saturated with the pain of severance, exile, and (in Mignon's case) abduction and abuse, they have also been blighted by a founding act of incest.

This story is in most respects a classic recognition narrative, reminiscent of models such as Iphigenia among the Taurians, Perdita in Shakespeare's *The Winter's Tale*, or (more directly) Cervantes's *La Gitanilla*. It is also, one might say, an archaic strand that sits uneasily with the nascent *Bildungsroman*, even at the fundamental level of narrative organization. Mignon's final appearance, her death, the telling of her story, and the death of the Harpist take up considerable space in the last three chapters of the novel, much more than the question of Wilhelm's own future. Yet their recognition plot is entirely separate from Wilhelm's, except in so far as he had become acquainted with both characters and offered them help. If one imagined an alternative narrative where *their* story was the principal focus of attention, Wilhelm would play only a contingent role. It is true that Mignon's affection for him is the immediate cause of her death; but this potential love story is itself only intermittent. Mignon disappears for long stretches of the narrative, and this narrative neglect is reflected in the careless, even offhand way in which Wilhelm treats her after his initial generous act in rescuing her from the itinerant tightrope walkers. The correspondence between Schiller and Goethe during the final stages of composition shows, moreover, that Goethe accepted Schiller's advice to rewrite part of the denouement in order to remove the almost shocking sidelining of Mignon's death once the funeral is over.[9]

There thus appears to be a mismatch between the narrative promise of the Mignon strand and its realization. However, this narrative shortfall is compensated for by the sheer intensity of the episodes concerning Mignon and the Harpist, an intensity which is encapsulated in the songs they sing. In the reception history of *Wilhelm Meisters Lehrjahre*, these songs have carried more weight and been more widely diffused than any other aspect of the novel. And from the outset, readers were struck disproportionately, in relation to the narrative space it occupies, by the pathos of the Mignon strand.[10] One obvious way of reconciling these apparently incompatible features is to read Mignon and the Harpist as figures of poetry and music, in other words as part of the allegorical schema referred to above. They take their place here neatly enough on the margins of the theatrical scenarios which dominate the novel. Wilhelm wants to be a writer, he writes dramatic poetry himself, and he also translates the fictional Italian original of 'Kennst du das Land?' into polished German verse. In this reading, Mignon and her fate are relevant only as the embodiment of a theme: the aesthetic and emotional intensity of lyric poetry and music, like theatre, is in the end to be left behind in favour of a higher moral vision. This, in fact, is the way Novalis read the novel. In the years following its first appearance, he launched a scathing attack on *Wilhelm Meister* as a text written against poetry,[11] while composing his own novel of romantic enlightenment, *Heinrich von Ofterdingen*, in which poetry and music are assigned an unambiguously transcendental and redemptive role.[12]

Despite the allegorical function that the Mignon story acquires in the overall economy of *Wilhelm Meister*, it remains the case that it is condensed and, as it were, impacted on the primary narrative construction. One sign of this is the double motivation of certain of the songs. 'Kennst du das Land?' refers to a grand house of classical design containing statues; this, for Mignon herself, is presumably the house she lived in as a child, but the novel features other similar houses, all of them connected with Wilhelm's story, not Mignon's. One of them in particular plays a crucial role in the unravelling of the plot and is the site of a double recognition: it contains the statues and other artworks which had belonged to Wilhelm's father, and it proves to be the residence of the 'Amazon' (Natalie).[13] The case of Mignon's second song, 'Nur wer die Sehnsucht kennt', is in some ways even more instructive, if more muted and subtle. The song is sung by both Mignon and the Harpist as a duet, so that the words, with their yearning for a lost home and a lost loved one, have to be attributed to both characters, not just to Mignon. There is a hidden irony and pathos here which is only available to the reader who already knows how the story will end. Although they are not aware of it, and never will be, they are father and daughter: it is not, for them, a love song, but a song of unfulfilled yearning for recognition. Yet the song is introduced at the end of a chapter where Wilhelm is daydreaming about the 'Amazon', whom he has recently encountered for the first time. The text tells us that 'He fell into a dreamy state of yearning' ('Er verfiel in eine träumende Sehnsucht'), and at that very moment he hears Mignon and the Harpist singing the song with great feeling.[14] The *Sehnsucht* expressed by the song thus not only belongs to the essential character of the Mignon strand, but also reflects Wilhelm's perceptions and Wilhelm's strand of the plot, especially as the object of his yearning will be the woman who leads him across the threshold into his 'mastership'.

This 'overdetermination', as one might call it, again demonstrates the plurality of the recognition plots of *Wilhelm Meisters Lehrjahre* and their unusual juxtaposition: instead of being gathered into a single interconnected set of life-histories, they are separate, pointing in different directions, and they *collide* with one another rather than becoming integrated. The same feature has a further consequence: since Mignon has her own recognition plot, she cannot be regarded as having a purely symbolic role in the novel, and that in turn means that her marginalization is more disturbing than that of the other women Wilhelm mistreats. She is condemned to remain forever an exiled other, a foreign body that the novel can finally only expel in order to reach something approaching closure.

George Eliot's interest in *Wilhelm Meisters Lehrjahre* and in the *Bildungsroman*, which she shared with George Henry Lewes, is well established.[15] It was particularly intense in the 1850s, just before she began to write her own fiction, and she apparently re-read Goethe's novel in the early 1870s, when she would soon begin work on *Daniel Deronda*.[16] Some of her other novels have been analysed as instances of the *Bildungsroman*,[17] but *Daniel Deronda* is acknowledged to be the prime example.[18]

It is not difficult to see why. Like Wilhelm, Daniel is an 'apprentice', a character in search of a role in life; the place of the *Turmgesellschaft* is taken first by the shadowy figure of Kalonymos and then by Mordecai, whose intense belief that Daniel is his chosen successor determines Daniel's accession to a lasting purpose in life, a mission even. As with Wilhelm, chance encounters with women also prove to be critical in Daniel's quest for an identity: Mirah and Gwendolen both need his help; both represent possible — but sharply contrasted — destinies for him.

So much is uncontroversial. Yet there has been one striking omission in critical discussion of *Daniel Deronda* as a *Bildungsroman*. If Daniel's role is analogous to Wilhelm's, one would expect Mirah to be compared with Mignon: both are foreigners, exiled from their physical and spiritual home, both have been abused as children, both are rescued by the titular protagonist, and both sing in a way which immediately calls forth a sympathetic response from their audience. This parallel, however, is virtually never mentioned.[19] In order to show not only that Mirah is indeed a variant of Mignon, but also that she is conceived, partly at least, in contradistinction to Mignon and her position in the plot of *Wilhelm Meister*, I propose, as a first move, to focus briefly on the scene in *Daniel Deronda* where Daniel discovers Mirah on the riverbank and rescues her.[20] The episode is a major turning point in the plot, the moment at which Deronda finds the beginning of the thread which will lead him eventually to the discovery of his own identity and vocation. It is thus proleptic, anticipating future recognitions through a series of questions which are asked and which remain only partially answered at this stage in the plot.

The essential point is that George Eliot appears to rewrite the rescue in such a way as to negate certain aspects of the Goethean model. Mirah asks, for example, whether Daniel is a man of the theatre, and he responds categorically that he is not.[21] In the rescue scene itself, the allusion has no immediate motivation, and it could equally be read as the conscious refusal of too close a parallel with *Wilhelm Meister*, given the importance of the theatre as theme and setting in Goethe's novel and Wilhelm's own obsession with drama and acting.[22]

Similarly, Daniel is reluctant to press Mirah for details of her story, leaving Mrs Meyrick eventually to elicit them for him: 'Deronda was mute: to question her seemed an unwarrantable freedom; he shrank from appearing to claim the authority of a benefactor, or to treat her with the less reverence because she was in distress';[23] above all, he is deeply conscious of his responsibility towards this fragile young woman and carries it out in an exemplary way. By contrast, as we saw earlier, Wilhelm's initial act of ostentatiously public bravery in facing down the brutal leader of the travelling acrobats is followed by relative neglect of Mignon, punctuated by occasional moments of fleeting interest.

In such ways, by a procedure that one could think of as a kind of narrative *praeteritio*, George Eliot uses her novel to correct the ethics of Goethe's.[24] At the same time and by the same token, she corrects the plot: the Mirah strand is firmly embedded in the overall recognition structure of the novel. Like the Mignon strand in *Wilhelm Meister*, it is apparently entirely separate from Daniel's: the family she seeks to recover is unconnected genealogically with his, and her troubled childhood with her abusive father was as unlike Daniel's protected and privileged upbringing as it is possible to be. Yet the ultimate convergence of her destiny with his is in fact prefigured at the very first moment of the rescue, while Mirah is still on the riverbank:

> The agitating impression this forsaken girl was making on him stirred a fibre that lay close to his deepest interest in the fates of women — 'perhaps my mother was like this one'.[25]

After the rescue, Deronda will immediately conceive the idea of finding Mirah's mother and brother and thus restoring her to her origins (unlike Wilhelm, who ignores Mignon's hint that he might one day take her to her home in Italy); in the process, Deronda will be led into a closer knowledge of Jewish society, customs and religion, and will meet Mordecai and learn of his prophetic mission. In this way, he will be prepared for his meeting with his own mother and his recognition of Jewish identity. It is as if Wilhelm, in attempting to reunite Mignon with her own family, had been brought to the *Turmgesellschaft*. The discovery and rescue of Mirah utterly change both Daniel's destiny and hers, creating two closely connected narrative paths, each with its own culminating *anagnorisis*. The merging of the paths is completed when Deronda recognizes that she loves him, a recognition that Wilhelm never achieved in relation to Mignon.

One of the consequences of this rewriting of the *Bildungsroman* and its recognition structures is that, like Mirah, music is rescued and fully validated. The musical strand is written deeply into the plot from the moment that Klesmer arrives on the scene to provide a benchmark of musical authenticity. Gwendolen's shortcomings in this respect foreshadow her moral inadequacy, and her movement towards a recognition of what is authentic in both spheres is a further essential strand in the construction of *Daniel Deronda* as a *Bildungsroman*. Mirah, of course, has perfect pitch from the start, and the episodes that stage her singing mark her re-emergence into positive social relations and her recovery from the trauma of being forced to sing too much and too soon. George Eliot was not the lyric poet that Goethe was, and she wisely avoids inventing words for Mirah to sing; instead, Mirah sings real songs, or fictional musical settings of real poems. Reversing Goethe's insistence on the priority of words over music, Eliot allows music to have the upper hand. Rather than an occasional moment of intensity, as in *Wilhelm Meister*, it becomes a symbol for spiritual sympathy and understanding and hence one of the circuits by which the recognition plots are connected together.

The relation of music to memory and to originary experience is a key component of this circuitry. Mirah's earliest memory is of her mother singing a Jewish lullaby to her. Although Daniel has no such memory, he might have had: his mother, as we have seen, was a famous singer, and he himself as a child had a beautiful voice. His first unconscious contact with his Jewish origins, in the Frankfurt synagogue, is mediated above all by music,[26] as is his first contact with Mirah.[27] And when Mirah, on two separate occasions, sings a setting by the fictitious composer Joseph Leo of Leopardi's patriotic ode in praise of Italy, she transforms Mignon's famous song into a celebration of the homeland the Jewish people yearn for — or at least that is how Daniel perceives it:

> Deronda had never before heard Mirah sing 'O patria mia'. He knew well Leopardi's fine Ode to Italy (when Italy sat like a disconsolate mother in chains, hiding her face on her knees and weeping), and the few selected words were filled for him with the grandeur of the whole, which seemed to breathe as inspiration through the music. Mirah singing this, made Mordecai more than ever one presence with her. Certain words not included in the song nevertheless rang within Deronda as harmonies from one invisible — [...] they seemed the very voice of that heroic passion which is falsely said to devote itself in vain when it achieves the godlike end of manifesting unselfish love. And that passion was present to Deronda now as the vivid image of a man dying helplessly away from the possibility of battle.[28]

Mignon dreams of a journey that she will never make to her lost homeland; Daniel will take Mirah, beyond the end of the novel, to *her* spiritual home which has also become his own. The refrain 'Kennst du das Land?' would seem to be echoed with a special resonance here.

Finally, the rescue and rehabilitation of Mirah also connote the rehabilitation of Jewish culture and identity in the perception of the English novelist and of her presumed readers, many of whom have in fact been notoriously slow to respond to this aspect of the novel. Mignon is not by birth a gypsy or a travelling acrobat, and her rescue was meant to deliver her from such abjection; virtually none of the nineteenth-century versions of her story will revalidate that part of her experience. But Mirah, even leaving aside her earlier life in the theatre, belongs to an ethnic group whose marginalized position, as seen from the point of view of European society, is exactly analogous to that of the gypsy or the acrobat.[29] In that sense, too, George Eliot has gone to the heart of the problem posed by this recognition plot and performed an extraordinary reversal — as indeed she had done earlier in 'The Spanish Gypsy', which exactly inverts the plot of *La Gitanilla*.[30]

We shall shortly be looking at characters from the margins of society as, taking centre stage, they appear in Angela Carter's *Nights at the Circus*. Let us return first, however, to Goethe's novel, bearing in mind the adversarial model of 'influence' that I have sketched out here. It may in fact be plausibly argued that a similar process of oppositional repetition was at work in the relation between the 'apprenticeship' plot of *Wilhelm Meisters Lehrjahre* and the archaic recognition plot in which Mignon features, the mythopoeic plot that continues to haunt latter-day narratives despite all rationalizing attempts to evacuate it. By a narrative *praeteritio* which is at least partly verb is always in the first person, which indicates that the pronominal function continues to be dominant.

13. In other words 'moi as a substantive'. I use this formula in order to distinguish the grammatical instance of moi as a noun from the disjunctive pronoun on the one hand, and on the other from the expression le moi in its epistemological, ontological, phenomenological and other senses. This move was crucial in the original French version of Pré-histoires; in English, one is obliged in any case to use expressions such as 'moi as a noun' ('the self' cannot of course refer to the grammatical instance of the French pronoun). However, I have preserved it here in order to draw attention to the grammatical as opposed to the conceptual frame of reference.

14. The expression 'le moi' occurs three times in this fragment. See also the commentary of the Port-Royal edition, reproduced in a note in Philippe Sellier's edition of the Pensées (n.p.: Mercure de France, 1976, where this is fragment 494), p. 268, note 3. According to this commentary, 'Le mot de MOI dont l'auteur se sert dans la pensée suivante ne signifie que l'amour propre. C'est un terme dont il avait accoutumé de se servir avec quelques-uns de ses amis.'

15. It should also be noted that this discourse takes the form of a dialogue, thus following one of the key formal preferences of the author of both the Provinciales and the Pensées. In fragment 688, the interiorization of the dialogue no doubt corresponds to the movement of introspection required by the quest for the self, or at least by its definition.

16. René Descartes, Metaphysical Meditations II.14. I have here translated Descartes's original Latin text rather than the French translation which was published in his lifetime.

17. In keeping with seventeenth-century conventions, Pascal uses masculine pronouns throughout this fragment. In translating it, I have used some feminine ones in order to bring out the implied narrative elements.

18. It goes without saying that it also recurs in discursive texts generically close to the Pensées such as La Rochefoucauld's Maximes.

19. On this translation, see Marc Fumaroli, La Diplomatie de l'esprit, pp. 204–09; also Nicholas Paige, Being Interior: Autobiography and the Contradictions of Modernity in Seventeenth-Century France (Philadelphia: University of Pennsylvania Press, 2001).

20. That moment, however, also has its pre-history: see below, pp. 153–54.

21. I am here thinking in particular of the thought experiments of Derek Parfitt in Reasons and Persons (Oxford: Clarendon Press, 1984), although of course science fiction itself often raises similar question in a purely narrative form.

22. John Locke, An Essay Concerning Human Understanding, 2nd edn (London: Thomas Dring and Samuel Manship, 1694), Book II, ch. 27, §15, p. 340.

23. See my study Recognitions.

24. See for example Paul Ricœur, Oneself as Another, trans. by Kathleen Blamey (Chicago and London: University of Chicago Press, 1992; French original, Paris: Seuil, 1990), chs 5–8; this idea is already present in the seminal study of Alasdair MacIntyre, After Virtue: A Study in Moral Theory (London: Duckworth, 1981), ch. 15. See also my study 'Fictional Identities'. Galen Strawson's 'A Fallacy of Our Age: Not Every Life is a Narrative' (Times Literary Supplement, 15 October 2004, pp. 13–14) shows ex contrario how far the linking of identity and narrative has become a modern doxa.

25. The name of Montaigne is of course here a metonym for the Essais: this is the sense of the first 'dans' at least, although presumably when Pascal says 'dans moi' he is making an introspective gesture and not only referring to the work he is composing.

26. My translation of Dictionnaire de la langue française, p. 589(b). On this point, see also Ferdinand Brunot, Histoire de la langue française, vol. II (Paris: Armand Colin, 1967), pp. 414–15.

27. Desportes, Complainte, in Cartels et Mascarades, Epitaphes, ed. by V. Graham (Geneva: Droz, 1958), p. 107. Littré also quotes two other occurrences in Desportes's poetry (Amours d'Hippolyte xxi, Chanson: 'Ce seroit cesser d'estre moy, Que de cesser d'aimer ma dame'; ibid. xxiii: 'ô moy, pauvre insensé') which if accepted would mean that the change of function would have to be dated as early as 1572–73. These instances are a great deal less convincing, since neither implies necessarily the existence of a noun form 'le moi', but they perhaps indicate the route the pronoun took in order to emerge eventually as a substantive.

28. Marie-Luce Demonet has pointed out to me a further interesting case in a late work by Jacques

Peletier Du Mans, the *Euvres poetiques [...] intitulés Louanges*, published, like Desportes's poem, in 1581 (Paris: R. Colombel, 1581). An explicitly reflexive poem entitled 'Remontrance, A Soi-Même' in the *Louange de la Sciance* contains for example the following lines: 'Ainsi c'est moi, qui à moi fais outrance, / Ne respectant moi ni ma remonstrance'. Although one cannot claim that any of these three instances of *moi* could count as *moi[S]*, the third comes remarkably close, and the intensity produced by the repetition of the pronoun is striking. The years 1580–81 thus seem to mark a critical moment in the pre-history of *moi[S]*. One would of course need to conduct a thorough search of works published between Desportes and Descartes in order to determine whether and how often *moi[S]* recurred during that period.

29. Gisèle Mathieu-Castellani, *Les Thèmes amoureux dans la poésie française 1570–1600* (Paris: Klincksieck, 1975), pp. 238, 244, 264, 266.

30. *Essais*, pp. 189–90.

31. The same metaphor is used in a key passage of 'Sur des vers de Virgile' (see above, p. 141).

32. *Essais*, p. 188. It should be remembered that the two parts of the sentence were added in the Bordeaux copy in two stages. Cf. also this sentence: 'Le secret que j'ay juré ne deceler à nul autre, je le puis, sans parjure, communiquer à celuy qui n'est pas autre: c'est moy.'

33. See above, notes 3–4. Montaigne adds the Aristotelian model in two successive passages of the 1595 edition: 'O mes amis, il y a nul ami', and especially 'leur convenance n'estant qu'un' ame en deux corps selon la tres-propre definition d'Aristote' (p. 190): this is the *heteros autos*, but without a substantivized pronoun.

34. *Essais*, p. 193; Horace, *Odes* II.xvii.5.

35. It will be noted that Montaigne first uses the etymological equivalent of Horace's 'partem', then makes explicit that only *half* remains. On the phenomenon of quotations that are anticipated before they are added, see Mary McKinley, *Words in a Corner*.

36. On the *topoi* of friendship that were current in Montaigne's day, see Ullrich Langer, *Perfect Friendship: Studies in Literature and Moral Philosophy from Boccaccio to Corneille* (Geneva: Droz, 1994), pp. 14–20, 164–76.

37. Augustine, *Confessions* IV.6.

38. The phrase 'ille alter' ('another him') also recalls the Ciceronian model.

39. Villey asserts that Montaigne seems not to have known the *Confessions* (*Les Sources et l'évolution des 'Essais' de Montaigne*, 2 vols (Paris: Hachette, 1933), I, 75); but see Richard Regosin, *The Matter of my Book* (Berkeley: California University Press, 1977), pp. 23–28 (in particular note 11), and above all Gisèle Mathieu-Castellani, 'Les *Confessions* de Saint Augustin dans les *Essais* de Montaigne', in *Lire les 'Essais' de Montaigne: perspectives critiques*, ed. by Noël Peacock and J. J. Supple (Paris: Champion, 1998), pp. 211–26. Mary McKinley (in *Les Terrains vagues des 'Essais'* (Paris: Champion, 1996), p. 100, note 1) offers some helpful bibliographical information on Montaigne's readings in Augustine. For a more general synthesis, see Pierre Courcelle, *Les Confessions de Saint Augustin dans la tradition littéraire* (Paris: Études Augustiniennes, 1963).

40. The most elaborately developed presentation of this hypothesis is Gérard Defaux's *Montaigne et le travail de l'amitié* (Orleans: Paradigme, 2001).

41. On the relations between *imitatio* and the writing subject, see *The Cornucopian Text*; Compagnon, *La Seconde Main*; Greene, *The Light in Troy*; Michel Jeanneret, *Perpetuum mobile: métamorphoses des corps et des œuvres de Vinci à Montaigne* (Paris: Macula, 1997), pp. 267–80.

42. See *The Cornucopian Text*, pp. 42–43, where the coinage is erroneously attributed to Erasmus; the priority of Poliziano is acknowledged in the preface of the French edition (p. 6, n. 2).

43. In Joachim Du Bellay, *La Deffence, et illustration de la langue françoyse*, ed. by Jean-Charles Monferran (Geneva: Droz, 2001), p. 293.

44. *Essais*, p. 1055; cf. III.5, p. 875. See also above, pp. 39–40, 45–46.

45. Seneca, *De ira* I.vi.5.

46. Montaigne, *Essais*, I.26, p. 152.

47. Pascal, *Pensées*, in *Œuvres complètes*, no. 689. See also above, p. 135.

48. Seneca, *Epistulae morales* 16.7.

49. See Kathy Eden, *Friends Hold all Things in Common: Tradition, Intellectual Property, and the Adages of Erasmus* (New Haven and London: Yale University Press, 2001).

50. *Essais*, III.12, p. 1056.

51. *Essais*, III.5, p. 847.
52. *Essais*, III.5, pp. 846–47.
53. See 'Le Récit montaignien: un voyage sans repentir', in *Pré-histoires*, pp. 164–76.
54. Morgan, 'Developing the Modern Conception of the Self', is also relevant here.

4

Fragments of a Future Self:
The First Person and Narrative in Rabelais

I turn now, moving against the chronological stream, to a specific cluster of instances of the first person singular in Rabelais's writing. These are drawn from the prologue of the *Tiers Livre* and from the two parallel episodes in the third and fourth books on the death of Guillaume Du Bellay.[1] First, however, it will be necessary to sketch out a rough typology of uses of the first person in the four authentic books as a whole.

The instance that is the most visible to the reader occurs where a first person singular pronoun refers to the actual or supposed author. In these cases, the author speaks to his readers about his book, tells them what to expect, how to read it, how not to read it, and so on. This authorial or paratextual instance is found above all, of course, in the prologues, but it also occurs, for example, at the end of *Pantagruel*, where future instalments of the story are announced, and in the first chapter of *Gargantua*, where the author recounts how he recovered the manuscript of the 'Fanfreluches antidotées'. To these cases may be added those where, within the fictional narrative proper, the author intervenes to assure his readers of the truth of a given episode or feature.

The second instance is that of the narrator as commentator: in a number of episodes, the narrator intervenes in order to add a commentary on an aspect of the matter narrated. Examples of this category are found in *Gargantua* 9 (on the colours blue and white), in *Tiers Livre* 1–2, on the right way to establish a colony, or towards the end of the *Tiers Livre*, in the description of Pantagruélion. Here, the author speaks above all as an expert, as one who has inside knowledge. Unlike the 'authorial instance', this type of first-person discourse does not lie along the axis author–book–reader; the commentary does not bear on the nature of the book or its veridicity. It remains the case, however, that the 'narrator as commentator' sometimes makes asides to his readers, which creates an overlap between these two categories (for example in *Gargantua* 9, where he says, 'J'entends bien que lisans ces motz, vous mocquez du vieil buveur' [I'm well aware that, as you read these words, you're laughing at the old boozer]).

The third instance occurs where the first person is a character within the story, as in the episode in *Pantagruel* where the narrator accompanies Panurge in his quest for 'pardons', or more famously, later in the same book, where Alcofrybas ventures into Pantagruel's mouth. This category is virtually absent from *Gargantua*, but it returns in *Tiers Livre* 49, where the narrator says that he saw Pantagruélion being loaded on board for the voyage in search of the 'dive bouteille'. It then reappears in the *Quart Livre*, in the Papimanes episode (twice), and in the 'frozen words' episode.[2] To these instances should no doubt be added the uses at various points in the *Quart Livre* of a first person plural ('nous') which implies the presence of the narrator among the travellers.

It is important to note that the first person as character in the fiction occurs only intermittently and as if randomly, without sequence, consequence or coherence. On the other hand, the appearance on the scene of this narrator–character seems to mark particularly important moments, or at least ones where the Rabelaisian imagination is particularly intense.

Finally, for the sake of completeness, we may add the (apparently) banal use of the first person by characters in the fiction in direct speech, whether it be Pantagruel, Panurge, Frère Jan, Picrochole, Homenaz or any other of the dozens of speaking characters in Rabelais's fiction. Banal the category may be, but it includes some strange and interesting variants to which we shall return shortly.

It has often been remarked that, from the *Tiers Livre* onwards, the name of Alcofrybas Nasier is replaced on the title page by that of François Rabelais, a change that obliges readers to modify their image of the author.[3] It is true that this change is not immediately apparent at the beginning of the prologue of the third book: not only does the figure of the author still speak with a jocular, comic voice, he also invokes by means of a series of rhetorical flourishes an antique model (Diogenes), just as the author of *Gargantua* had invoked Socrates. Both these manoeuvres may moreover be understood as variants of the *captatio benevolentiae* that is a standard feature of literary prologues in the early modern period.

A slight but critical shift occurs, however, in the initial staging of the *Tiers Livre* prologue. In 1534/35, it is the *book* that is compared with Socrates, with the Sileni, with the marrowbone and with a bottle; in 1546, the author compares *himself* with Diogenes. This analogy in fact serves as a fulcrum for the structure of the whole prologue, which turns on the syntagm 'Je pareillement' [I likewise]. At the same time, from one book to the other, the decor is transformed. The story of how Diogenes reacted to the activities of his compatriots sets the scene for the entry of an author who finds himself confronted with an external, contemporary reality, in which war features as the archetypal embodiment of duty and commitment. Never in the course of the first two books had the author proffered an image of himself that was so closely linked with history; never, indeed, had the 'je' been the subject of actions outside the world of the book or its narrative. Nor is this shift an isolated or accidental phenomenon, since Rabelais's books will henceforth carry paratexts (the prologue of the 1548 *Quart Livre*, the 1552 dedication to the Cardinal de Châtillon) which feature a pronominal subject grappling with an extra-literary world.

Let us however first follow the formal order of the text and re-read the sentence that begins 'I likewise':

> Je pareillement, quoy que soys hors d'effroy, ne suis toutesfoys hors d'esmoy, de moy ne voyant n'estre faict aulcun pris digne d'œuvre, et consyderant par tout ce tresnoble royaulme, deça, dela les mons, un chascun aujourd'huy soy instantement exercer et travailler.[4]

[I likewise, although I have escaped from fear, have not escaped from distress, seeing that no worthy act has been done by me, and considering the way in which, throughout this most noble kingdom on both sides of the mountains, each man at this very moment is setting himself assiduously to work.]

The initial 'je' provides a striking instance of the survival of the older, non-enclitic first-person form; it may in fact be regarded as one of Rabelais's deliberate archaisms. Montaigne would certainly have written 'moy pareillement'. This 'je', then, emphasized by its isolation from the verb of which it is the subject, attributes to itself a shifting emotional state ('effroy', 'esmoy'). The marked assonance of the two nouns serves to link these states as aspects of a psychological turbulence for which no context or explanation has yet been supplied: we *hear* this affective unease before we understand it, especially as the diphthong 'oi' also occurs in 'quoy', 'soys' and 'toutesfoys'. The assonance is then immediately taken up again ('de moy voyant'), linking the disjunctive pronoun closely with the emotional disturbance of 'effroy' and 'esmoy'; at the same time, the prior position given to 'de moy' assigns to the pronoun a prominent role in the structure of the sentence. Thus, from 'je' to 'moy', the first person emerges progressively from the phonic substance of the sentence as the focus for a disquieting affect. At a purely structural level, one might easily be tempted to consider this sentence as a kind of pre-echo of the Pascal–Montaigne(–Seneca) series we looked at earlier.[5]

An explanation is now supplied: the 'je' is troubled by his lack of participation in the collective activity of the French; he has been excluded, moreover, because he was judged to be 'trop imbecille et impotent' [too feeble and infirm]. He thus suffers from a feeling of inadequacy, incompetence and guilt, and this self-accusatory tone continues through the ensuing passage. The explanation still remains incomplete, however, especially as new cryptic allusions are added. He has not been employed, he says, even to perform menial tasks: 'tout m'estoit indifferent' [Everything was indifferent to me]. What is this 'indifference'? Is it a mere lack of commitment or a philosophical state of mind, a Diogenic ataraxia?[6] The mystery is compounded when the first person declares that he is ashamed that he has not drawn on what little remained of his own personal resources ('[...] ce rien mon tout, qui me restoit'). What is this small but precious resource that he still clung on to, and after what? A personal catastrophe, presumably, since he appears to have lost everything else. But what catastrophe?

A partial answer to these questions may be inferred from what follows:

> Prins ce choys et election, ay pensé ne faire exercice inutile et importun si je remuois mon tonneau Diogenic, qui seul m'est resté du naufrage faict par le passé on far de Mal'encontre. (p. 349)

> [Having made this choice, I thought I would not be uselessly and unhelpfully employed if I shook my Diogenic barrel, the only thing left to me from the shipwreck I suffered in the past at the lighthouse of Ill-Encounter.]

The close similarity between the phrase 'qui seul m'est resté du naufrage' and the earlier 'ce rien mon tout, qui me restoit' provides a specific subject for the verb 'rester': it is the author's 'Diogenic barrel' which was saved from the shipwreck, and the context provided by the remainder of the prologue, and by the fact that this is

a prologue to a new comic fiction after a gap of some twelve years, allows one to
infer that the barrel is Rabelais's book, or his capacity as a writer. The catastrophe,
too, is given a name; at the same time, however, the embryonic trace of a personal
narrative which seemed to be on the point of establishing itself is swallowed up
in the traditional narrative mode of allegory. A whole moralized life is contained,
potentially, in this allegorical nucleus, which evokes a voyage, the hoped-for shelter
of a port, a reef with its warning lighthouse, and then a catastrophe that explains
the narrator's loss of virtually everything. But when a first-person narrative takes
allegorical form, it moves from the mode of inalienable individual experience into
the public domain: hardly has the story begun to emerge than it disappears again
into the most well-worn of traditional narrative formulae.

We turn now to a different but also strikingly idiosyncratic use of the first person
in the two episodes of the later books where the death of Guillaume Du Bellay is
evoked by the characters in the story. In the first of these episodes (*Tiers Livre*, chapter
21), Pantagruel advises Panurge to consult the old and dying poet Raminagrobis,
arguing from the neo-Platonist theory of poetic inspiration:

> les poëtes qui sont en protection de Apollo, approchans de leur mort ordinaire-
> ment deviennent prophetes, et chantent par Apolline inspiration vaticinans des
> choses futures. (p. 415)

> [poets who are under the protection of Apollo, when they are close to death
> regularly become prophets and sing by Apolline inspiration, foretelling things
> to come.]

This prophetic gift is further extended, according to Pantagruel, to all old men who
are close to death, and this leads him to cite, not ancient examples, but a recent
one, that of

> Guillaume Du Bellay, seigneur jadis de Langey, lequel on mont de Tarare
> mourut le .10. de Janvier l'an de son aage le climatere et de nostre supputation
> l'an .1543. en compte Romanicque. (p. 416)

> [Guillaume Du Bellay, sometime lord of Langey, who died on the Mont de
> Tarare on the 10th of January, in the year which was the climacteric of his age
> and, by our reckoning, the year 1543 according to the Roman calendar.]

The insertion of this historical and biographical reference into a humanist discourse
constructed largely of *topoi* is striking in itself; it also recalls the structure of the
Prologue, where the *exemplum* of Diogenes leads into a reference to the war
between France and the Holy Roman Empire. What is yet more striking is that
this movement across the textual frontier between humanism and present-day
concerns is made possible — indeed the frontier is rendered almost invisible — by
a strange dislocation of the first person pronoun. Up to this point, Pantagruel has
used the didactic 'je' characteristic of the humanist pedagogue: 'J'ay daventaige
souvent ouy dire' [I have furthermore often heard it said], 'Je ne vous allegueray
exemples antiques [...] seulement vous veulx ramentevoir le docte et preux chevallier
Guillaume Du Bellay.' [I shall not cite ancient examples to you [...] I only want to
remind you of the learned and valiant knight Guillaume Du Bellay]. But already,

in this last sentence, which includes the reference to Du Bellay's death, an event of 1543 is evoked as a *memory* by characters who, one had previously supposed, belonged to a fiction. This telescoping effect is no doubt not especially anomalous in Rabelais's writing, where chronological and narrative plausibility are regularly given short shrift. What is exceptional, however, is the precision of the reference: the narrator insists on the strictly historical moment and place of Du Bellay's death. Rather than a vague reminiscence, which might equally be textual like the classical *exempla*, what we have here is an immediate, local memory.

The phrase that follows, moreover, removes any possible ambiguity by assuming that the memory is a personal, subjective one, since the use of the first person plural attributes it solely to Pantagruel and to those who were eyewitnesses to the event:

> Les trois et quatre heures avant son décés il employa en parolles viguoureuses [...] nous prædisant ce que depuys part avons veu, part attendons advenir. Combien que pour lors nous semblassent ces propheties aulcunement abhorrentes et estranges, par ne nous apparoistre cause ne signe aulcun præsant prognostic de ce qu'il prædisoit. (p. 416)

> [He used the three or four hours before his death to speak in vigorous language [...] predicting to us what we have in part already seen and in part expect to come about, even though at that time these prophecies seemed in some way abhorrent and strange, since no cause or present sign appeared to us that prognosticated what he was predicting.]

In chapter 26 of the *Quart Livre*, the procedure is almost identical, although here divided between the speech of two characters. Pantagruel makes a Platonizing speech on the death of Heroes, then Epistemon interrupts him to add the example of the death of Du Bellay, presented once more in the first person plural: 'Nous (dist Epistemon) en avons naguieres veu l'experience on décés du preux et docte chevalier Guillaume du Bellay' [We, said Epistemon, formerly experienced this as eyewitnesses at the death of the chivalrous and learned knight Guillaume Du Bellay] (p. 600). It is no doubt significant that the word 'experience' is used instead of Pantagruel's 'exemple' in a sentence which is otherwise remarkably similar: that which we witnessed was an experience rather than a quotation.

The Du Bellay dossier returns one last time in chapter 27. Pantagruel indicates his personal presence at the deathbed, as he had done in the *Tiers Livre*: 'ce que veismes plusieurs jours avant le departement [...] du docte et preux chevalier de Langey' [As we *saw* several days before the demise [...] of the learned and valiant knight de Langey], and Epistemon goes on immediately to say 'Il m'en souvient' [I remember] (p. 602). This confirms that both were present, as if the dying man had been surrounded by the characters of Rabelais's fiction as witnesses to an extraordinary death that bordered on the supernatural.

It is thus surprising that, in the list of eyewitnesses provided by Epistemon immediately afterwards, all the names belong to a strictly non-fictional category:

> De mode que les seigneurs de Assier, Chemant, Mailly le borgne, Sainct Ayl, Villeneufve laguyart, maistre Gabriel medicin de Savillan, Rabelays, Cohuau, Massuau, Majorici, Bullou, Cercu, dit Bourguemaistre, François proust, Ferron, Charles girad, François bourré, et tant d'aultres amis, domesticques, et

serviteurs du deffunct tous effrayez se reguardoient les uns les aultres en silence
[...] (pp. 602–03)

[So that my lords of Assier, Chemant, Mailly le borgne, Sainct Ayl, Villeneufve
la Guyart, Master Gabriel, doctor of Savillan, Rabelays, Cohuau, Massuau,
Maiorici, Bullou, Cercu known as Bourguemaistre, François Proust, Ferron,
Charles Girad, François Bourré, and many other friends, servants and members
of the household of the deceased, were all gripped with fear and looked at one
another in silence [...]]

The absence in this list of any of the names of Rabelais's fictional characters, and of
any Greek or allegorical name such as Epistemon's, here produces an extraordinary
'reality effect': the accidental, irreducibly individual character of the proper names
places them unequivocally in the non-fictional domain. The fact that modern
commentators have found some of the names in the archives serves only to confirm
this effect, since the text is itself already structured by the fiction–reality opposition
and by its erasure.[7] The presence of Rabelais's name, placed discreetly in the middle
of the list, provides conclusive evidence of this, since the reader needs no archive
or other special form of knowledge in order to know that Rabelais is a historical,
extra-literary name.[8]

The naming of Rabelais gives yet another twist to the logic of the first person
in these episodes. Since Rabelais's characters had appropriated 'je' or 'nous' in their
recollection of a critical event in Rabelais's life, it is in fact normal that Rabelais
himself should be referred to in the third person as a simple co-witness.

It is therefore also logical that Epistemon, the possessor of subjective knowledge
('experience'), should be the first to voice an affective response:

Il m'en souvient (dist Epistemon) et encores me frissonne et tremble le cœur
dedans sa capsule, quand je pense es prodiges tant divers et horrificques les
quelz veismes apertement cinq et six jours avant son depart. (p. 602)

[I remember, said Epistemon, and my heart still shudders and trembles in its
chamber when I think of all the various horrendous prodigies we clearly saw
for some five or six days before his departure.]

It is only subsequently that this terror spreads among the other 'friends, servants and
members of the household of the deceased'. While the name 'Rabelais' is at it were
only one among several signatures on a document, the fictional character displays
his personal, emotional involvement in the national catastrophe embodied in the
death of Guillaume Du Bellay.[9]

One further detail, which has its effect at more than one textual level in this
cluster of episodes from Rabelais's later writings, will bring us back to the Prologue
of the *Tiers Livre*. Pantagruel's initial commentary on the prophetic gift of old men
drew on the metaphor of a spiritual voyage:

Car comme nous estans sus le moule, et de loing voyans les mariniers et voyagiers
dedans leurs naufz en haulte mer, seulement en silence les considerons, et bien
prions pour leur prospere abourdement: mais lors qu'ilz approchent du havre, et
par parolles et par gestes les saliüons, et congratulons de ce que à port de saulveté
sont avecques nous arrivez: aussi les Anges, les Heroes, les bon Dæmons [...].[10]

> [For just as we, standing on the harbour wall and seeing the sailors and travellers
> in their ships far out to sea, only contemplate them in silence and indeed pray
> for a happy landing; but, when they are close to harbour, we greet them and
> congratulate them with words and gestures on their safe arrival in our midst;
> so too the Angels, Heroes and good Daimons [...]]

This micro-allegory, well worn as it is, looks strangely like a pre-echo of the
narrative journey of the *Quart Livre*. More precisely, it anticipates the insertion of
a historical deathbed scene into the framework of a happy landing after a highly
literary (and allegorical) storm. That storm, which constitutes one of the best-
known and most dramatic episodes of the *Quart Livre*, can be explained, according
to Macrobe, by the death of one of the Heroes of the Isle of the Macraeons: 'croyons
[...] que hier en soit mort quelqu'un. Au trespas duquel soyt excitée celle horrible
tempeste que avez pati' [we believe [...] that one of them died yesterday, and that
his death provoked the terrible storm that you suffered].[11]

These fictional scenes are linked, then, to the allegorical nucleus of the *Tiers Livre*
Prologue, that is to say the 'shipwreck at the lighthouse of Ill-Encounter', except
that the characters in the primary narrative land safely, whereas the author claims to
have undergone a wreck that deprived him of virtually everything. From this may
be drawn a preliminary conclusion: the unexplained suffering and fear mentioned
in the Prologue are already the half-suppressed echo of the disaster that took place
in January 1543 on the Mont de Tarare.[12] Inversely, the emotions evoked on the
threshold of the *Tiers Livre* reverberate throughout the third and fourth books: on
each occasion, the pronoun subject is surrounded by signs of disturbance, terror,
despair; on each occasion, it is associated with storms and shipwrecks.

One final example: in chapter 7 of the *Tiers Livre*, Panurge has stopped wearing
his codpiece 'en laquelle il souloit comme en l'ancre sacre constituer son dernier
refuge contre tous naufraiges d'adversité' [in which, as in a hallowed anchor, he was
accustomed to invest his faith as a last refuge against all the shipwrecks of adversity]
(p. 372). The exchange that takes place here by the attribution to Panurge of the
allegory of a sea voyage and the theme of a refuge in times of trouble, is exactly
parallel to the dislocations we have already considered; at the same time, it has
the effect of associating Panurge's anxieties very closely with those of which the
authorial first person sometimes allows us to catch a glimpse.[13]

This cluster of themes may even be detected at the level of structure. The mere
fact that the reference to Du Bellay's death occurs in both books suggests that they
are constructed around the memory of a literally shattering event. That the first
version of the *Quart Livre* ends abruptly as *Pantagruel* and his companions make
their 'happy landing' after the storm, just before the subject of the death of Heroes
is raised, is only the most dramatic indication of this kind of fragmentation. A
fissure appears in the composition of the book which will be only partially and
provisionally erased in the 1552 version.

The dossier of intratextual references is complemented by the title pages of these
two books. Rabelais not only uses his own name, rather than the pseudonym
Alcofrybas Nasier; he also advertises his profession ('docteur en medecine'). On the
other hand, he adds an identification which is purely fictional: the author claims

to be 'Calloïer des Isles Hieres'. In the sixteenth century, these islands (real islands off the south coast of France, not far from Marseilles) served as a refuge for exiles and escapees; the 'caloyer', from the Greek *kalos hieros* ('a good and saintly man') is a hermit who lives on an island or in a similar refuge; and the juxtaposition of 'hieros' and 'Hières' produces a semi-hidden Rabelaisian pun.[14] Frank Lestringant has shown that an 'île du Caloyer' frequently figures on contemporary maps; it is always difficult of access, having the form of a mountain, but on its summit is found a sheltered and peaceful area, a place of refuge. In other words, such islands have a distinctly allegorical form, recalling the topos of the Rock of Virtue.[15] Consequently, when Rabelais disguises himself as a 'caloyer', he is already entering the world of allegory; the identification is moreover entirely in line with the micro-allegory of the Prologue. In both instances, one finds a seascape, a threat of disaster, an escape and a refuge where only meditation and writing (as opposed to public action) are possible.

On the title page of the 1552 edition of the *Quart Livre*, the mention of the 'caloyer' has disappeared. The *Quart Livre*, especially in this later version, is the story of an episodic sea voyage with frequent landfalls on islands. Among these, the most prominent is the visit to the archipelago of the Macraeons, aged though venerable men who have known decline and deprivation, and who might easily be regarded themselves as 'caloyers'. It is thus no longer necessary for the author to identify himself as such: the 'caloyers' have become characters in the story thanks to an exchange of functions which is now beginning to look systematic.

It is not my intention here to establish some kind of Rabelaisian psycho-biography. The evidence of a textual disturbance that opens a window on an extra-textual experience has a historical and anthropological importance, not a personal one. The pages of Rabelais's later books that we have been looking at constitute a structured object that carries traces of its provenance and use: our task is to draw from that object, in the most delicate manner possible, valuable information that one cannot get from other sources about modes of thought and feeling in mid-sixteenth-century France.

One may begin by restoring the 'object' to its place in the broad history of uses of the first person in narrative. On the one hand, considered retrospectively, its fleeting appearance at the heart of Rabelais's third and fourth books produces a perceptible crack in the surface of the early modern text, allowing us to identify a procedure that looks familiar to us: the narrator, speaking in the first person, presents us with a narrative that blurs the borderline between fiction and reality. Since the eighteenth century such procedures have in fact been central to the functioning of autobiographical fiction. In that kind of narrative, however, it is used consistently, so that we are able to reconstruct the story and the psychology of the narrator as a kind of surrogate for the historical author. This is the case, for example, in Benjamin Constant's *Adolphe*, and it depends on the existence of a fully-fledged mode of 'non-fictional' life writing, as in Rousseau's *Confessions*. Rabelais's readers had of course no such reference point for their understanding of what Rabelais was doing.

This deliberately anachronistic perspective may be counterbalanced, on the other hand, by invoking the genre of allegorical narrative as Rabelais and his readers knew it. In narratives such as the *Roman de la Rose* or Jean Lemaire de Belges's *Concorde des deux langaiges*, for example, the first-person figure is maintained consistently while identifying himself (or herself) with the allegorical landscape. Such figures hide nothing: their dreams, their loves, their disappointments, their suffering, the stages of their journeys are all narrated; furthermore, they make no gestures towards the world 'outside' their story which are not immediately absorbed into the logic of the story itself.

Seen in relation to these two contrasting models, the Rabelaisian first person is marked by signs of uncertainty, in particular its intermittent appearance, together with a kind of dislocation or redistribution of narrative materials and functions. These two elements are already present in the key sentence of the Prologue of the *Tiers Livre* which encapsulates an allegorical micro-landscape. It would be easy enough to write this sentence out as a standard allegorical narrative, preserving its first-person form, but this is not what Rabelais does. Conversely, when he turns this same landscape into the décor of the *Quart Livre* as a whole, the pronoun subject becomes marginal, a figure who appears here and there, especially at the beginning of chapters — except that, by means of a further reversal, the pronoun will appear in the middle of an episode, in an imaginary archipelago, taken over by characters who act as if they no longer belonged to the fiction but to the world inhabited by the historical Rabelais.

I suggested earlier that one might read the fragmentary phrase 'hors d'esmoy, de moy voyant' from the Prologue of the *Tiers Livre* as in some sense an anticipation of the series of echoes carried by the words 'moy' and 'voy' from Montaigne's *Essais* to fragment 689 of the *Pensées*. It is important here to specify the conditions under which such a suggestion might be something more than an idle speculation. In each case, but especially in the whole series considered as a set of instances, one may identify an effect which we hear as the return of a melodic fragment. The melody sounds familiar to us, but it is not sustained or developed; it is rapidly reabsorbed into the background noise of other discursive patterns and habits. The similarity of sounds is accompanied by another similarity at the thematic level which returns insistently in both the pre-history and the history of the self: the shadow of uncertainty, of possible guilt, and thus of self-defence which surrounds the emergence of the pronoun subject in its reflexive form. In Rabelais's *Tiers Livre*, the apologetic *topos* of the Prologue is connected first to the figure of a literally insular hermit, then to that of an idler who can make no contribution to the national preparations for war. In the *Essais*, confession and repentance are converted into metaphors of a secular laying bare of the self.[16] It is hardly surprising that Pascal, with his Augustinian perspective, should have understood what was at stake in Montaigne's variant and conceived a counter-variant of his own.

Such a comparison has no value unless one rigorously respects the differences: in Rabelais, the intermittence of the first person and its tendency to revert to allegory; in Montaigne, the increasingly substantial and consistent use of the first person as a guiding principle, but without the particular articulation conferred by a continuous narrative structure. It remains the case that the Rabelaisian configuration, as a textual disturbance opening on to a specific and local experience of the world, may be said to belong to the pre-history of the self and of its narrative possibilities.

Notes

1. This section was originally meant to be read in conjunction with 'L'Ombre de Guillaume Du Bellay' in *Pré-histoires*, pp. 87–93; the same materials are treated at greater length in the last essay of Part II above ('The Death of Guillaume Du Bellay'), which overlaps at certain points with the present section (no further cross-references will be supplied here).

2. This passage is the subject of a brilliant commentary by Tournon (*'En sens agile'*, pp. 9–16), who remarks on precisely this unfamiliar presence of the narrator as character.

3. See for example Screech, *Rabelais*, p. 279; in Screech's account, this change is grounded in the serious and philosophical character of the third book.

4. *Tiers Livre*, in *Œuvres complètes*, ed. by Huchon, p. 348.

5. Little has been written about the self in Rabelais, for reasons which are no doubt self-evident. Those who are interested above all in the history of ideas have tended to identify the (implied or actual) Rabelaisian subject with the medical, philosophical, religious and other beliefs of the historical figure François Rabelais; those who have explored Rabelais's comic imagination regard the 'je' of the prologues and elsewhere primarily as an authorial persona: see for example Dorothy Coleman, in *Rabelais: A Critical Study in Prose Fiction* (Cambridge: Cambridge University Press, 1971), especially ch. 4. Alfred Glauser devotes the opening chapter of his *Rabelais créateur* (Paris: Nizet, 1964) to the 'presence of Rabelais' and compares Rabelais's 'moi' at various points with Montaigne's; the lines of this study are however blurred by a certain lack of historical precautions and of grammatical and rhetorical distinctions. For some helpful comments in a historical context, see Defaux, *Rabelais agonistes: du rieur au prophète* (Geneva: Droz, 1997), pp. 358–60.

6. In Stoic philosophy, all externals are in themselves 'indifferent', i.e. value-free; they only acquire the power to disturb when humans project on to them their own desires, fears and emotions. The Stoic sage achieves tranquillity of mind by perceiving this and avoiding any such projections.

7. See Richard Cooper, *Litterae in tempore belli: études sur les relations littéraires italo-françaises pendant les guerres d'Italie* (Geneva: Droz, 1997), pp. 51–61.

8. For a similar list, see *Tiers Livre*, in *Œuvres complètes*, ch. 34 (p. 460). Here, both Ponocrates and Epistemon claim that they were present at the performance of the 'morale comœdie de celluy qui avoit espousé une femme muette', together with the character Rondibilis and also a number of historical individuals, including 'François Rabelais'. See André Tournon's remarks on this performance in 'Un silence signé Rabelais', *Cahiers Textuel*, 15 (1996), 77–87.

9. One may however note that the 'real' characters, who say nothing, *reflect*, and that the narrator can tell us what they were reflecting on: 'tous effrayez, se reguardoient les uns les aultres en silence, sans mot dire de bouche, mais bien tous pensans et prevoyans en leurs entendemens que de brief seroit France privée d'un tant perfaict et necessaire chevalier à sa gloire et protection.'

10. *Tiers Livre*, in *Œuvres complètes*, ch. 21, pp. 415–16.

11. *Quart Livre*, in *Œuvres complètes*, ch. 26, p. 599. On this link between Rabelais's later books, see also Krailsheimer, *Rabelais and the Franciscans*, pp. 128–29.

12. The link between the Prologue of the third book and the two episodes featuring the death of Guillaume Du Bellay is corroborated by another verbal echo: Du Bellay is referred to three times by variants of the formula 'le docte et preux chevalier', while the Prologue speaks of 'tant vailans, disers et chevalereux personnaiges, qui en veue et spectacle de toute Europe jouent ceste insigne fable et Tragicque comedie'. Langey, if he had lived, would no doubt have counted as one of these 'characters'. The shift from fiction to historical reality and back is also apparent both in these formulas, which belong to epic and chivalric romance, and in the reference to theatre.

13. The resemblance between the voice(s) of the narrator and that of Panurge are studied by Myriam Marrache, *'Hors toute intimidation': Panurge ou la parole singulière* (Geneva: Droz, 2003), chapter IV. In the light of the frequently made assumption that Pantagruel is Rabelais's mouthpiece, it is especially useful to have this counterbalancing evidence.

14. On these various elements, see Lestringant, *Écrire le monde à la Renaissance*, pp. 178–84, and Huchon (ed.), Rabelais, *Œuvres complètes*, pp. 1360–61.

15. See my article 'Reading Rabelais: Variations on the Rock of Virtue', in *Literary Theory / Renaissance Texts*, ed. by Patricia Parker and David Quint (Baltimore and London: The Johns Hopkins University Press, 1986), pp. 78–95.
16. See 'Le Récit montaignien: un voyage sans repentir', in *Pré-histoires*, pp. 164–76.

like Charles Taylor's, whether prominence is given to the Cartesian *cogito* as a founding moment, to the phenomenology of a self as a vector of *cogitationes*, or to the ways in which pre-Freudian culture anticipates the theory of a self divided between the conscious and the unconscious — whatever the perspective, cultural historians speak of a progressive interiorization of identity that constitutes one of the most essential foundations of modern Western consciousness. A subjective sense of identity has no doubt been expressed by other cultures and by other phases of our own. What we in particular seem to have invented is a thing called 'the self'[7] which is the location of a kind of gradual and indefinitely extensible proliferation of individual characteristics, habits, preferences, feelings, reflections, experiences and the like: a thing which seems to have a natural affinity with the byways of narrative and which is always ready to surrender to the pleasures and pains of the 'talking cure'.

To capture the uncertainties, the discontinuities, the backslidings, the sheer untidiness of this segment of cultural history without retrospectively projecting on to Montaigne, Descartes or Pascal the exotic blossoming of the modern self, which they could not have foreseen even in their worst nightmares, is a difficult and delicate task. Mainstream history of ideas is of limited assistance here: it speaks primarily of what can be said to be *expressed* in philosophical discourse, and is thus not well equipped to handle implicit instances; it tends to presuppose that rational discourse is always in some sense a level playing field; above all, its questioning of the past is often explicitly teleological, seeking to reconstruct an 'evolution' and its 'source' — the title of Charles Taylor's book provides a convenient example, even if the use of the plural 'sources' brilliantly problematizes the question from the outset.

Instead, one may consider a reverse, 'upstream' movement which, at every point on the route, strives to erase the traces of the future. In order to read Pascal or Descartes, one should ideally consign to oblivion not only the Hegelian and Freudian juggernauts but also the memory of Diderot, Rousseau and Locke. In order to read Montaigne on *le moi* (about which, as we shall see, he doesn't in fact speak), one needs equally to leave behind the particular uses of the word by Descartes and Pascal. And so on. Descartes and indeed Montaigne himself would then lose their status as points of origin for the modern self: the *cogito* would emerge as a strange and unexpected singularity in the philosophical field, the *Essais* as an exorbitant variant of an established sixteenth-century practice of writing. Such textual instances would furthermore appear as isolated moments in the sedimentation of the self rather than as episodes in a story that was always waiting for them. This effect would be even more striking for the period preceding Montaigne. Once one has left behind the dossier provided by the *Essais*, saturated as it is with both grammatical and thematic uses of the first person, one finds oneself picking one's way amid much more fragmentary traces which cannot be reduced to conventional forms of historical coherence. We shall be looking shortly at the humanist theory of *imitatio* and the question of the Rabelaisian 'I'; other traces of the subject (in both senses) may be identified in sixteenth-century lyric poetry and its classical and Italian antecedents, but that is an archipelago we cannot explore further here.[8]

In what follows, I shall therefore examine a series of texts as a cluster of archaeological fragments showing signs of a family resemblance within the broader horizon of French culture between 1550 and 1650, without any claim to provide a definitive reconstruction of this family's genealogy. I shall begin with a fragment in the most literal sense, a textual instance preserved by chance from the shipwreck of history: short but highly structured, it carries within that structure relatively clear traces of its provenance. It goes without saying that such traces lend themselves to analysis as elements in a philosophical discourse, but they may also be read according to the principles of literary analysis, paying attention to figurative, dialogic or narrative features. In this way, a fragment of textual evidence becomes the object of a poetics, on condition that it is a poetics turned in its entirety towards the singularities of history. The text in question is fragment 688 of Pascal's *Pensées*, and its title is admirably suited to our purpose here: 'Qu'est-ce que le moi?'

'What is the self?'

> Un homme qui se met à la fenêtre pour voir les passants; si je passe par là, puis-je dire qu'il s'est mis là pour me voir? Non, car il ne pense pas à moi en particulier. Mais celui qui aime quelqu'un à cause de sa beauté, l'aime-t-il? Non: car la petite vérole, qui tuera la beauté sans tuer la personne, fera qu'il ne l'aimera plus.
>
> Et si on m'aime pour mon jugement, pour ma mémoire, m'aime-t-on? *moi*? Non, car je puis perdre ces qualités sans me perdre moi-même. Où est donc ce *moi*, s'il n'est ni dans le corps, ni dans l'âme? Et comment aimer le corps ou l'âme, sinon pour ces qualités, qui ne sont point ce qui fait le moi, puisqu'elles sont périssables? Car aimerait-on la substance de l'âme d'une personne abstraitement, et quelques qualités qui y fussent? Cela ne se peut, et serait injuste. On n'aime donc jamais personne, mais seulement des qualités.
>
> Qu'on ne se moque donc plus de ceux qui se font honorer pour des charges et des offices, car on n'aime personne que pour des qualités empruntées.[9]

[Imagine someone who goes to the window to look at people walking past. If I walk past, am I entitled to say that she went to the window to look at me? No, because she isn't thinking of me in particular.

But imagine that someone loves a person because of his good looks: does she love *him*? No, because if he catches smallpox, which destroys the good looks without killing the person, she will cease to love him.

And if someone loves me for my judgement, for my memory, does she love *me*? No, because I can lose these qualities without losing my self. Where then is this 'self' of mine, if it is neither in the body nor in the soul? And how is it possible to love the body or the soul other than for these qualities, which cannot be what constitutes the self, since they are perishable? For would anyone love the substance of someone's soul in abstract, regardless of that person's qualities? That is impossible, and would also be unfair. Thus one never loves anyone as a person; one can only love qualities.

We should therefore no longer sneer at people who require others to honour them for their rank or office; for what we love in other people is never anything other than sham qualities.]

In order for Pascal to be in a position to ask the question 'Qu'est-ce que le moi?', it was necessary that *moi* should already be a noun, a *thing* whose nature and composition were open to investigation. By the 1660s, the substantivization of the pronoun seems indeed to have entered current usage: in Molière's *Amphitryon* (1668), a play written and performed for an audience which was highly literate but by no means erudite, the servant Sosie uses it to express the duplication of his identity by Mercury, the messenger of the god Zeus, who has himself taken on Amphitryon's identity in pursuit of his wife Alcmène.[10]

On the other hand, the shift is also relatively recent: both Pascal and Molière are using a neologism. The context in which it occurs emerges clearly if one unpacks the philosophical presuppositions of *Pensées* 688 concerning the nature of body and soul, and in particular the relation between enduring substance on the one hand and perishable qualities on the other (which implies that the essential self is immortal). These presuppositions already suggest that the fragment belongs to the aftermath of the Cartesian *cogito*. And indeed, in the *Discours de la méthode*, just before the *cogito* itself is formulated, the word *moi* occurs in substantival form:

> Je connus de là que j'étais une substance dont toute l'essence ou la nature n'est que de penser, et qui pour être n'a besoin d'aucun lieu ni ne dépend d'aucune chose matérielle, en sorte que ce moi, c'est-à-dire l'âme, par laquelle je suis ce que je suis, est entièrement distincte du corps.[11]

> [As a consequence of that, I knew that I was a substance whose entire essence or nature consists only in thinking, and who in order to exist needs no place and depends on no material thing, so that this self, that is to say the soul, through which I am what I am, is entirely distinct from the body.]

Here, then, is the ontology of the self that Pascal seeks to analyse, an ontology that identifies the self with the soul and insists on an absolute separation between the soul–self and the body. It is moreover essential both for Descartes's argument and for Pascal's that the substantivized pronoun be the first person singular, not the third.[12]

One may also note that Pascal presumes in this fragment that it would be possible to lose one's memory without losing one's self. The very fact that he presumes it in passing indicates that, for him, it is not a point on which debate is possible. Yet some forty years later, John Locke will make memory the foundation of his definition of personal identity, a philosophical move that will give rise, precisely, to prolonged debate (the question is taken up again in the eighteenth century by David Hume and Thomas Reid). Between the emergence of what I shall from now on call *moi[S]*,[13] Descartes's *cogito*, and that future debate, the Pascalian fragment occupies a precise and critical place in the history of the notion of 'identity' (as we would say today — that term was not yet in use in the seventeenth century).

A more detailed account of the context of Pascal's question would also lay emphasis on the features that connect it with the milieu of Port-Royal, and especially with a deep Augustinian distrust of all human values. This is evident, for example, in the equivalence established in the last paragraph of the fragment between love and worldly homage. It is on these grounds that Pascal is capable of affirming in fragment 597 that 'le moi est haïssable' [the self is detestable].[14]

Up to this point, I have followed the conventions of a localized history of ideas. As I have already indicated, however, the *Pensées* are not only a collection of philosophical, axiological or theological propositions. In the domain of what he calls the 'esprit de finesse', which we might translate approximately for our present purposes as 'the intuitive sense', Pascal draws explicitly on the resources of rhetoric and more generally on the set of devices that we would call literary. In those terms, *moi[S]*, given that it is the subject of a *title*, must be read as the first of a series of first-person grammatical forms. The whole of the first part of the fragment unfolds, in fact, on an axis which is at once pronominal and deictic: the singular position of the speaker becomes the focus of Pascal's question from the very first sentence. The theme of the fragment — where is the locus of personal essence to be situated? — is at once translated into an instance of subjective discourse.[15]

This aspect is all the more striking because the opening sentence stages an accidental encounter where the gaze of a stranger falls on the 'moi' as he or she passes by. Pascal here seems to be echoing a passage in Descartes's *Meditations* where the point at issue is the distinction between sense-perception and mental judgement (this is the famous passage about the piece of wax):

> I would [...] be inclined to conclude from this that we recognize wax by means of our eyesight, and not only by inspecting it with our mind, if it were not the case that, seeing by chance from a window some people walking past in the street, I say that I can see some people, just as habitually as I say that I can see some wax. Yet what do I see but some hats and coats, which might be worn by automata? But I still judge that they are people. And so I understand, solely by the capacity of judgement that resides in my mind, what I believed I was seeing with my eyes.[16]

It looks as if Pascal must have borrowed this analogy in order to dwell on its metaphorical value: how can one *see* the self? In his account, in fact, the visual interplay is progressively intensified. The accidental glance of the first sentence becomes the most deliberate and motivated of gazes, the gaze of love. A drama is sketched out: the beloved is disfigured by smallpox, or loses her (his) memory. What is more, the drama features a *subject*, a first-person figure: it is I who am the beloved object, at least up to the point where a loss of memory causes me to be rejected by my lover.[17] In this way, one could easily reconstruct a narrative movement which would begin with the glance (the *coup de foudre*) of the opening sentence and end in a crisis where love became inextricably entangled with, and eventually indistinguishable from, political ambition.

It is well known that in France, from the 1660s, this latter theme will be narrativized to an almost obsessive extent, whether in the tragedies of Racine or in prose fictions like Madame de Lafayette's *La Princesse de Clèves*.[18] More immediately pertinent for our discussion is the enormous impact made by a translation of Augustine's *Confessions*, first printed in 1649; its author was Arnauld d'Andilly, who belonged, like Pascal, to the milieu of Port-Royal.[19] The *Confessions* are of course a paradigm of narrativization of the self; what is striking here is that this model had to wait until the middle of the seventeenth century to deploy its full force.[20]

Another major coordinate for this set of questions is provided by the emergence of the problem of identity at the end of the seventeenth century as a focal topic for philosophers who characteristically invent narratives (or at least virtual narratives) in order to test their definitions. This strand of philosophical enquiry leads straight into the realm of science fiction — transplanted brains, androids who perfectly imitate an existing person, individuals reduced to a set of electronic information which is then transmitted to a distant place and used to reconstruct the same (but is it the same?) individual from different atomic materials.[21] In his chapter on the notion of a person, John Locke already imagines a similar case in order to show that the identity of a *person* should not be confused with that of a *man*, where the body plays a crucial role:

> should the soul of a prince, carrying with it the consciousness of the prince's past life, enter and inform the body of a cobbler, as soon as deserted by his own soul, every one sees he would be the same person with the prince, accountable only for the prince's actions: but who would say it was the same man? The body too goes to the making the man and would, I guess, to everybody determine the man in this case; wherein the soul, with all its princely thoughts about it, would not make another man: but he would be the same cobbler to every one besides himself.[22]

We need however to make a careful distinction here. Narrative has always carried implicit conceptions of identity: this is one of its most archaic and essential functions, as one can see from the number of narratives that end with a recognition scene.[23] The narrativization of the first person no doubt also presupposes a particular conception of the ontological or moral subject, even if that conception is hazy or difficult to elicit by standard interpretative procedures. But in the mid-seventeenth century, the future moment when philosophers (not to mention psychoanalysts) will define identity in narrative terms is still distant. *A fortiori*, it doesn't occur to Pascal to regard the self as constructed like a narrative, as theorists and philosophers of our own times have done.[24]

Such examples, once again, are recalled primarily in order to set them aside and avoid writing them into a teleological sequence where our early modern examples would appear as anticipations or points of departure. This one-way diachronic relation may be illustrated with particular clarity by means of *Pensées* 689, in other words the fragment that follows 'Qu'est-ce que le moi?': 'Ce n'est pas dans Montaigne mais dans moi que je trouve tout que j'y vois' [It's not in Montaigne but in myself that I find everything I see there]. We shall return to this fragment and its antecedents shortly; for now, it will suffice to point out that the juxtaposition of 688 and 689 on the same sheet of paper in the manuscript copies establishes an *a posteriori* connection between *moi[S]* and Montaigne, as if the question 'What is the self?' led one naturally to a reflection on Montaigne,[25] and vice versa. At the same time, the absence of *moi[S]* in 689, despite the movement of the first-person subject pronoun towards the disjunctive pronoun, reminds one that the gradual saturation of the *Essais* by a pronominal grammar of the first person singular is accomplished without the hypostasis of *moi[S]* as an object of enquiry or analysis.

The emergence of *moi[S]*

The next question is to determine when the pronoun *moi* began to be used as a noun in French. Robert's *Dictionnaire historique de la langue française* dates the shift to 1581, but without indicating the text on which this assertion is based. The 1889 Littré mentions an *Epitaphe* by the poet Philippe Desportes which we will quote later; furthermore, it situates the new form in the perspective of historical syntax:

> In early French, *je* was not or at least was capable of not being enclitic. However, when it became regularly used as an enclitic, early modern French began to use *moi* as a subject instead of *je*.[26]

So in the course of the sixteenth century, *je* is gradually replaced in its disjunctive function by *moi*, especially at the beginning of a sentence, and it is no surprise that the most extensive evidence of this shift is provided by Montaigne's *Essais*.

We need to remind ourselves that this lexical change may not in itself imply a shift in the way the subject is conceived. One may none the less assume that the substitution of an object pronoun for a subject pronoun carries with it at least the potentiality for an increased reflexivity: if one compares Montaigne's phrase 'moy qui me voy' (see below) with its hypothetical anterior form 'je qui me voy', the phonetic and formal difference between subject and object is eliminated in the former phrase in favour of a semi-repetition ('moy [...] me') which brings subject and object close together in a mirror relationship. The very large number of reflexive sentences of this type in the *Essais* tends moreover to corroborate the grammatical evidence, allowing one to posit a movement in this period — or at least in this text, which must by definition show what is possible in the period — towards the formation of a new instrument of thought.

What we are concerned with here, however, is the relationship between this shift in linguistic usage and the emergence of *moi[S]*. The lines from Desportes which Littré cites as evidence of the substantivization of the pronoun are as follows:

> La seule mort a causé ma tristesse,
> La seule mort y pourra mettre cesse,
> Ne m'empeschant plus longuement de suivre
> Cet autre moy, pour qui j'aimois à vivre.[27]

> [Death alone has caused my melancholy, death alone can bring it to an end, no longer preventing me from following that other self for whom I loved to live]

It must be conceded here that the notion of a 'first use' is problematic, since there may well have been other previous examples that have been lost, especially if one includes possible oral instances of which there can be no record. The only thing one can affirm — and it is by no means negligible — is that, if *moi[S]* was already in frequent use in the 1570s, it would indeed be strange that Montaigne never availed himself of it.[28]

In the *Complainte*, Desportes was writing in the name of a patron whose friend had recently died. In that context, the phrase 'Cet autre moy' might seem to be merely a vaguely neo-Platonist conceit, where the use of *moi[S]* is motivated by a discreet allusion to the Androgyne myth as interpreted by Aristophanes in the

Symposium. There is no trace of an inward-turned gaze, even less of a Montaignian project of self-representation. Thus the example is disappointing for anyone who was hoping to find in it a convenient point of departure for the history of the modern self. In that sense, the 'other self' of the *Complainte* would be an isolated case, even an inconsequential accident. Indeed, the fact that it is chronologically juxtaposed with the *Essais* would seem to demonstrate that Montaigne precisely did not require this new coinage in order to undertake his complex explorations of writing in the first person singular.

The self and friendship

And yet it is strange that this poem of mourning for a friend who is a faithful mirror of the *moi* and whose loss leaves no other perspective than death for the self who remains should have been published in the wake of the first edition of the *Essais*. For it is well known that Montaigne had initially intended to construct his book around an edition of Éstienne de La Boétie's *Discours de la servitude volontaire*, but that in the end he contented himself with a chapter ('De l'amitié') on their now posthumous friendship, accompanied by twenty-nine love-sonnets by La Boétie. Had the sonnets, removed in later editions but present in the 1580 edition, perhaps drawn Desportes's attention to that particular chapter? If so, his use of 'Ce moy' may not have been so fortuitous, and the hypothesis is corroborated by Gisèle Mathieu-Castellani's study of the textual relationship between the two writers.[29] Whatever the truth of the matter, it remains the case that in Montaigne's chapter as in Desportes's *Complainte*, friendship goes hand in hand with death, giving rise to unusually prominent and inventive uses of *moi*.

The grammar of the first person singular is developed with considerable intensity in 'De l'amitié'. Among the occurrences which are already present in the 1580 edition, the following is especially striking:

> Nos ames ont charrié si uniement ensemble, elles se sont considerées d'une si ardante affection, et de pareille affection descouvertes jusques au fin fond des entrailles l'une à l'autre, que, non seulement je connaissoy la sienne comme la mienne, mais je me fusse certainement plus volontiers fié à luy de moy qu'à moy.[30]

> [Our souls were so closely yoked together, they contemplated one another with such ardent and equal affection, mutually laid bare to their very entrails, that I not only knew his as I knew my own, but I would certainly rather have entrusted myself to him than to myself.]

The conception of a perfect identity between friends is here accompanied by a kind of physical interiority ('mutually laid bare to their very entrails');[31] saturated with a lexis of similarity, the sentence moves with ever greater intensity through a series of symmetrical expressions ('l'une à l'autre', 'la sienne comme la mienne') and culminates in a concentrated juxtaposition of subject pronouns.

Looking beyond the hypothesis of an immediate textual link between the *Essais* and the *Complainte*, one will of course want to take into account instances added after the first edition, and in particular the famous sentence 'Par ce que c'estoit luy; parce que c'estoit moy' [because it was him; because it was me], the symmetry of which seems again to encapsulate the notion of 'another self'.[32] The textual relation is in fact complicated here because similar formulations occur from antiquity onwards in reflections on friendship. In addition to the neo-Platonist myth of the Androgyne as a figure of twinned identity, the Aristotelian *heteros autos*, and the Ciceronian *alter ego*, all of which we have already mentioned,[33] Montaigne's imagination was formed in this area as in so many others by examples drawn from the Latin poets. Within the same movement of thought, he quotes a passage from Catullus on the death of a friend, and, more extensively, these lines of Horace:

> [B] Illam meae si partem animae tulit
> Maturior vis, quid moror altera,
> Nec charus aequè, nec superstes
> Integer? Ille dies utramque
> Duxit ruinam.[34]

> [Since a premature blow has taken from me that part of my soul, why do I, the other part, less beloved, less complete, still linger on? That day brought the ruin of both.]

The quotation was added in the 1588 edition, but it seems already to be foreshadowed, both in substance and in structure, in the 1580 text: 'Nous estions à moitié de tout; il me semble que je luy desrobe sa part [...] il me semble n'estre plus qu'à demy' [We went half and half in everything; it seems to me that I have stolen from him his share [...] it seems to me that I am now only half alive].[35]

Desportes must of course also have known these Latin models, which allows one to assume a textual relation that moves in more than one direction — from Horace to Montaigne, from Horace to Desportes, and from Montaigne to Desportes (even, perhaps, from Desportes to the Montaigne of 1588).[36] Another model that might have acted as an intermediary needs however to be considered here, a more problematic one, namely St Augustine's *Confessions*. In one of the chapters of his penitential biography, Augustine meditates at length on the death of a friend, an event that was the more traumatic because the friendship was exemplary:

> Et me magis, quia ille alter eram, vivere illo mortuo mirabar. Bene quidam dixit de amico suo: *Dimidium animae meae*. Nam ego sensi animam meam et animam illius unam fuisse animam in duobus corporibus; et ideo mihi horrori erat vita, quia nolebam dimidius vivere.[37]

> [And I was the more astonished that I could continue to live after his death because I was another him. He who called his friend 'Half of my soul' was right. For I felt that my soul and his were one soul in two bodies; and life was repellent to me because I did not wish to be only half alive.]

The phrase 'Dimidium animae meae' comes from another Horatian ode (I.3) which Montaigne certainly also knew,[38] although it is less relevant to Montaigne's context because the reference is not to the death of a friend but to the departure of Virgil on a journey. It would be tempting to imagine that Montaigne was familiar with Augustine's lament, but the evidence is not conclusive: the similarities could no doubt be explained by the currency of the *topoi* themselves.[39]

Let us return finally to Desportes's lines as a vehicle for the 'first' use of *moi[S]*. By demonstrating that, around 1580, the theme of a dead friend could give rise to an unprecedented grammatical transformation, they discreetly reinforce the hypothesis according to which that theme lies at the heart of Montaigne's writing.[40] Inversely, the major event that was the first publication of the *Essais* lends to this little-known poem an undeniable weight as a distant (yet also strangely close) echo of *Essais* I.28. However one interprets this textual conjuncture, it proves that the language of self-representation was on the move in this period, breaching the limits imposed on it by pre-existing linguistic and textual norms.

The self and *imitatio*

The theme of friendship is however by no means the only matrix for the emergence of *moi[S]* in the late sixteenth century. A phenomenon of this kind cannot be explained exclusively in terms of a biographical or psychological accident: it must presuppose a discursive context which is equally valid for Montaigne, Desportes and many others, that is to say the complete range of discursive resources that an educated vernacular writer had at his or her disposal around 1580. These of course include particular ways of talking about friendship, and the phrases and formulas that accompany that theme. *Imitatio* is the overarching matrix here, as was indeed indicated by our exploration of intertextual echoes in the preceding section.[41] It was the tension between the writer and his prestigious models, especially in the context of the debate over Ciceronian style, that gave rise to the Latin neologism *seipsum exprimere*,[42] and when Du Bellay came to defend himself in the 1550 preface to the *Olive* against excessive borrowing from classical and Italian models, his ultimate argument is a simple inversion of the poetics of imitation: 'Je ne me suis beaucoup travaillé en mes escriz de ressembler aultre que moymesmes' [I have not striven especially in my writings to resemble anyone other than myself].[43] Since Du Bellay, of all the mid-century French poets, was the one who most famously cultivated an individualized poetic persona, with its accompanying first-person grammar, it is not unreasonable to regard this formulation as at least a straw in the wind. It looks very much, in fact, like a moment in the pre-history of Montaigne's remarks on his own practice of imitation: one thinks, for example, of passages such as the one in 'De la phisionomie' (III.12) where, having conceded that the *Essais* may have the aspect of a mere anthology, he goes on to say that the last thing he wanted to do was borrow the voices of other writers: 'si je m'en fusse creu, à tout hazard, j'eusse parlé tout fin seul' [if I had had the confidence to do it, I would have taken the risk of speaking wholly on my own].[44]

One may track a similar development through the rewritings of a single sentence borrowed by Montaigne from Seneca and from Montaigne by Pascal. These sentences, given here in chronological order, constitute what may be regarded as a series of archaeological fragments, bearing witness to a marked displacement of the notion of intellectual property towards an introspective centre:

> Platonis argumentum adferam — quid enim nocet alienis uti ex parte qua nostra sunt?[45]

> [I have cited one of Plato's arguments — for what harm does it do to make use of other people's property to the extent that it is our own?]

> Ce n'est non plus selon Platon que selon moy, puisque luy et moy l'entendons et voyons de mesme.[46]

> [It's no more Plato's idea than it is my own, since he and I understand and see it the same way.]

> Ce n'est pas dans Montaigne mais dans moi que je trouve tout ce que j'y vois.[47]

> [It's not in Montaigne but in myself that I find everything I see there.]

To this series may be added a further variant from Seneca:

> De alieno liberalis sum. Quare autem alienum dixi? Quidquid bene dictum est ab ullo meum est.[48]

> [I make generous use of other people's property. But why do I say 'other people's property'? Whatever has been well said by anyone belongs to me.]

Seneca begins by making a simple gesture of citation ('Platonis argumentum adferam') which is positive and affirmative: Plato here preserves all his intellectual property rights. The qualification or justification that follows is defensive ('quid nocet') and is founded on the recognition of a limit ('ex parte qua'). The use of the first person remains within the conventions of philosophical style ('adferam') and is rapidly overtaken by a generalizing plural form ('nostra'). It is true that Seneca's other formulation erases the name of the textual source and at the same time gives a prominent position to a first person singular possessive adjective ('meum'). But it does so in order to affirm a common ownership of discursive goods rather than a transformation grounded in an individual identity.[49]

Montaigne takes a crucial step in this series by asserting himself actively as the subject and by attaching a negative particle to the name of Plato. No sooner is Plato evoked than he is set aside to make way for the first person, for the word 'moy' which is then repeated ('luy et moy'); this repetition is moreover prolonged by the assonance of 'moy' with 'voyons'.

Montaigne's version, however, remains at the level of a coincidence of perspectives: 'luy et moy l'entendons et voyons de mesme'. Plato's utterance has shifted to a new subjective position, but apparently without a change of content or value. In our micro-series, it is in fact Pascal who brings about the most radical transformation. The negation, transferred from Plato to Montaigne, is now more rigorous: the Pascalian subject absorbs and erases the whole of Montaigne (that is to say, of the *Essais*) and replaces it with his own content, his own 'property'. It follows that the relation of the subject ('moi') to what it sees ('voit') is reflexive and introspective: where one thought one was seeing a foreign text, one finds only oneself.

Pascal's sentence thus remains fully within the domain of *imitatio*, with its tension between writer and model. At the same time, this fragment on Montaigne, set next to the fragment 'Qu'est-ce que le moi?' as if it were a kind of gloss, indicates that Pascal's question of and about the *moi* is likely to have been prompted by his thorough, and thoroughly critical, reading of the *Essais*. In the chapter 'De la phisionomie', for example, Montaigne speaks more aggressively than he does in I.26 of his appropriation — and even his deliberate deformation — of other writers' texts;[50] Pascal merely takes that principle to its logical conclusion.

It goes without saying that all of these sentences remain anchored in their own historical moment. In order to return explicitly to the historical question while complementing this analysis of the textual relations between Pascal and Montaigne, we may introduce here a passage from the opening segment of the chapter 'Sur des vers de Virgile'. It contains the following well-known fragment of a sentence: 'moy, qui me voy et qui me recherche jusques aux entrailles [...]' [I, who see myself and pursue myself into my very entrails].[51] If one divides the fragment into two, one may describe the resulting segments as follows:

1. 'Moy qui me voy' consitutes the element of self-reflection which was absent from the sentence from I.26 we have just considered ('Ce n'est non plus...'), but which is present in Pascal's fragment 689, as if the later writer had also had this sentence in mind when he rewrote the one about the imitation of Plato;

2. 'et qui me recherche jusques aux entrailles': this 'exploration' is analogous to Pascal's enquiry in 'Qu'est-ce que le moi?', the gaze that successively removes the layers of the human personality in the search for its core, its 'identity' as we might say. And what Montaigne is talking about in this passage from III.5 is precisely the false appearances and 'fauces approbations' which emerge as the theme of the final paragraph of *Pensées* 688.

It therefore looks very much as if fragments 688 and 689 belong to a far more complex set of textual relations that comprises not only the sentence from I.26 but also the passage from III.5, together with further possible echoes of III.12 and no doubt many other chapters.

Without abandoning this textual pathway, we can take one further step by adding to our collection of examples the following lines which occur half a page earlier in III.5:

> En faveur des Huguenots, qui accusent nostre confession privée et auriculaire, je me confesse en publicq, religieusement et purement. S. Augustin, Origene et Hippocrates ont publié les erreurs de leurs opinions; moy, encore, de mes meurs. Je suis affamé de me faire connoistre.[52]

> [In favour of the Huguenots, who attack our private, auricular confession, I confess in public, religiously and purely. Saint Augustine, Origen and Hippocrates made public the errors in their opinions; in addition to those, I publish the faults in my patterns of behaviour. I am hungry to make myself known.]

Pascal's critique of Montaigne, it will be recalled, focuses above all on the self-absorption and self-advertisement of which the last sentence in the quoted passage is an exemplary instance. We thus remain here at the centre of the intertextual field in which the writings of Pascal and Montaigne mirror and oppose one another. At the same time, the opening sentence connects these remarks to their own specific historical moment. By a reflex which is entirely natural in the 1580s, when the question of confession, auricular or public, was highly topical, Montaigne chooses to model his secular confession on a heterodox religious practice. Yet the reference is clearly not intended to be read theologically: on the contrary, it is metaphorical, as can be seen from the fact that Hippocrates is named in the same breath as Augustine and Origen. The whole thematic nexus of the chapter 'Du repentir' (III.2) turns on this deliberate secularization, as I have shown elsewhere.[53] It would be unwise, however, to conclude from this that Montaigne has liberated himself at a blow from the weight of censorship imposed by Christian (especially Augustinian) authority and tradition on autobiographical narrative and on the self as an object of reflection. Indeed, the genre that much later became know as 'autobiography' carried the name of 'confession' long after Montaigne's lifetime. As for Pascal, his role in this regard is primarily to restore and reinforce the ideological frame of reference evoked with such insouciance by Montaigne, while emphasizing by antiphrasis (or by antiperistasis) the quasi-imperialist power of the *moi*.[54]

Notes

1. See OED, art. 'self'.
2. See in particular Charles Taylor, *Sources of the Self: The Making of the Modern Identity* (Cambridge: Cambridge University Press, 1989), Part II. A similar assumption is made by new historicists in the wake of Stephen Greenblatt's *Renaissance Self-Fashioning* (Chicago and London: University of Chicago Press, 1980); it is hardly necessary to add that Shakespeare and his contemporaries play a key role in this account.
3. *Ad Atticum* III.15.4; *Ad familiares* VII.5.1; *De amicitia* 80. The only extant example in the nominative case is in fact the 'alter idem' of the *De amicitia*; in other words, the expression *alter ego* in the nominative is not found in the writings of Cicero or of any other classical Latin author.
4. *Nicomachean Ethics* IX.9.10. The 'alter idem' of Cicero's *De amicitia* is clearly a translation of Aristotle's phrase. The form *allos ego* occurs in a sentence attributed to Zeno in the writings of Diogenes Laertius.
5. The ancient Sanskrit grammarians derived from the word the name of an important category of semi-reflexive verbal forms (*âtmanepada*) roughly equivalent to Latin deponent verbs, but originally, it appears, closer to the Greek middle voice.
6. On the appearance of *sich* as a noun in Middle High German texts of the fourteenth century, see Ben Morgan, 'Developing the Modern Concept of the Self: The Trial of Meister Eckhart', *Telos*, 116 (1999), 56–80.
7. I use the English word 'self' throughout this section as a direct translation of the French *le moi*, but the difference between a first-person and a third-person pronominal noun is often critical, not least in the parallel but not synchronous histories of the self and *le moi*. I shall therefore revert to the French word where confusion might otherwise arise.
8. Among recent studies in this area, see especially Jean Lecointe, *L'Idéal et la différence: la perception de la personnalité littéraire à la Renaissance* (Geneva: Droz, 1993); François Rouget, *L'Apothéose d'Orphée: l'esthétique de l'ode en France au XVIe siècle de Sébillet à Scaliger, 1548–1561* (Geneva: Droz, 1994), pp. 87–99; Perrine Galand-Hallyn, *Les Yeux de l'éloquence: poétiques humanistes de l'évidence* (Orleans: Paradigme, 1995), especially I.1 and III.3. It goes without saying that I am also leaving aside here the whole question of Petrarch's use of the first person, which is itself often regarded as a point of origin of the modern 'self'. To follow the traces that lead back to Petrarch and beyond would require a dauntingly large dossier and set of scholarly skills, and would be most appropriately carried out by a closely coordinated team of researchers.
9. Blaise Pascal, *Pensées*, in *Œuvres complètes*, ed. by Lafuma, p. 591, no. 688. I have also used this passage as the starting point of an essay on 'Fictional Identities' in *Identity*, ed. by Henry Harris (Oxford: Clarendon Press, 1995), pp. 99–127.
10. *Amphitryon* II.1, lines 736 *et seq.*
11. René Descartes, *Discours de la méthode*, ed. by G. Gadoffre (Manchester: Manchester University Press, 1961), p. 32.
12. In *Meditations* II, Descartes makes intensive use of the phrase *ego ille*, which seems in some cases to come close to functioning as a noun. Where it is the subject of a verb, however, the